The Triple Struggle
Latin American
Peasant Women

by Audrey Bronstein

South End Press   Boston

For my mother, Frances Shaw, with love.

"Well, I want it to reach the poorest people, the people who don't have any money. It's for them that I agreed that what I am going to tell be written down. It doesn't matter what kind of paper it's put down on, but it does matter that it be useful for the working class and not only for intellectual people or for people who only make a business of this kind of thing."
 — Domitila Barrios de Chungara, *Let me Speak!*
Testimony of Domitila, a woman of the Bolivian mines,
Stage One, London 1978

Additional research for this publication was funded by War on Want
Photographs are the author's except for p. 14 (Jenny Matthews), p. 32
(UNICEF photo by Bernard Wolff), p. 39 (WHO), p. 182 (Luis Silva), p. 189
(United Nations), p. 204 (S. Salgado, courtesy of Christian Aid).

Cover Design by Carl Conetta
Maps by Jan Brown

Library of Congress: 83-06017
ISBN paper: 0-89608-179-6
ISBN cloth: 0-89608-180-X

ACKNOWLEDGEMENTS

This book is the result of the support, energy and commitment of many women and men both in England and in Latin America. Without them, it would never have happened.

My first thanks go to Inter-Action and the United Nations Fund for Population Activities for providing the financial assistance which made my trip to Latin America possible. In particular I want to thank Ed Berman and Tarzie Vittachi for encouraging me at the start of what seemed a daunting task.

Dozens of people working in the field in Latin America helped me to meet and talk with women. I am especially grateful to Caroline and Magedelano Avila, Jerry, Glynni, Sister Francisca, Sister Lorraine, Dolores Padilla, Gil Santian, Anna Lund, Barbara Henszey, Maria Sara de Paez, Francisca Mayer, Blanca Figuero, Ameilia Villaneuva, Bea Koster, Phil Blair, Bambi de Arrellano, Yara Carafa, and field staff at the Institute of Peruvian Cooperative Education and UNICEF.

To Jenny Smith de Cuevas, Marianne and Noel Dunne, Alex Chavez and Cecilia Grenadino — for their friendship, hospitality and help with the work — but more, for just being there — a very special thank you.

I am grateful to everyone at Inter-Action for being so understanding during those long periods when I was nowhere to be seen. Thank you for carrying my share of the work. I also want to thank Catherine Cahn and Keith Smith whose support throughout the last several months I truly appreciate. Thanks also to Jane Woodhead for her eleventh hour assistance.

Kate Young, in addition to writing the Foreword, also provided valuable and helpful insights.

To WOW Campaigns Ltd., my thanks for publishing the book and giving these women the chance to be heard. Particular thanks to Helen Allison, whose energy and ideas have contributed so much, and Luis Silva for supporting the publication.

Jenny Pearce has been a support and inspiration every step of the way — from her substantial contribution of political and economic information on Latin America, through to helping me in those times when I couldn't write one more word.

Andy Chetley has spent many long hours as editor of this book. His professional assistance, friendship, constant encouragement and support, and the strength of his belief in the importance of this project have served as a life line to me.

I cannot name all the women whose thought and feeling are the heart of this book. It is to them that I am most deeply grateful.

CONTENTS

FOREWORD

Despite the fact that the literature on women's situation in Latin America is increasing rapidly, there are few accounts which include the actual voices of women themselves. The few that do — such as Domitila's account of her life and struggles in the Siglo XX mines — are deservedly popular.

In her book Audrey Bronstein has attempted to bring us the voices of perhaps the most silent of all Latin Americans — peasant indigenous women. Not only silent but in many cases silenced both by cultural patterns that make men the public representatives of women, and by the marginal place that peasant and subsistence producers are given in the management of national affairs.

The interviews in many cases suffer from the awkwardness and hesitancy encountered when people begin to think aloud about the unquestioned, to talk about the untalkable. Issues of poverty, lack of resources, and injustice are relatively easy to recount; more personal matters — domestic tyrannies, blighted hopes — come less easily to the fore. The book thus raises those same questions that have been the source of heated debate for over a decade: is there a universal feminist problematic? Do Third World women consider "bread and butter" issues to be their only concern?

From this account of conversations with women from differing Latin American countries we can get an idea of the magnitude of their problems — the daily and common struggle of women and men against unremitting poverty — a poverty from which others benefit; the secular presentation of women as being of a different quality of humankind than men, which prevents them from taking an active part in the allocation and sometimes even the enjoyment of scarce or valued social resources. Despite the representation of social differences between the genders as being securely founded in nature, Audrey Bronstein's discussions with many of the women show that this "natural" inferiority is coming to be challenged.

And here I think a useful lesson can be drawn from the book: that it is probably rather easy to leap to the wrong conclusions about what women such as those interviewed feel about their own lives and their priorities if we assume that they have actually had the possibility of reflecting deeply upon their situation. Rather what the book highlights is the need for the creation of the conditions under which they can begin to place their own experience within a wider context, and to discover and celebrate their own needs and quiet yearnings. This is the strength of Audrey Bronstein's attempt, which is matched by the evident desire of many of the women to communicate to her across the massive barriers of differing culture and language.

Kate Young
London 1981

PREFACE

Women comprise 50% of the world's population, do two-thirds of the world's work hours, receive 10% of the world's income and own less than 1% of world property, according to the International Labour Organisation. As unjust as that global picture may be, when the situation of Third World peasant women is examined, it becomes apparent that they are one of the most oppressed social groups in the world today.

They suffer in three ways: as citizens of underdeveloped countries; as peasants, living in the most impoverished and disadvantaged areas of those countries; and as women, in male-dominated societies.

The result of this triple oppression is that Third World peasant women are amongst the least articulate and least heard members of the global society. Development has been measured in terms of social and economic change affecting the male population. Social scientists and development technicians have shown little interest in the specific needs of women. The factors affecting women's ability to participate fully on a social, economic and political level have been ignored.

The growth of the women's movement in industrialised nations and the launch of the International Decade for Women in 1975 have begun to focus more attention on the role of women in both underdeveloped and developed societies. Yet there is little information available to enable us, in the industrialised nations, to appreciate the specific problems of our sisters in the Third World. There is less information offering a woman's perspective, and almost nothing from the peasant women themselves. Basic questions about whether their problems are in any way similar, or whether the debates in the women's movement here have any relevance to the needs of women in the Third World remain unanswered.

I wanted to hear for myself the opinions of these women on the nature and context of the situation in which they lived, their role within the family, the economic process and the social and political structures.

In 1978, I applied for a United Nations grant and a sabbatical from my employer, Inter-Action Trust, a London-based community development organisation.

I wanted to talk with women with whom I already had some bond and attempt to bridge the enormous gulf between our different cultures. As a community worker, and a long-term member of an organisation run loosely along the lines of a cooperative, I looked for contact with women who were involved in development projects, cooperatives and the learning process. And, as a spinner and weaver myself, I chose a region renowned for its women weavers: Latin America.

In London, I had been working with a group of six women from Kentish Town, who were exploring the extent of underutilised skills among women in the area, and identifying new areas of education and work, previously inaccessible to them.

They set up a local women's workshop with an emphasis on self-help community education and new work ventures. This experience had served as a personal springboard for each of the women to move into further education or employment, that is, to begin to make changes in the pattern of their lives. They all said that before becoming involved with the project, they lacked confidence and had not known how to even think about personal change, let alone where to start.

I wanted to learn from the Latin American peasant women about how they felt their "development" experiences had affected them. My objective was not academic. I didn't want to "study" them or development in Latin America. I hoped to speak with women, who, within a peasant, macho society, rarely speak, or give their opinions publicly on anything, much less on their own living conditions and the changes introduced by both foreign and indigenous development agencies.[1]

I hoped to learn about the role of women in the struggle for social and economic change in the Third World, and I wanted to compare the concerns of Third World women with our own in industrialised nations. I also wanted to learn more about the issue of sex and class: how far is the oppression of peasant women in the Third World related to their subordination by a male-dominated society and how far to their position as peasants, victims of underdevelopment and the unequal distribution of wealth within and between nations?

Most of the women were involved in some kind of organised cooperative income generating activity or new community development initiatives.

------

1. The names of all the women interviewed have been changed, and in some cases their villages have not been identified, to prevent any unfortunate reprisals or repercussions.

They included women who were members of cooperatives (weaving and other crafts, jam-making, bread-making, agricultural), women who had attended various training and community development courses (health, nutrition, cooperative development), women who were leaders within their own communities, as well as women who were not involved in any special community, social or economic activity outside of their traditional roles as wives, mothers and subsistence farm workers.

I visited Guatemala, El Salvador, Ecuador, Peru and Bolivia. The women I interviewed in Ecuador, Peru and Bolivia lived in the Andes mountains. In Guatemala, I spoke primarily to Indian women living in the northern highland regions. The few non Indian or *ladina* women whose words appear in the book are from the same highland region. In El Salvador my travels were restricted to a small area in the eastern region of the country.

I spent an average of three months in each of Guatemala, Peru and Ecuador. Because of the impending coup in Bolivia and the growing civil war in El Salvador, I spent only a few weeks in those countries.

I hope the book will be of interest both to members of the women's movement here, as well as to those women and men interested in development issues and the struggle for change here and in the Third World.

The book is an attempt to aid in the process of education and understanding, and to encourage strong international bonds amongst both women and men who are concerned with the changes that must occur in the lives of women all over the world.

Audrey Bronstein
London, November 1981

*"The division of labour among nations is that some
specialise in winning, and others in losing. Our
part of the world, known today as Latin America,
was precocious: it has specialised in losing ever
since those remote times when the Renaissance
Europeans ventured across the ocean and buried
their teeth in the throats of the Indian civilisations.
Centuries passed, and Latin America perfected its
role . . . our region still works as a menial. It
continues to exist at the service of others' needs."*
— Eduardo Galeano,
The Open Veins of Latin America

INTRODUCTION

Geographically, Latin America extends from the Rio Grande of Mexico to
the Tierra del Fuego of Patagonia. It includes Mexico, six Central American
republics plus newly independent Belize, 10 South American republics and
in the Caribbean: Cuba, the Dominican Republic and Haiti.

Apart from Brazil, which was colonised by the Portuguese, and Haiti,
which was taken over by the French, most of the region came under Spanish
rule in the 16th century.

At the time of the Spanish conquest, the main centres of indigenous
population were in Central America — where the Aztecs and Mayas
predominated — and in the Andes, where the Incas had established a
flourishing civilisation not long before the conquest. The Indians were
decimated by the conquest, either through warfare, disease or forced labour
in the mines in Mexico and what is today Peru and Bolivia.

Despite the decimation, Indians are still the majority of the population in the rural areas of Guatemala, Peru, Ecuador and Bolivia. In Guatemala there are over 20 Indian languages. In Peru, Ecuador and Bolivia, the Indians speak Aymara or Quechua. Primarily the Indians speak their own languages, although some know Spanish, the official language of all these countries. In El Salvador, the population is mainly mixed Indian and white (ladino). They all speak Spanish.

In other areas of Latin America where the Indian population was smaller at the time of the conquest, the European influence is much stronger. In Argentina and Uruguay, for instance, where there has also been considerable European immigration, the population is almost totally European.

Racial differences still affect social status and economic opportunities in Latin America. The whiter a person is, the more likely that she or he is to be found in the upper echelons of society. The Indians invariably occupy the lowest position on the social scale.

Underdevelopment

Latin America is part of the underdeveloped or Third World. There are, however, wide variations in the level of development throughout the region. Brazil, Mexico, Venezuela and Argentina are the most industrialised countries of Latin America. Their per capita income is considerably greater than that of the countries I visited:[1]

Brazil	$US 1,570	Bolivia	$US 510
Mexico	1,973	El Salvador	660
Argentina	1,910	Peru	770
Venezuela	2,910	Ecuador	880
		Guatemala	910

For comparison: United States, $US 9,590; United Kingdom, $US 5,030

Even in the most industrialised countries of the region, the benefits of economic growth have reached only a minority of the population and malnutrition, infant mortality, illiteracy, unemployment and underemployment are very high throughout Latin America.

The United Nations estimates that 50% of Latin America's 330 million people are destitute. In all countries the unequal distribution of wealth is very great. The model of development pursued in most of Latin America today stresses economic growth rather than redistribution of wealth.

————

1.   *World Development Report*, The World Bank, 1980

Everywhere the results are the same — increasing poverty for the poor and greater concentration of income for the wealthy.

Latin America's underdevelopment is not accidental. Latin America was brought into the world market by the Spanish and since then has existed to serve the needs of the developed world. Eduardo Galeano, the Uruguayan writer, has called Latin America's history since the conquest, "five centuries of the pillage of a continent".

First, the region's silver and gold riches were systematically plundered and shipped back to Europe. Later in the 19th century, Latin America supplied Europe with the raw materials and minerals needed to develop Europe's industries.

In the 20th century, many Latin American countries took advantage of disruptions in the world economy, such as the Depression and the World Wars, to embark upon a process of industrialisation. But in most countries the process was soon exhausted by the need to import much of the fuel, machinery and technology, and by the small size of the internal markets.

Where manufacturing industries did develop, such as in Brazil, the most dynamic sectors were taken over by American and other foreign multi-national corporations seeking cheap labour and new markets. Even today, most Latin American countries remain dependent on a few primary commodities or cash crops for their foreign exchange earnings. They have no control over the prices they receive for those commodities as they are subject to the fluctuations of the world market.

Political developments

Dependency and underdevelopment have also affected social structures and political developments in Latin America. A small minority of the population have benefitted from an alliance with foreign interests which has concentrated wealth and political power in their hands.

The ruling elite in Latin America is determined not to share its privileges. The struggle for social justice in the region is intense and frequently violent. Peasant organisations, trade unions and political parties which represent the underprivileged are illegal in many countries in Latin America and are often met with repression.

The military are a powerful force throughout Latin America. Since 1959 they have been trained and armed by the United States in a determined attempt to prevent "another Cuba". Once in power, the military nearly always begin their rule by "purging" the country of all those in the factories, the shanty towns, on the rural estates, in the universities and churches who have fought for social change. The organisations these people have built up to defend themselves also come under attack. Thousands have been killed, tortured and "disappeared" in recent military coups in Chile (1973), Uruguay (1973) and Argentina (1976).

The ruthlessness of the ruling elite in suppressing all forms of popular organisations and the lack of any peaceful avenues to change — elections are notoriously fraudulent — have resulted in open civil war in El Salvador and imminent civil war in Guatemala.

In Bolivia, where the tin miners in particular have a long history of struggle, a military coup in 1980 prevented the election of a centre-left government and suppressed all political activity.

Peru and Ecuador have only recently emerged from long periods of military rule and now have civilian governments. The military still remain in the background, however, ready to intervene in case of a real challenge to the present socio-economic system.

Peasants and the land

Nearly one third of Latin America's population lives in the rural areas where poverty, inequality in income distribution and the lack of medical and educational facilities are at their most extreme.

The system of land ownership lies at the base of many of the conflicts in Latin America, and indeed in much of the Third World. According to an Oxfam report:[2]

> "Unjust land tenure systems and the political, economic and social policies which enable these systems to prevail are the chief causes of hunger and poverty in the Third World today."

Like the general underdevelopment of Latin America, the system of land ownership has its roots in the Spanish conquest. Although there have been some minor variations over the centuries, the basic structure of land ownership has not really changed since that time.

The majority of prime agricultural land is owned by a tiny minority of the population, who are known as *latifundistas*, while the majority, the *minifundistas*, live on small, infertile, eroded plots of land.

At the time of the conquest, the Spanish crown assumed the right to distribute conquered lands and peoples as it saw fit. It rewarded the *conquistadores* with land grants and large estates, including the right of

---

2.   Claire Whittemore, *Land for People,* Oxfam Public Affairs Unit, Oxford, 1981, p.1.

control over indigenous settlements. This also included the right to receive tribute from the native population and allowed the new land owner to make use of the native population for labour and personal services. In return, the land owner was supposed to look after the spiritual welfare of the population and ensure they became Christians. This system was known as the *encomienda*.

After the initial conquest of the Indians by force, attempts were made in several countries to give legal protection to those who survived. The Indian communities were saved from complete extinction, but were driven into subsistence agriculture on the barren mountain slopes while the *conquistadores* took over the more fertile valleys and coastal lowlands.

As time passed the *encomiendas* gradually declined, but the system of labour duty persisted. Periodically labour was transferred from the native settlements to the mining, agricultural and public works of the Spanish.

However, as the Indian population declined, it became necessary to ensure a permanent labour force on the large estates. This was done by either taking over the Indian's subsistence plots, making them dependent on the large estates for survival, or by a system of debt peonage, which was a legal provision obligating a debtor to repay his debt through labour. It was frequently used to establish a permanent state of bondage. Where the Indian population were allowed to keep their communal or individual land rights, labour duty was still frequently used by the church and by local administrators and imposed on the community as a whole.

At the end of colonial rule, more and more members of the local *creole* elite (of pure Spanish ancestry) sought social status and wealth through control of the land, and continued the expropriation of Indian land. The Indians were once again incorporated into large estates where they received a subsistence plot in return for services and labour.

These service-tenure relations took a variety of forms and were given different names in different countries: *huasipungo* in Ecuador; *colonato* in El Salvador; *inquilinaje* in Chile, and *cambao* in Brazil. The labour involved was primarily agricultural, but the services required ranged from work in the house to providing daughters for the sexual pleasure of the landlord.

The system was usually enforced by violence or the threat of violence. The land owners worked closely with the local police, the military and the church. These three institutions dominated Latin American political and economic life for centuries, and, in many areas of Latin America they continue to wield enormous power.

The *latifundio-minifundio* system was thus established by force over the centuries. Its legitimacy, however, has never been accepted by most of the

Indian populations who lost their lands in the process. Periodic rebellions have occurred such as the one led by Tupac Amaru in the Andean highlands at the end of the 18th century. These rebellions have always been suppressed with considerable brutality.

Agrarian reform

By the end of the late 19th century changes began to occur as large scale commercial crop production was introduced, and wage labour gradually became the norm in many countries.

The "changes" were not beneficial to the peasants, however. They were evicted from their land and many peasants were forced to become landless labourers. Others became tenant farmers or small holders, paying rent for their land. In these cases, the plots were often so small, overworked and depleted that the peasants were forced into seasonal migration to sell their labour to the large cash crop plantations.

Even though the *latifundio* system has proven to be inefficient and unproductive, the land owners have always resisted any kind of agrarian reform, often aggravating the situation by leaving large parts of their estates idle, to ensure themselves a regular labour supply each year.

There have been attempts at agrarian reform in Latin America. In the four major revolutions — Mexico, 1910-17; Bolivia, 1952; Cuba, 1959; and Nicaragua, 1979 — agrarian reform was introduced. However, only in the latter two cases did a government come to power prepared to involve the peasants in the redistribution. In Cuba and Nicaragua, steps were also taken to ensure that infrastructural support was provided so that peasants could purchase equipment to improve the land and production.

Gerrit Huizer points to Mexico and Bolivia as examples of where the "effects of the more successful radical peasant movements were usually limited, in the end, after a new, middle-sector elite had established itself in power with peasant support."[3]

In Mexico a new type of commercial farming class has gradually emerged, taking advantage of greater access to credit and markets, while the majority of the peasants have fallen back into conditions not radically different from those before the revolution. In Bolivia, the reform merely succeeded in creating impoverished *minifundistas* lacking the financial and technical means to improve their productivity and standard of living.

————

3.   *Peasant Rebellion in Latin America*, Penguin, Harmondsworth, 1973

In other countries where agrarian reforms have been carried out, they have usually been introduced from above, aiming mainly at modernising the rural sector, expropriating some of the more traditional and inefficient land owners and encouraging them to invest their compensation in other areas of the economy. Rarely have the peasants themselves been involved in the process and rarely have their lives been greatly improved as a result of the "reform".

During the 20th century, the pressure on the land has increased tremendously, due to rapid population growth and the inadequacy of the land available to meet the needs of the mass of the rural population. Despite the large amount of fertile, arable land in Latin America, the agrarian sector is considered to be in crisis, and is unable to produce sufficient food for its population.

Most international development agencies have tended to attribute this to agricultural backwardness rather than to the unequal structures of land ownership. The Oxfam report criticises this approach:[4]

> "In the agricultural sector 'modernisation' is the key word . . . The implication is that until now the rural poor have been left behind in the process of modernisation. All that needs to be done is to draw them into it. In practice this is a self-defeating aim . . . Often modernisation itself makes them poorer by strengthening the resources of the rich."

In the 1950s and 1960s, encouraged by models of development put forward by several of the agencies, many land owners began to introduce labour-saving machinery on their estates. They also continued to commit increasing amounts of land to growing cash crops for export rather than to feeding the local population.

Thus lack of land and declining employment forced many thousands of peasants to migrate to the cities in search of a livelihood. These internal migrations continue today and Latin America is now the most urbanised region of the Third World.

Its cities show all the outward signs of modernity such as highways, skyscrapers, supermarkets and department stores, but in reality they are centres of poverty and deprivation. Dominated by foreign corporations, concentrating on capital intensive rather than labour intensive production, industrialisation has not kept pace with the rising population and the massive migration to the cities.

––––––

4.   Claire Whittemore, *op. cit.*, p.1

Many of the peasants who find their way to the cities are forced to eke out an existence as street vendors, shoe-shiners, servants and prostitutes. But even the slimmest possibility of survival in the city is considered a better bet than survival in the rural areas.

Women in Latin America

The position of women cannot be isolated from the wider circumstances in which they live. For Latin America as a region, and for each of the countries looked at in this book, an examination of the economic and political structures is essential to provide the background and understanding of the situation of Latin American women. The history of exploitation has created the forces still at work which relegate all Latin Americans, and particularly poor women and men, to their modern day state of servitude.

Women of all classes in Latin America are further affected by the particular values and stereotypes which assign them to an inferior position in society simply because they are women. In a region of the world where oppression is usually brutal and violent, the more subtle forms of oppression of one sex by another, even through affection and love, are rarely given much importance.

The Church in Latin America, on the one hand, has become a leading force in championing the cause of the poor. Traditionally, the power and influence of the Church had been used to support the status quo. However, this role has been increasingly challenged by priests who, working closely with the poor and oppressed, have come to support their efforts for social change. Liberation Theology, which stresses the Church's social and political role in addition to its spiritual function, has had a great impact on the Latin American church.

Some priests, such as Camilo Torres, killed fighting with the guerrillas in Colombia in 1967, have joined the armed struggle to fight for change, while others work through peasant and worker organisations. Some members of the hierarchy, such as Dom Helder Camara, Archbishop of Recife in Brazil and Archibishop Romero of El Salvador, who was assassinated by a right wing death squad in March 1980, have also taken the side of the poor.

When it comes to the women's struggle, however, the Church has continued to use its power and influence to reinforce and transmit traditional values which place women in a secondary role in society. In the Epistle to the Ephesians, St. Paul wrote: "The husband is the head of the wife, just as Christ is the head of the Church."

The image of the woman as passive, maternal, self-sacrificing and long-suffering has much to do with the Catholic Church and permeates Latin American culture and society. It reinforces the cult of the male known as *machismo* — that brand of sexism deeply rooted in the Latin culture that not only encourages, but also demands superior, aggressive and authoritarian behaviour from men, and general acceptance of this behaviour by women in all social classes.

Machismo has been more specifically defined as:[5]

> *"an expression — sometimes at the level of caricature — of the patriarchal system. It consists in establishing a certain superiority of men over women, by which men feel themselves to be privileged beings, both in society and in the family. This serves to consolidate a certain 'specialisation', a division of functions, attitudes, capacities and qualities which are then attributed to one sex or the other . . . Both implicitly and explicitly, women have been used to the advantage of men."*

Most women, as well as men, come to believe that their roles are somehow "natural" to them — the woman's place is in the home and she must defer to her husband in all matters outside it.

Within the family, women are in charge of the daily domestic chores and raising the children. They usually have some autonomy in this domain, but it is never translated into any kind of autonomous position in the wider world. Work in the house is not considered productive because it is not paid employment, even though through this, the women make a clear contribution to society. Their low-status work within the family is a cheap and effective way of reproducing and sustaining the labour force.

The legal structures and customs in Latin America perpetuate women's subordination. Divorce is rare in the region and, where it is allowed, it safeguards the interests of the men rather than the women. In order to qualify for alimony, for instance, a woman must usually show evidence of "good conduct". She must also usually wait a certain period of time before she can remarry. In any case, divorce proceedings are expensive, and therefore not available to poor women. In some of the poor urban and rural communities, legal marriage is a rarity. Here the women have no protection when, as frequently happens, they are left alone with their children, having been abandoned by their husbands for another woman.

Abortion is illegal throughout Latin America. Here again, the Church's

---

5.   Latin America and Caribbean Women's Collective, *Slaves of Slaves*, Zed Press, London 1980, p.7

powerful influence works against change. In spite of this, women continue to seek abortions. The yearly estimate in Mexico is 800,000 and in Colombia it is 280,000, even though in both these countries, women can be imprisoned for having an abortion. Most of these abortions are carried out in very unhygienic conditions. For Latin America as a whole 30% to 50% of all maternal deaths are from improperly performed abortions. The poor suffer particularly as they are unable to pay the price of a safe, even though illegal, abortion.

Birth control is a controversial issue in Latin America. This is because many birth control programmes launched by the American and international development agencies in the region are aimed primarily at direct population control rather than giving the woman the right to control her own fertility. The view behind these programmes is that underdevelopment and poverty are caused by population pressure, an analysis which blatantly ignores the part played by the developed countries themselves in creating underdevelopment. In addition to the political controversy surrounding a woman's right to choose, many birth control programmes have also gained reputations for testing unsafe contraceptives on poor Latin American women or for enforced sterilisation.

A recent report on women by the North American Congress on Latin America (NACLA) stated:[6]

> "Dalcon shields were distributed by (the U.S. government) Agency for International Development (AID) to Third World countries through agencies (like Planned Parenthood), despite knowledge of their dangers, until they were banned in the United States in 1974. AID still uses its channels to dump high estrogen-content birth control pills for drug companies that have found their US market reduced. And Depo-Provera[7], an injectible contraceptive known to cause myriad harmful side effects, including cancer, can be bought over the counter in Central America."

The Peace Corps, the US volunteer programme which sends out young Americans to work in the Third World, was expelled by the Bolivian government for its alleged activities in sterilising peasant women without their knowledge. The Peruvian government followed suit in 1974 for similar reasons.

———————

6.   North American Congress on Latin America, *Women in Latin America*, Vol. XIV, No.4, 1980, p.6

7.   The use of DP as a contraceptive is banned in the United States, and its use in the U.K. is restricted. For more information see *Depo-Provera*, Campaign Against Depo-Provera, London 1981.

The planning behind both international and domestic birth control programmes usually ignores the social and economic reasons for large families amongst the poor such as the high rate of infant mortality and the need for extra hands to contribute to the family's income.

Women's participation in the paid labour force is still very low. Only one in five women (20%) in Latin America, excluding the Caribbean, is part of the paid labour force. A study by the International Labour Organisation in 1970 showed that of those women who are in paid work, 17.4% are employed in agriculture, 20.3% in industry and 59.5% in services. The "service sector" is often no more than a euphemism for low-wage, non-unionised jobs such as street vending or domestic work. Women are rarely involved in union matters and their level of political participation, as members of the labour force is very low.

According to the NACLA report:[8]

> *"one-half of the women in the service sector, or one of every three women doing non-agricultural work are employed in domestic service. Latin America has the highest percentage of household employees in the world, and they are almost exclusively women . . . young migrant women predominate. Two out of every three migrant women wind up as servants."*

In fact, the high percentage of poor migrant peasant women working as servants is one way that other wealthier women are able to free themselves from domestic responsibilities.

Thus there is a sexual division of labour even outside the house. Women in the labour market are usually relegated to certain "female tasks". But while there are certain aspects of the role of women which affect women of all classes in both the urban and rural areas, it is clear that each of these groups also face very particular and different sorts of problems.

Peasant women

Most of the difficulties for Latin American women presented here so far are also experienced by the peasant women. But because they are poor, of the peasant class, they are further deprived of the satisfaction of basic human needs, as well as many more rights and freedoms.

The standard of living and the quality of life is very low for women, men and children living in the rural areas. Malnutrition, disease, lack of access to

---

8.   North-American Congress on Latin America, *op.cit.*, p.9

basic services such as clean water and electricity, lack of access to even the simplest educational and medical facilities are common to most Latin American peasants. But it is the women who suffer most. It is the woman's responsibility to ensure that her children are healthy, that there is enough food every day, to cure children of disease. The women, themselves, are physically very weak given their work load, pregnancies every 1½-2 years, breast feeding of newborn babies and generally low standards of nutrition.

According to the World Health Organisation, over half the people in the Third World do not have clean water to drink. Figures for rural Latin America are well in excess of that. In Guatemala, 84%; in Ecuador, 87%; in Peru, 83%, and in El Salvador, 66% of the rural population are without clean water.

In all of these countries it is the job of the women and young girls to provide the family with water. For all of them it means daily trips to the local source of water, often at great distance from the home.

Illiteracy figures for Latin America are higher for peasants and higher still for peasant women. Few peasant women can read and write. Because there has been little importance given to peasant women when information and statistics are gathered, exact figures are difficult to obtain.

The role of the peasant woman living in the rural mountainous regions of Latin America is clearly defined. The tasks she performs vary only slightly from country to country. She is involved in agricultural production as well as having the primary responsibility for domestic duties. She, alone, is responsible for the care and education of the children. But the man is recognised as the head of the house and makes all major decisions.

As the tendency towards growing cash crops for export has increased, peasant men now spend much of their time as wage labourers working away from the family plot. This leaves the peasant women solely responsible for the cultivation of their own small bit of land to feed the family. In spite of this essential role played by women in agricultural production, they are largely ignored by the development planners. It is the men who receive training, new technology and credit.

The women also contribute to the economy of the household by raising and selling small animals, the production of foodstuffs for local sale, and the production of handicrafts for sale on the tourist market. On the whole, women are ignored in this too, having to rely on traditional methods without access to time and labour saving devices.

Peasant women suffer further limitations in their activities outside of the home and agricultural duties. Their subordinate position in the home is translated to a parallel subordination in the wider sphere. The development of agricultural and craft-based cooperatives over the last two decades, particularly in the rural areas, has at least brought peasant women new opportunities to earn cash.

All cooperatives, functioning as legal trading entities, have to conform to a set of strict, complicated laws. These are different in every country and govern the type of management structure to be set up, the nature and constitution of committees, the distribution of financial resources and membership requirements, to name but a few legal specifications. Generally, however, the participation of women in any capacity other than as a worker is limited. Even as workers they are relegated to a subordinate position.

In Ecuador, for example, women are legally bound to obtain written permission from their husbands before they can join a cooperative as a full member. In Peru, only widows are considered eligible for full membership in agricultural cooperatives. All other women derive semi-member status through their husbands, or if unmarried, as a temporary worker. Whatever their status, they are always paid less, and are rarely elected to positions of responsibility or leadership.

In terms of the general community life, a woman's place is not in village meetings, not as a community or local leader, not having access to educational or further training facilities and not enjoying the full social life of the village. The low status accorded to the peasant woman and accepted by her, restricts her ability to contribute to the social, economic and political life of her society.

The facts of women's subordination were borne out in the difficult process of actually trying to arrange the interviews.

The Interviews

For most of the women I talked with, it was the first time that anyone, especially a foreigner, had specifically sought them out to ask what they thought, and how they felt about anything, let alone such a wide range of issues as we covered in the interviews. There had been visitors to their villages before, but very rarely were the women involved in these encounters. The official greetings, meetings and socialising all tended to be exclusively the concern of the men.

This was true, too in villages where women's courses and projects were being run. Even the initiatives for establishing women's projects often came from the men in the community. The men would perform the official opening and closing ceremonies; they would receive the visitors, show them around, and then present them to the women. The men were almost always present during the courses.

If the husbands were around when I arrived, as was usually the case, I had to ask their permission, even before asking the women if they would agree to talk to me. In fact, the second request was sometimes superfluous, since if the husband said, "yes, all right," that was it ... the interview was arranged with no more discussion or decisions to be taken, whether the woman wanted to do it or not.

Speaking to the women without their husbands was not easy. The men were both eager to "join in" and reluctant to leave the women alone with me. I used to explain quite openly that it would be better to talk to the women alone, because if the men were present, the women would say nothing. I could direct all my questions to the women, but the answers would always come from the men. The more enlightened amongst the men would nod their heads seriously and agree, "Yes, that's true". But they still didn't want to leave us alone.

After some difficult treading of the fine line between joking insistence and rudeness, and because I was a crazy *gringa* (foreigner), the men would reluctantly agree. We would be left alone, or remove ourselves to another location.

One man reappeared at the doorway to his house every 15 minutes to see if we needed him, the unstated question being, "how could we manage without him?" The fourth time, afraid of being rude, and possibly causing difficulties for his wife, I said that we had finished. He came in and proceeded to dominate the conversation from that point on. She did not say another word.

In group situations, too, all the women would stop in mid-sentence if a man appeared within earshot; and they often did, as they were curious to see what was going on. I was always the one who had to ask them to leave.

There were similar problems with young girls and their mothers, and young women with older women. Several times, I had quite open conversations with young, unmarried girls of about 15 or 16, or young, married women, until the mothers or older women came to join us. The younger girls and women would then say either nothing or exactly the opposite of what they had been saying to me. And all women, regardless of age, stopped talking or lowered their voices to an almost inaudible whisper, if we were discussing birth control and another woman appeared.

A Peruvian woman told me at length about her lack of confidence in friends and neighbours:

> *"Not unless you really trust someone will you talk to them about things like this. And it is very rare here, to be able to trust someone. Because, for example, I might have confidence in a* señora, *and I*

will tell her everything. And tomorrow, she might go and tell everything to another woman.

"And even a sister of mine. She thought that I had taken something not to have any more children. 'Well, really,' I said, 'honestly, I haven't taken anything. I don't know about things like that.' 'Well,' she said, 'why don't you have more children?' 'Ah,' I said, 'I don't know why.' I couldn't really take her into my confidence, and tell her that we just didn't have relations."

Time was often a problem too. The women were working from the moment they got up very early in the morning, until they went to bed at night. Sitting with me for one or two hours was a luxury that was difficult to justify. Occasionally, in order to interview cooperative members, I paid the hourly rate to the cooperative so that the women would not lose money for having taken time off.

Other discussions took place while women cooked, spun, wove, knitted, worked in their fields, led their animals to pasture, tended sick children, did their buying and selling in the market, or washed clothes, dishes and children. I talked and listened to women wherever and whenever possible. We were almost always surrounded by at least three or four babies and very young children, and often the older children of the family as well. It was difficult as the women didn't want to talk about subjects such as marriage and birth control with the older children present. They also could not talk for more than a few minutes without being disturbed by the younger ones. Conditions were rarely easy.

Because so few rural Indian women in Guatemala, Ecuador, Peru and Bolivia speak Spanish, (they speak their Indian language), I would occasionally have to use translators. But this was unsatisfactory. If translators were men, not known well by the women, this obviously inhibited the freedom and range of the conversation we could have. But even with female interpreters, there were difficulties. If the interpreters were of the professional class, from the city, their prejudices and the peasant women's feelings of inferiority prohibited an open exchange. And, at the same time, the interpreters provided me with their personal analysis of the women's comments, so I was never really certain what had been said by whom. If a local *campesina* (peasant woman) did the interpreting, we would occasionally have the problem of women not wanting to speak openly in front of someone from their own village.

As a result of these circumstances most of my conversations were restricted to women who not only spoke Spanish, but who were also not afraid to talk to me. The two factors usually operated together, as women who spoke Spanish often had more contact with people from outside the village.

The interviews were sometimes painful for both of us. These women wanted to talk to me. They wanted to be able to tell me what they felt, and find out about me. But many times, because of their difficulties with the Spanish language, particularly the Guatemalan women, they would only repeat apologetically that they did not know, or they had nothing to say, and maybe I should talk to their husbands after all.

It was suggested to me more than once, however, that being a foreigner was an advantage, in that my relationships with the women were not hampered by the traditional class barriers. Peruvian *campesinas*, for example, would not talk openly to another Peruvian woman whom they did not know well, especially were she middle-class, well-educated and from the city. The fear of being laughed at would always be there.

But the real difficulties arose from the nature of the discussion we were having. Questions about how women see themselves, what kind of changes they'd experienced, or changes they thought were important — whether general or specific — brought long pauses. It wasn't the language barrier that caused the problem, but rather the concepts quite alien in manner and substance to the way that most of the women thought.

Most peasant women tend not to look at themselves in terms of independence, rights and freedoms, much less think about change and choice for themselves as women.

And to talk of change and choice in a situation where people are operating daily on a penny economy, where children cannot go to school for lack of a pencil and notebook, where children die from malnutrition and little or no access to health services is, on the face of it, somewhat absurd. For many women, the only "choice" they have, is who they will marry, and when; and for some, even that choice is not theirs.

But I did meet women who had become leaders, and who had strong opinions about the situation of women . . . women who emphasised the need for others to develop their self-confidence and to begin to take on responsibilities outside the domestic duties of the home.

My role, my intervention, posed a dilemma for me most of the time. Was I raising issues of interest to me as a feminist from a developed country which were not of major concern to these peasant women?

It often seemed that if I did not raise certain issues such as wife-beating, relations in the home, or men's attitudes to women, the subjects might not have come up as often as they did. But once the women realised I did have some knowledge and understanding of their reality, they spoke very openly.

To them, I was a slightly crazy *gringa* — an oddity — a 33-year old single woman with no children, travelling on her own, in a society where rural women marry in their mid to late teens, have five or six children by the time they are 30 and rarely go anywhere on their own. They were always curious about me and women in "my country" . . . how did we live, what work did we do, why did we have so few children, what were the men like, what could I teach them, why wasn't I married, where was my mother?

They showed a tremendous affection towards me. Whatever the problems in understanding each other, whether due to words or ways of thinking, we seemed to make contact for the short time we were together. I found in them a real vitality and strength. We laughed a lot, and they would often say how much they enjoyed the conversation because they never had a chance to talk about the kinds of issues we covered.

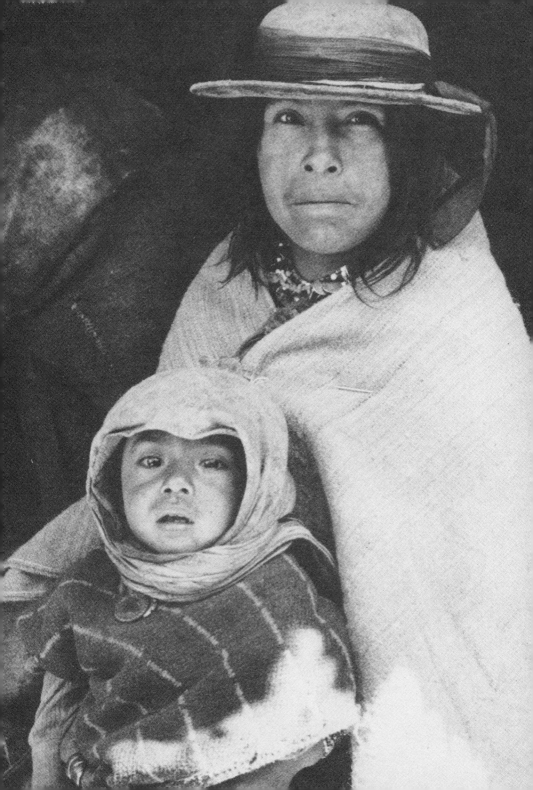

"The women are the heroes . . . in the sense of being mothers and raising a family. To be able to endure seeing so many of your children getting sick and suffering — that takes a lot of courage."
— Margarita, president of a cooperative

ECUADOR

Ecuador is a small Andean country deriving its name from the Equator, which passes a few miles to the north of the capital, Quito. Before the Spanish conquest, it was part of the Inca Empire. Today, Indians make up roughly half the population of eight million.

Ecuador gained its independence from Spain in 1822, but like the rest of Latin America, it did not gain economic independence at the same time. From the 19th century to the present, Ecuador has gone through a series of "boom and bust" cycles corresponding to world demand for the particular commodity it was exporting at the time.

From the end of the 19th century to the 1920s this was cocoa. Competition from alternative sources of supply helped force down prices and this was followed by the Great Depression in the 1930s which led to a fall in demand and a severe crisis in the economy.

In the 1940s, there was a banana boom which lasted until the late 1950s when the US banana companies which controlled production turned to cheaper sources of supply. Nevertheless, banana exports still make an important contribution to Ecuador's export earnings.

In the 1970s, the most recent boom came with the discovery of oil in the eastern (*Oriente*) region. This is now the country's main export earner.

The ups and downs of the Ecuadorean economy are reflected in the country's turbulent political history which includes at least 14 military coups since independence. They also contributed to the rise to power of

Velasco Ibarra, a populist, demagogic leader who dominated Ecuadorean politics for four decades.

He appeared on the political scene in the 1930s, basing his power on the emerging group of migrants, mainly Indians from the highlands, who could no longer survive on their small plots. They flooded into Ecuador's cities in the Depression years to find work in the service sector or in street vending. Velasco came to power five times between 1932 and 1972 but each time proved incapable of solving the country's socio-economic problems and was overthrown by a military coup.

Land ownership

One of the key elements in Ecuador's political development is the power of the large land owners. Despite land reform efforts in the 1960s and 1970s, the land tenure system is characterised by inequality. A mere 5% of farms occupy 52% of land.

Large scale agriculture for export dominates, with much of the best land in the coastal regions being used for banana, cocoa, rice and coffee cultivation. In the highlands, or *sierra*, subsistence or semi-subsistence farming prevails on small plots — the *minifundia*. Here the main crops are potatoes and barley for local consumption.

As in other Latin American countries, from the time of the Spanish conquest, land began to be concentrated in the hands of the new colonists, with the Indian population used as virtual slave labour. It was not until 1918 that the *concertaje*, a form of bonded slavery, was abolished in Ecuador. It was replaced by the *huasipungo* system, where land owners gave the Indians small subsistence plots, usually of poor quality, in return for work on the landlords' fields.

The *huasipungo* was finally abolished in 1964 by the military junta which came to power in the previous year. The junta had a developmentalist strategy aimed at attracting foreign investment, giving incentives to industry and introducing tax reforms. At the same time, it repressed the workers and peasants who demanded real, structural reforms.

It was a strategy promoted by the United States in the hopes that sufficient reforms from above would prevent revolution from below. Known as the Alliance for Progress, it was developed in response to the Cuban revolution.

The nature of the objectives help explain why the agrarian reform hardly touched the unequal distribution of land in Ecuador. Only those lands which had been abandoned for 10 years or more were subject to expropriation. The result was to create a mass of *minifundia* on which survival was extremely precarious. By 1968, an estimated 40% of Ecuador's total population was dependent on *minifundia* production.

The preservation of traditional land ownership patterns has created problems for the Ecuadorean economy. The *latifundios*, or large estates, are extremely inefficient and unproductive and the country has a serious problem of inadequate food production.

A military government which took power in 1972 under General Rodriguez Lara, again made the commitment to agrarian reform and a programme of modernisation. The land owners immediately rallied to defend their own interests, accusing the government of "communist infiltrations". Peasants and workers also began to organise to demand an effective reform.

When the reform was announced in October 1973, it was again a disappointment. The land owners were too powerful, and the other wealthy classes, such as the coastal planters and the newly emerging industrial class were all unwilling to challenge the power of land holders in case it resulted in the sharing of their own privileges with the poor. In 1976, Lara was overthrown by a right-wing military coup.

Although the 1973 law did not improve the position of the peasantry, it did herald the modernisation of many large estates into more productive enterprises using machinery rather than Indian labour, thus creating further problems of rural unemployment.

Faced with little prospect of producing enough food on their own tiny plots, and little work in the rural areas, many of the peasants have been forced into migration to the coastal regions in search of temporary work on the plantations. Some have gone to the *Oriente* region, where large areas of virgin land have encouraged settlement. However, lack of both resources and legal title to the land have made this an insecure existence. A more permanent form of migration has taken place to the main towns, particularly Quito and Guayaquil, as the peasants look for work in the cities.

Lara's government had plans to use the country's oil wealth to develop industries. Industrial production grew by 14% between 1973 and 1974, but foreign capital quickly penetrated the industrial sector. This has led to the establishment of capital intensive industries which are inappropriate to the country's growing unemployment problem. The dependency on foreign imports of machinery and technology to develop industries suits the needs of foreign interests, but does little to improve domestic unemployment.

The working class did grow during these years. Like the peasantry, it was badly hit by the rapidly rising cost of living, particularly of food costs in the early 1970s, as the oil boom benefitted the already wealthy. By 1972, the total earnings of the top 1.8% of the population equalled those of the bottom 79%. Because of the increased demand for consumer goods, foreign controlled manufacturing within the country also increased. The accompanying inflation worsened the living standards of the rural and urban majority.

In 1976, the most radical sector of the working class formed a trade union confederation — Central Ecuatoriana de Organizaciones Clasistas (CEDOC), whose main affiliate was the National Federation of Peasant Organisations (FENOC). In 1977, 150,000 workers and peasants participated in a general strike which called for 50% wage increases, the nationalisation of oil and the implementation of an agrarian reform. The strike was met by heavy repression. In October of the same year, 120 sugar workers at the Aztra mill were killed when police attacked a demonstration.

Nine years of military dictatorship ended in June 1979 with the election of the social democrat, Jaime Roldos. Roldos was later killed in an air crash in 1981 and his vice-president, Oswaldo Hurtado took over. Although Roldos came to power on a programme of reform, the conservatives control Congress, and few of the promised reforms have so far materialised. The intolerance of the wealthy elite to a redistribution of wealth in favour of the workers and peasants, coupled with the influence of the military, makes real change "from above" unlikely. But at least under the civilian government, the peasants and workers have been able to organise more freely. This will be important in future struggles.

Position of women

In the Ecuadorean highlands the extended family, (usually husband and wife, married and unmarried children and perhaps a nephew or niece), is the basis for subsistence production. Women play an important role within the family both in production as well as reproduction. They are involved in all aspects of the work: weeding, sowing, and harvesting as well as looking after the animals.

Few women are wage earning workers, although under the old *huasipungo* system, women would provide certain services, such as labour in the fields or milking cows for the land owner in return for the subsistence plot. Despite the introduction of machinery for many functions and the modernisation of many estates, land owners continue to employ milk maids, (although in the most modern estates they will operate milking machinery) and they are paid a small remuneration. A few women are brought into the market economy in that way.

Another way is through the marketing of any small surplus from the family plot. There has been a noticeable increase in the number of former *huasipunueras* marketing their products. Produce is usually sold to a middle man or retailer in the nearest village, and it is usually the wealthier peasant women who go most frequently to sell at the market place. In addition to this, women complement the family's subsistence income through income generating activities which vary from region to region. Most of the women interviewed were involved in handicraft production, or localised cottage industries.

Economic changes within the country have in many ways increased the importance of women's work on the family plot. The men will often migrate to the large estates or to the cities in search of work. Usually only younger, single women will undertake the move to the city, looking for work as servants. This leaves the married women in charge of the plot and all the activities necessary to sustain the extended family. This contribution of the peasant woman, or rather her maintenance of the subsistence economy, is often neglected by development planners who place the emphasis on involving men in projects for increased production.

Peasant women face further barriers to development. Statistics show that rural women are less well educated than rural men. Illiteracy is a critical problem in rural areas of Ecuador. A government sponsored report in 1977 showed that illiteracy amongst rural Ecuadorean men was 38.4% and amongst women 60.7%. And, too, it is the women who bear responsibility for the children and have to confront most directly the problems of malnutrition, disease and inadequate health care facilities, endemic in the rural areas.

Awareness of the specific problems of women has been growing in Ecuador although the women's movement is still mainly concentrated in the urban centres. In 1980, the Union of Women Workers (UMT), an affiliate of CEDOC, held its first congress. Part of its programme is aimed at incorporating women workers into trade union struggles, centering its demands around day care centres in factories and equal opportunities at work. The UMT is also making attempts to organise peasant women, trying to create an awareness and understanding of the economic and political factors shaping their lives.

ECUADOR

The country:
Area: 283,520 sq. km.
Main cities:
  Capital: Quito (pop. 600,000)
  Guayaquil (pop. 1 million)
  Cuenca (pop.. 105,000)

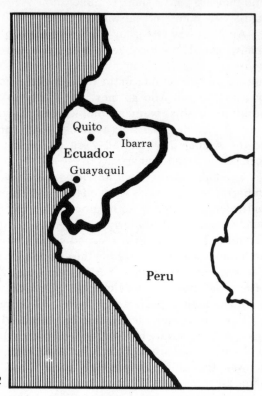

The people:
Population: 8,021,000 (1980)
  Women: 4 million (mid-1980)
Rural: 59%
Annual rate of population growth:
  3.3%
Race: 45% Indian, 40% mestizo, 10%
  European, remainder black or Asian
Language: Spanish, but Quechua spoken
  amongst Indians

Social indicators:
Life expectancy at birth: women, 62
  years; men, 58 years
Infant mortality rate: 83/1000 live
  births, 0-1 year
**Population without access to clean
  water:** rural, 87%; urban, 18%
Population without sanitation: rural,
  89%; urban, 37%
Adult illiteracy: women, 30%; men,
  22%

The economy:
Gross National Product: US $7 billion
  GNP per capita: US $880 (1978)
Distribution of Gross Domestic Production:
  (1978)
  Services: 44%
  Industry: 35%
  Agriculture: 21%
  Manufacturing: 17%
Economically active population (aged 15+):
  51.5% (1970)
  Women as % of total labour force: 21% (1980)
  Women employed in agriculture: 16% (1975)

The government:
Civilian constitutional rule
Central government expenditure: (1979)
  Education: 31% of total budget
  Public health: 9.3%

NO MEN ALLOWED

Rio Negro was a pioneer town settled in the 1930s as part of the peasant move to the east in search of land. The long, dusty main street was one of the four routes to the jungle, about five hours further east by road. All day and night, buses and lorries rattled through the town, and in almost every doorway, there was always someone watching the world go by. When the noise of the traffic subsided, the thunder of the river could be heard as it passed through one side of the town at the foot of the mountains surrounding the village.

Seven years earlier, the main crop of the area, a fruit called *naranjilla*, had been completely wiped out by disease. So most of the families living there had had to make two starts in life; the first when they came to stake out their land to settle the village, and the second, 30 years later, when the main source of income failed.

Now, over a dozen women were making a third start by establishing a co-operative to produce and sell marmalade from the guava fruit, still in abundance in the area. With the help of a woman Peace Corps volunteer, who suggested a "no men in the group" policy, the women were well-organised, enthusiastic and in the process of applying for grants to build their own small factory. They had been using the kitchen of one of the members, but needed to expand their production. They were at the same time negotiating with the local authority to set up a kiosk at the side of the road, to sell to travellers going to and from the jungle.

This was the first group I'd met with a clearly stated policy of discriminating against men. Most of the women felt that it was a good idea in order to create the kind of safe environment needed for women to participate. This "isolationist" approach, quite common in the women's movement in the developed world, but almost unheard of in rural Ecuador, gave rise to much comment about *machismo*, and its own particular brand of oppression.

> *"For me, the cooperative is neither a step forward, nor a step backward. I want to get involved but my husband doesn't want me to spend time working there. He wants me here in the house. He arrives home, and the minute he arrives, he wants his food; he wants to be served. And if not, he shouts and gets very angry. The*

only time I can go out is on Sundays. I sometimes go and sell the
marmalade in the markets. He doesn't seem to mind so much then
because he is resting. But I can't really earn much doing that
becasue I only earn a percentage of what I sell, not an hourly wage.

"Other women I know have trouble with their husbands, who say
they have to stay home with the children."

Anna-Maria, 28 years old, four children.

Another woman had her own view of what the women's movement might
mean for people in Ecuador:

"Here in Ecuador, we don't have what do you call it — this women's
liberation. That is what we lack in Ecuador (laughing) — liberation
of the women. I think it is a good idea — most of it. But it depends on
what you do, and how you do it. Because some people say that this
women's liberation . . . means that the wives beat their husbands or
that the wives give the orders instead of the husband. I think that
would be a bad idea. The way that I think is the Christian way. It
says that the man is the head of the house, and the head of the wife.
That is what the Church says . . . the way that Christ was the head
of all the disciples."

Margarita was the founder and president of the cooperative. She moved to Rio Negro when she was 11, with her parents and seven brothers and sisters.

She finished primary school, but wasn't able to attend secondary school. The school was in another town, and her mother would not let her leave the village on her own. So Margarita stayed in Rio Negro, and went to a sewing school for two years. She left early, one year before graduating, to get married.

She is in her late 30s and has three children.

I know my work with the cooperative is a sacrifice to my family. It takes me away from them, but it's important to work and survive with your own force.

I don't know what the others feel, but I think that some of the others don't have the same drive to work — no matter what happens. It was me who had the idea to put up the kiosk to sell marmalade to the tourists and people passing through the town. And I said that if no one else wanted to do it, I'd run it. I want to work. To be able to work, for anyone here, but especially for a woman, is wonderful.

With the cooperative, we haven't had a big economic benefit. In time, I know it will grow. I hope it will be strong enough to involve more women in the village. It would be wonderful to have all the women here working.

My notion is to give courage to all women so they could move forward and stop thinking they are less than other human beings. We are always in the position of serving — if not in one way, then in another. A way to play another role is to fulfill yourself through work. The first thing I would like to do is create sources of work so that the women could be more . . . so they could work.

I think that if a woman is working, and earning some money, her husband won't have to look after her completely. Knowing this makes a big difference. That is a large part of the problem . . . that the man works and the woman lives only to bear children and eat.

That is why so many women are so submissive and timid, not only outside the home, but inside too. Because the day that the husband decides not to give her any money for food, they would all die of hunger. So we must work to be able to have our own way of sharing the responsibility of the family. Then the men can't behave like our bosses . . . we are stronger women.

If the women themselves see they are earning and helping to earn, they too have the right to say: "Well, it isn't just you sacrificing to support the family . . . I am sacrificing too — so why do you treat me like this, like your servant? I am your wife, and you should respect me." In some houses, the women are treated just like slaves — they even have to wash their husband's feet.

Of course, you have to do all your work in the house. That's the woman's job, but it isn't her job to be ordered about by the man like a servant. Each has to fulfill their obligations, but there should be understanding, discussion and agreement. But some women can't do anything — only the men have rights.

It is still the man who is in charge. He is the head of the house. That is the way our beloved country is. My house is a little different — we are like a mutual society — my husband and I. If I say something, and he doesn't agree, he will explain or show me why. And then we discuss it. But we are lucky to have this understanding . . . it is an equality.

We both believe that I am worth as much as him, and vice versa. I don't have to make up for being a woman. I don't feel I am worth more or less.

My mother was always very happy at home. I could say that she was my example. Because my father respected my mother . . . and they both had the same idea . . . that they should share the responsibility of the family. So I must have learned it from them.

Everyone is different — it depends on each person. There are some women who are very strong — and they don't care about anything. But in general, women are — well the men are more powerful. We are more feminine, possibly weaker.

But in the sense of being mothers, and raising a family, we are much more courageous — to be able to endure seeing so many of your children going without good food, getting sick, and suffering — that takes a lot of courage. The women are the heroes. The fathers usually don't concern themselves with this. Very rare is the father who will think, "I must go and look after my daughter because she is sick." It is always the mother. It seems impossible for the men to be able to do this. But when you are poor, as a woman, you have to be able to withstand a lot. It is very difficult, when the man doesn't have regular work, and only earns a small amount daily. It is your job to try to manage with what he earns.

Some of the husbands are in agreement with the cooperative. They help and collaborate with us. Some of them though, cause trouble. One day we were in a meeting, and one of the husbands was passing by. His wife hid behind the door. It was funny, but I felt sad and it bothered me. I said to her, "This isn't good. I don't agree that you should come here and have to hide behind the door. I don't know how we are going to resolve this. Either you stay or go — one or the other." She said that it wasn't his fault, but her fault because she was so timid and she was afraid that he would be angry.

So I went to see him. He wasn't there, but I said to his mother — she still has a lot of influence over him — I tried to make her see and understand what we were trying to do. I said that we weren't earning a lot, but we had hopes for the future. And I tried to explain what his wife could lose just because of his whims and ideas.

Shortly after, I saw him, and he said that he wasn't the problem . . . that the problem was the children. He got very angry and said that she couldn't carry on because of the children.

But he must have changed his mind — because he sends her now. He said, "There is a meeting. Why haven't you gone." And she said, "Well, I knew you were coming back, and if I wasn't here when you got here . . . " And he said, "Ah, you should have gone and not worried about it." I don't know why he changed his mind — I have no idea. He supports us now . . . not a great deal . . . but he doesn't cause trouble like before. Before, she couldn't cook with the rest of us . . . she couldn't do anything.

We don't have too many problems with the others. Sometimes they get angry because the women will spend the day here, cooking and packing the marmalade instead of being at home. But they still don't understand what we are trying to do.

About a week ago, a few women were complaining about their husbands, and I said, "You have to explain to your husbands that we aren't trying to teach the women to be different — to be less obedient. We are trying to learn and do something to make life better for our children — for the family."

We have been thinking of calling a meeting for all the husbands to talk to them and see whether they are willing to support us or not. I want to know what they think and whether they will agree to have their wives working.

In the meetings we've had — you look at how much you spend going to school or college — or to send your children to learn something — and we are learning free of charge — all kinds of useful things. I've said to all the women — for example, the two that are learning book keeping — they are learning something here — how much would it cost them and how many years of study to learn something like that? It is a great benefit to everyone to learn about business.

I've tried to explain to the women that what we are doing is like a school — and we are learning things that, really, even the men don't know. They will be better educated than their husbands. Still each one is more timid than the next, but little by little they are moving along. Now they talk. Before, some of the women wouldn't open their mouths. It is good for us to be united and working together. Someone puts an idea forward, and you learn from each other.

The men aren't the problem really. As soon as they realise that the woman is actually bringing money into the house, they would understand. The problem is the children. Because of the way things are here, we don't have a nursery where we could leave the children. It is essential, but the women believe that the children will be badly looked after if they are left in a place like that. But it doesn't have to be a young girl whom they don't trust . . . it could be one of the women themselves. You must have something like that if mothers are going to work.

People are quite far behind too in the area of birth control. I think the husbands must be a large part of the problem. They don't have any understanding with their wives so that they could talk to each other. If they did, they could both go to a doctor and learn how to avoid children.

They have crazy ideas — many of the husbands. It isn't a problem for me . . . my husband is a good man. But I have heard that — well — they are really very *macho* here. They think they are such "big men" that they can support all the children their wives have. They are very jealous and think that if the women don't carry on having children, they won't obey the way the men want.

One of the women in the cooperative has that problem with her husband — the young one with nine children. She wants to look after herself and he says no. After this last child she had, I told her that I would loan her the money to go and visit a doctor to arrange for some kind of control. Everyone is afraid of doing anything here in the village, so you have to go somewhere else.

She spoke to her husband, but he said that he didn't want her to use anything because she might get cancer. I think that the men are, in fact, really afraid of cancer, but only in part. They use it as an excuse so their wives won't use anything. If he is really afraid for her, he should suggest that she has an operation. That is the most feasible way of doing it without having more problems. They are very poor and they have so many children.

I know there are operations for men too, but no one here would ever suggest that, and much less do it. There is one case of a man here who had the operation. He is single. But I think that is a very rare example. The men won't let their wives have an operation like that and they would certainly never have it themselves . . . not in a country like ours.

When I was thinking of trying not to have any more children, I went to the priest and he said that the Church still doesn't give its agreement to this, but in the circumstances, he thinks it is up to each individual's conscience what to do. He said, "You are a responsible mother, and you think that you don't want any more children . . . it is only between you and your conscience. It depends on how you think. If you are thinking that you don't want more children because you don't want to serve your husband as a wife . . . and you want to abandon him and live a free life . . . if that is the way you are thinking, not even God will consent to that. But if you are only thinking of your family, then it is all right."

I want my three children to have a profession, so they can earn their way in life. These days you must study to make it through life. The only inheritance we can give them is the chance to study and learn.

You have been travelling and talking to women in other countries, and you live in a country where there have been improvements for women. How can we organise better — how can we understand people better? How can we move on from where we are, so that people have a dynamism to be able to work — to want to work? We need help in so many things — mainly in an understanding of people. Because sometimes you think that you understand and know someone, but most often you really don't know the depth of their ideas, and you are often deceived.

It is a real problem if you are going to try and work in a cooperative. Of course, everyone has a certain character that they show to everyone else . . . but how do you really understand? For example, my *compañeras* (comrades) — most of them like to work, and work hard, but the problem is that they believe we are all going to have tremendous gains from the cooperative now — in their lifetime. They still don't understand that we all have to work — we all have to cooperate so that something successful will result eventually. And they also seem to think that someone else is the boss, and that they should be paid just like any ordinary worker.

I suppose I am guilty of the same thing, because I am already losing hope. I am thinking . . . I want them to change after only a few months. I want them all to say now, "Well, this is our cooperative." I have said to them, "This belongs to all of us. Suppose I go — I won't take this with me . . . it stays with you. It is as much yours as mine. So why don't you have the same interest in working now for future benefit or our families?"

They think that all they have to do is the cooking or the packing. They don't worry about all the other things we have to do — all the legal problems, trying to get the kiosk and the land. There are always problems. No one really wants to hurt anyone else, but one little wrong word, and people are angry with each other. And one *compañera* will start to resent another.

If there were — if we had — well, we have to organise . . . but you need a lot of patience for that. What is important is that all the *compañeras* have that patience — and know how to carry on. I would like us to have more talks about *cooperativismo*. I believe very strongly in this way of working together — but it is very difficult. We have taken on a difficult task.

It is more difficult because here . . . well . . . perhaps in other societies, there are changes. But here, for the *campesino*, there is no change at all. And that is more true for the women. We are carrying on the way it has always been — like in the olden times. I think that in the cities there is probably a better understanding of this "women's liberation".

Without a fundamental understanding of the principles involved, something like this "liberation" becomes . . . well, ignorance and lack of understanding. It means that some people want to talk about liberation of the women . . . but all they mean is amusement.

I went to see some women friends, and they said, "No, don't be silly . . . now there is no problem. We have this women's liberation now. Why are you going to stay and wait until your husband arrives . . . let's go . . . finished." But this way of doing things without any real kind of understanding about the meaning of women's liberation will only fail. If my husband thinks it is just so I can go and have more fun, he won't understand and he will be against it . . . and there would be problems like there are in a lot of homes.

Señora Carmen was not a member of the cooperative,
although she ran a small business buying crates of guava
fruit from local women who went up the mountain to pick it.
She then resold it to the cooperative or other buyers, making
a small profit.

Although her husband worked full-time as a labourer,
she was the primary income earner in the family. She had
one of the several small general stores in Rio Negro, selling
drinks, sweets, tinned goods and household supplies. Another
of her sidelines was making bread and cheese which she also
sold in the shop.

She was 47, had been married for 30 years and had nine
children. With the eldest being 30, and the youngest only six,
family planning had always been a problem for her. She
began to talk about her unsuccessful efforts to have fewer
children.

I had two failures. There was a doctor here who did the cure for not having children. He charged me 1,300 sucres (£26), and the next month I was pregnant. I went to complain, and he said that it wasn't possible — but I was pregnant. Then I went to another doctor — a woman doctor, and she charged me the same amount and I had lots of injections, but the next month, I was pregnant again and I went to complain to her, too. She said that it wasn't possible. I said, "Look, I have had eight children. Do you think I don't know when I am pregnant?"

She said, "Wait and see for a couple of months." After that I didn't go back for any more treatments. But I did have to pay both times. I said that they should give me my money back because I didn't get the results I paid for. But they said that it must have been the wrong time for the first injection, or something like that — but what did I pay her for? If I had only known about this first injection, then I wouldn't have had the last two.

There was a time when one of the doctors wanted to put coils in everyone. He said that all the women should have them. He said they were very good, and not dangerous, and that everyone should have them. He even convinced me to have one. But I got an inflammation inside and I went right away to the other doctor. The other doctor said it wasn't good to give them to everyone, because some people couldn't use them, and that sometimes they gave you cancer. And he took it out.

A few women here use the pills. I used to use the pills . . . but I had terrible headaches. My head hurt all the time . . . and I told the doctor that I wasn't going to take them any more. The doctor said I should have the operation, but I was afraid of what it might do to me, so I didn't have it. I have had so much trouble trying not to have children, and I still had nine.

The doctor said there were some methods where you didn't have to take any pills. You just had to count the days of your menstruation — and there were some safe days. He gave me a book about it. Since then, I haven't taken any pills and I am still fine. Now I am 47, and I don't know if I could still have children or not. They say that when your period doesn't come, there is no danger of having children, so maybe I will be safe.

It is always the mother who suffers. The men don't have much interest in all this, and they certainly don't worry about it. The one who has to face the situation, and put up with it all is the mother.

For women, there really isn't anything more than having a family. If their fate is to get married, then they will get married.

Here there aren't many girls over 20 who aren't married. Most marry at 18 or 19. Sometimes it is because of the neglect of the parents; sometimes the carelessness of the girl herself. It would be better to have some work that the girls could do, but they are with their boyfriends so young . . . and then married . . . and then children.

When I came here — when my father brought me here, I was 14. I thought I would be equal with my older brother, but I had a very hard life. I didn't know my way around here; I didn't know anyone.

They used to send me to the hills to collect the *naranjilla* with a machete. It was 1½ hours from here, and I didn't know the way. I hadn't been to school much . . . only up to the third grade. I wanted to study more, but I couldn't. My parents were very poor. There wasn't any school or anything here, so I had to go and work in the fields.

I didn't know what else to do besides get married. It was almost a whim . . . It was the only way I had to get out of the house. So I did what I didn't really want to do . . . and I got married at 18. That is the way that life frightens you; the way it makes you suffer.

I have said to my daughters that they should enjoy the life of a single person while they can, and that really, it would be better to be single. I say that is what would be preferable, but real life is a different thing. I can tell my daughters things, but girls are always the same, and when they get things into their heads, you can't tell them anything. You can try to make them see, but that is all.

A woman's life is like a slave's life. The men have much more freedom. I want all my children to be able to study . . . and especially the girls. I want them to study something they like, and want to do. Because here, the women never know anything — about life, or other ways of living. They never learn anything, and they never know anything.

Before, our parents never used to think that it was important for their children, boys or girls, to do anything other than work on the mountain in the *chacra* (fields) with their parents. But now, the parents are thinking that they don't want the same thing happening to their children as happened to them.

I think that my daughters should know something about sewing, or embroidery . . . something that they can work in . . . if they want to go to live somewhere else, so they can earn a living. It would have been better if they could have studied to be a book keeper or a nurse, but we didn't have enough money for that. So at least if they know how to sew, they can make shirts and dresses and sell them. It really is the only thing for women to do here in the village.

I don't really have any hope for me that my life is going to change. Maybe for my daughters. That's why I said it was so important for them to have work outside of the house — to know something about how to help themselves. The one thing I have never known how to do is sew . . . it might have been different if I could have done that. Because if you can do that, you can earn your way. You can do repairs; you can make shirts; you can sell dresses — up to 120 sucres (£2.40), these days. Then you have something to go forward with.

It's a different system for the boys . . . for the men — it's different from women because of the suffering that women go through in life. I think it might have been better to be a man. (She laughed.)

The man leaves the house, goes to his work. He can find work more easily. A man goes where he wants, and finds work, and they pay him . . . even though it isn't very much. He can even get a job as a *cargador* (stevedore) to earn money.

A woman can't do that. You have to look for a house to work in, and you have to be careful, because in some houses, the people aren't very nice. If the girl is very young, and sincere, and not very wide awake or aware, it is worse — because there is no one to look after her. People will certainly take advantage of her.

When the men come home from their work at night, everything has to be ready for them . . . everything in the house done. Women have to be in the house all day, washing, cooking, ironing . . . all the things we have to do and look after so many children too. But the men go . . . without worrying too much about what is happening in the house . . . if the children have clothes or not.

It is always the same here . . . the men have luck in finding work and the women don't. But it is true for the men too, that unless they study something that will give them a profession . . . the only thing they can do is work in the fields. Of all my children, only one is in college — in Quito — and that is because he is living with my brother. I haven't been able to send all my children to study . . . so their fate is the same as everyone else's.

I have been thinking of having them study by correspondence . . . because I can't afford to send them away — everything is so expensive now. Renting the room, the food — it just isn't possible. I heard something about a school where you can study by correspondence. I think it is in Los Angeles de California. My brother wrote a letter, but the papers haven't arrived yet.

I think we should have studies by correspondence in this country. Up to now, not one president has recognised this. I think they should have certain places all over the country where you could go to get help with this kind of studying, and at the end it would be valid . . . they could set certain standards. Because if we carry on as we are now, nothing will ever change. We are too poor to send our children to school, and we aren't going to get any richer.

Before we used to have enormous *naranjilla* crops, but a plague came and killed every single one of the plants, and we haven't had even one since.

That was seven years ago. Everyone had to find another way to earn a living. Some of them just left their houses here and went somewhere else. Those of us who had nowhere to go, and no money at all to do anything with . . . we had to stay here and suffer, and wait for whatever was going to happen. Almost everyone in the village lost everything.

You had to do whatever you could to try to earn something — both those who left and those who stayed. I had never worked like this before, but I had to do something, so I learned how to make bread and built the oven. I set up my little shop, selling Coca Cola, and beer, and whatever else I could.

I think I am going to give up making the bread . . . It is a lot of work, and there isn't much profit. A quintal of flour costs 300 sucres (£6), butter is 25 sucres (50p) a pound. The yeast is 15 (7½p) a package, and then there is sugar, wood for the fire . . . everything costs. And it isn't like before. Flour used to cost 200 sucres; sugar cost 125 sucres, and now it costs 350. Butter used to cost 15, and now it is 25. To make the bread I need a quintal of flour, five pounds of butter, two packets of yeast, and sugar — and there is no profit and it is very hard work.

I have never really worked out exactly how much I earn in the shop. Before I didn't have the refrigerator. I only got it this month, and now I make ice-creams too. To make them everything costs about 22 sucres and I sell them for 33 in total . . . so I make about 10 or 12 sucres profit. It isn't much.

I also earn money by buying guava in season from the women who go to collect it on the mountain, and then I sell it to another *señora*. I can earn about two sucres a box. I have to find whatever methods I can to earn money, especially if I stop making bread. Before, when I was younger, I could make the bread more easily. When you are young, you can work harder. But now, I don't have the same strength . . . and I lose more as I grow older. Without making a profit, it isn't worth the trouble . . . now that everything is so expensive. I can't buy anything with the small profit I make.

My husband went to Quito to look for work, wherever he could. Now he has work nearby, and earns a monthly salary. Now we don't suffer like we did at the beginning when there was nothing . . . there wasn't anyone or anything to give us work to do. No one had anything.

My husband earns about 1,800 – 2,000 sucres (£36-40) per month. It isn't very much, either, but it pays for the fridge. And whatever is left, he gives to me and I decide what we need. I am in charge of all the money. It isn't the same with all the couples here, but I know that in many, the women don't give their money to their husbands. They keep it to buy what they need. So if you have to buy shoes, or clothes, you have money.

It is much better if you have work to earn some money. The women in the marmalade cooperative ... now they are moving forward — they are earning and learning. In their meetings they are talking, giving their opinions and thinking. It is much better. Because with one idea and one head, you aren't really thinking — not the same as when there is a group of you. And you have to learn to agree with each other, and find solutions to your problems together.

The cooperative really is a step forward for the women here ... because the women had nothing before and now they have work and enjoy themselves. Here the land is very poor and we don't earn much from the land, so we need something else. In other places, if you can't do one thing, there is always other work, another job, another thing ... like in the jungle or in the city. If you don't like one thing, you can change and find something else — washing or ironing or being a cook in someone's house. But here there isn't anything like that, and we, mothers, can't just leave our children to go and work in someone else's house. We have to be here all the time.

The only other work there is, is to collect the guava when it is in season. It is worth about 10 sucres (20p) a box. But what can you do with 10 sucres? You might be able to buy some noodles and sugar, but you can't buy oil to cook the noodles with, or matches to light the fire.

Alicia was 26 years old, and worked as the nurse in the local health centre. Her family had moved to Rio Negro 14 years earlier, in an attempt to escape the high cost of living in the city. As a result, there was enough money in the family to send her to secondary school and on to a professional nursing course in Quito, an unusual opportunity for a young country girl.

She was even more unusual in that she married "late" at 24, and to a man four years her junior.

We talked while she was on duty one morning in the health centre. The centre was new, and had excellent facilities — a separate examination room, two hospital beds and a dentist's surgery. Unfortunately there was no dentist.

There was also no one in the centre that morning. We talked about the role of women in Ecuador, while her six-month old daughter slept in the next room.

I am happy to be a woman. But maybe it is because I have always had more liberty than the others even when I was young. I have been able to do what I wanted even though I was a woman.

In this area, women do get married very young. I think it is for lack of money. They can't afford to go to school, so they stay at home, and then get married, and look after their children. Maybe I'm different because of the way my father thought. He wanted us all to have a profession so that we would live better and have an easier life than my mother had.

When I was young, I never liked children, and never wanted to have any. But when you are married, there is something missing if you don't have children. It gets boring if it is just you and your husband. But with a child, it is totally different. It is an amazing change — very difficult for the couple but it is a new life that you have brought into the world.

When I was pregnant, I didn't want the baby at first. It wasn't the same as before. I couldn't go out; I couldn't do anything, but stay in the house. I got angry that I was carrying this burden. But little by little, I got used to it.

When I had the baby, I had been hoping for a boy, and it was a girl. What a disappointment. I wanted a boy so badly, and everyone had told me, "Yes, it will be a boy." It was an obsession to have a boy, and my husband wanted a boy. When they told me it was a girl, I got angry, and then I cried and cried. I guess I thought that men were worth more than girls too. It was awful. I didn't know how my husband was going to react. But he was happy.

In the first few days, I used to look at my new daughter, as if it were her fault that I felt like a failure. I really thought it would be better if she died. But only two days later, I changed. After all you forget everything, and you realise that it is something in your head that you have to change.

Now, I look at all children as if they were my own. I thought that I would be a failure as a mother, that I wouldn't be able to look after my child, or worse, that my child wouldn't be as I wanted it to be. But I am very happy, and my husband is too.

It is so hard to raise children. I am lucky because I have someone to help me. Even with the girl, I have too much to do. I want my daughter to have an easier life. I want her to have the best — everything I didn't have. My father had to work very hard to find the money we needed. Because there were five of us, and three in secondary school, there were a lot of expenses. Our lives weren't all that easy as students. I think when you are studying, money helps to resolve some of the problems you have. But we didn't have much money.

I don't want my child to lack for anything. I want her to have an easier life than the one I had — without any deprivation. I would like her to have a profession before she marries, and be a little older than most of the girls around here. When she is ready, in all senses, I would like her to get married.

That is the life of a woman here. Women expect to get married. There are a few who stay single, but I think it is much more difficult if you are single. When your father and mother die, you are alone, without anyone who can look out for you. You are lonely, and not happy.

I will tell her about family planning before she gets married, so she knows all the details. I don't want her to arrive at marriage with her eyes closed. If she doesn't know about all of these things, her marriage will be a failure.

For example, other mothers know about it, but they don't tell their daughters. For them, it is a bad thing if their daughters know about family planning before they are married. Their minds aren't open enough to accept these things.

When I started to work here, I wanted to give talks about family planning but there was no acceptance amongst the mothers. I spoke first to the mothers to see if they would agree that their daughters could come to the health centre for classes. I wasn't going to give classes in sex education. I was just going to talk about health, hygiene and menstruation . . . things young girls should know. But the mothers said no, because I was going to open their daughters' eyes too young. So the girls reach marriage without knowing anything. That's why they get pregnant immediately, and scarcely is the first child one year old, and they have another one. And they carry on like that.

The older women aren't interested either, because they are afraid. Other women have told them that if you take contraceptives, it hurts your head, and you might get cancer. That is why they are afraid. They say that God puts us here to create children, and they will have as many as He gives.

There are only a few women who use family planning. I have tried to promote it all the time that I have been here, but without much success. Whenever the women come in, I talk about it. For example, when a mother comes in with her baby for a health check, and the baby is six months old, I talk about family planning, and tell her it isn't good for her to get pregnant again.

I know they don't want so many children. After the second or the third, they are already very tired. They tell me this, and I show them all the controls they could use. They say they don't want more because there are so many problems, and life is so expensive. But when it comes to actually deciding what to use, they change their minds.

I think the husbands are mostly against it. I tell the women to go and talk with their husbands, and tell them about it, explain it, so they will understand. They do tell their husbands, and the husbands say, "No, I'll work harder to earn more money." They won't let their wives use anything.

Only a few men ever have vasectomies, even though it is easy. The other men would make fun of them if they knew about it. The women have heard that there is an operation for them too, but that after you have had it, you can't work as hard as you used to. You can't go up the mountain, or carry wood, and of course, the husbands say no, because they want the women to carry on working. The pill costs 5 sucres (10p), and the coil costs 10 sucres, but if we know people can't afford if, then it is free.

But the men and women here don't really talk about it, or even agree to have another one. Just suddenly, she is pregnant again, and it is a shock, because she doesn't want any more. The woman is subject to what the man decides.

He is the one who rules always. Here in Ecuador, we don't have this famous women's liberation.

I have spoken to other *compañeras* about that — not here but in Ambato (nearby, larger town). We have meetings, other nurses and I, and we talk, and we see that things are developing in other places. It isn't any longer just what the husband says. But here in the *campo* (country), there isn't really any understanding of that sort of thing.

To try to change that . . . it would be hard for the husbands. I am always telling the women, as a joke, "Now is the time to adjust your skirts, and not let yourselves be so dominated by your husbands." One woman went home, and told her husband what I'd said, and he told her that she could never come to the health centre again, because I was teaching her bad things.

In our society, they give priority to the men, as the father is the one who decides everything. And the women . . . they just stay in the house, get married, and that's it.

It is very difficult for women to leave the house and find work, unless it is something that they already know how to do — like cooking, washing, ironing. Or maybe in a factory. But it has to be something that doesn't require great skill, because they aren't prepared.

Here now, it is the season of the guava. The women collect and sell it. But it is only one or two cases that they can manage, and that isn't much. When there isn't much around, they can earn 100 sucres (£2), but it takes a long time. When there is a lot, they only earn 10 or 20 sucres (20 or 40p) per box.

The problem is still the husbands. They don't want them to go out and do other things. Some women in the cooperative have this problem.

I think the women are enthusiastic about the cooperative, and they want to work and earn money — but the husbands cause problems. They say that they are good enough men to work and maintain their families, and the women don't have to work.

I think it is a source of work for some women who have decided to work. It gives them some economic help. But the women still have to sacrifice, because they go home after the cooperative, and they still have to do all their other work. The husbands shout because the food isn't ready, and why is this child crying, and why has the other one fallen down?

I don't really think it makes them stronger, or more courageous. It is a source of work. Although, I have noticed that the women talk more . . . at least, they have a new theme of conversation. Before, all they could talk about was husbands and children. Now when they come to the centre, they are talking about cooperative problems, selling and meetings.

The mothers go to the meetings in school, representing their husbands. But when a decision has to be made, the women can't make it. They say, "I don't know; I have to talk to my husband." This really bothers the teachers. They say that if the women come representing their husbands, they have to come ready to take a decision. Or if there is an election for a committee, and someone is named to it, she can't accept because she doesn't know what her husband will say. She has to talk to him first before she can accept, and if he says no, then she can't. Just one little word.

My work is very important to me. I get up at 5:45 a.m., and start to cook the lunch. Then I get the baby ready, and have my coffee. I have to be at the centre by 8 a.m. If there are no patients, I leave at noon, heat up my lunch, eat, and go back to the centre by 2 p.m. If there are patients, I can't leave until 1 p.m., and then it is a rush. I work until 6 p.m., go home and make dinner. Sometimes, I cook both lunch and dinner in the morning. In the evening, I do all the laundry — all the nappies.

At the beginning, when I first had the baby, my husband wanted me to stop working. I had a girl helping me, but the baby was always crying, and this really bothered my husband. But I said no, because especially with a baby, our expenses were going to be more. Now I don't worry about it. I haven't stopped. I have another girl who helps me with the baby, and she is better. We will probably have another child, but not for another two or three years. It will be well planned.

My husband teaches in a school in the jungle. He comes back every weekend. We have a very good relationship. He gives me all the money, and I look after it. What usually happens here is that the man earns the money, and gives some to his wife — more or less what she needs, depending on the man. The rest he spends on drink, and whatever else. I don't know what else. My case is different, I don't think there are many who do it as we do it.

Life here is difficult. The women work very hard . . . in the house all the time, looking after so many children. But the man has to go up on the mountain, in the rain, or the hot sun, and often without eating. So in that respect, the man's life is a little more difficult.

If I were in charge of the country, I would punish all the bad husbands. (She laughed.) I would try to change the mentality of the men and the women too. Because if the women don't change, then their husbands never will. If the woman is strong and intelligent, quietly, she can begin to take the "reins" in the house. But if she is humble and meek, and doesn't speak for herself, it will be like I said before . . . the same from generation to generation.

I think we could start by having classes for the women. But you have to choose a good time, for example, in the afternoon, and with plenty of warning, so they can plan their work in the house. It shouldn't last more than one or two hours, because if they aren't back in time to prepare the supper, their husbands will be angry.

I have read about China . . . women there have many children, but there is work for them to do. They go to school, study, and are prepared to do things. There is also a nursery for the children. So I guess they are better off.

They say that here, in our Ecuador . . . how many millions or thousands of children are malnourished? I read it in the newspaper, that there is an incredible number of children who don't have the proper food to eat. And they say that the young people are the future of the country . . . so they should all eat properly, and get an education. I think that the adults have to eat too, but the young people need it much more. If the country is full of starving children, what kind of future can we expect? We will be a country full of sick people, probably backward mentally, too. We won't develop very much . . . but if we have strong well-fed people, healthy in all respects, our development will be healthy too.

I think, like everywhere, people who have money, are the ones who succeed, and they give a good education to their children. There is the upper class, the middle class, and the lower class. The upper class and the middle class don't have too many problems, but the lower class . . . people who don't really have the economic resources . . . it is the same for them all over Ecuador. And I think it will always be the same.

Now we have a new president, and they say that he will pay attention to the working classes. But in the end, I don't think so. The government doesn't really look after the poor people. And I don't think a new government will be any different.

THE CHANGING MARKET

Artesania del Norte, based in Ibarra, in northern Ecuador, was another cooperative providing work and income for rural women. It had been set up with the help of a Peace Corps volunteer 13 years earlier, and became, for a time, the most successful craft cooperative in the country. Its products included embroidered shirts and dresses, and hand-knit sweaters.

Now it was suffering badly due to decreased demand for its work, both overseas and locally. The foreign craft market is complicated, highly structured and constantly changing. Most peasant women, given their limited experience and lack of education cannot hope to compete effectively when the demand for their product changes, as it is almost certain to do, and the foreign volunteer is no longer there to help.

The women of Artesania del Norte were unable to find new markets for the garments they produced, or to create a more marketable new product.

As one of the women told me:

> *"We need another kind of project or business. Before, when we were able to sell the embroidery, and the dresses and shirts, we were earning money and working together. But now, we can't sell the embroidery and we don't know how to do anything else."*

This was the most common thread linking the craft cooperatives I visited. Whether in Ecuador, Bolivia or Guatemala, when the success of the cooperative depended on its ability to compete in the international craft market place, on a long-term basis, failure was common.

With this particular cooperative, women were losing faith in it as a steady source of income. The philosophy of *cooperativismo*, working together and market strength through unity, would not put food on the table. And so, many were turning back to the more exploitative situations of selling to the commercial intermediaries, the owners of tourist shops, who would buy low, and sell at prices of up to 300-400% profit. But at least this was "cash in hand" for the women who needed the money to feed their families.

I spent a week with Señora Hilda, a former president and founding member of the cooperative. It was to have been a short visit, but that week, in many towns in Ecuador, Ibarra included, national strikes and riots broke out as a protest against increased bus fares. As a result, it was dangerous, and impossible to travel anywhere.

It was a strange feeling to stay in Señora Hilda's house . . . I'd seen her so many times before — or, rather, women like her: short, plump women with round "motherly" faces, sitting in their open doorways . . . knitting. And there we sat together for almost a week . . . knitting.

In the early years of the cooperative, Señora Hilda had a lot of contact with the Peace Corps volunteers working in that area. She began to tell me about some of the attitudes of local women to the idea of using family planning.

Can you imagine the problems that women have, when one child is very small and another is about to be born, and there is yet another, only a little bigger than the last? Some women who were pregnant said, "No, leave me alone. I don't want to use such things." But then after they had all those children, some of them changed their minds.

There were so many cases where women used something to not have children, and they got very sick. I don't know what they used, but they probably did it without consulting a doctor. They might see a doctor once, but then not again. They were asked who had told them about birth control, and the women said, "the Peace Corps" — because this was their work before. They used to talk to women about not having children . . . "You have so many and you should go to see your doctor to find out about family planning." But the women said they were afraid it would make them crazy. The Peace Corps people said it would be worse if they had so many children that they couldn't give them food or education.

Many of the women went to the doctor and had the *espiral* (IUD) put in, but they never went back to see the doctor again. They got infected and began to rot inside. But this was the fault of the women who decided to do it, and even more, it was the fault of the Peace Corps and the doctor, who didn't teach the women that they had to go back for check ups.

Women here are afraid and shy, so they won't go to doctors easily. People are very Catholic and religious, and say, "Well, God says I should have all the children who come to me, so I won't use these things."

But they need it, and what they need, too, is a doctor close by. If the village is two or three hours from the doctor, the people aren't going to pay for the bus rides to go and see the doctor all the time, because they have to pay whatever the doctor charges, too. And often the men don't like it. But there aren't too many against it. They have to go with their wives to the doctor so they understand what it is all about.

I was living in another village, near here, about 15 years ago. There was a Peace Corps volunteer there, and we were starting the sweater cooperative then. The Peace Corps volunteer was the one who was talking about family planning. She spoke to me. I didn't need it any more, but she didn't know that. I had had three children, and one bad birth, and then I had an operation. I couldn't have any more children.

She said to me, "You already have three children. You shouldn't really have any more because you won't be able to feed and educate them." And I asked her about it, because I'd heard someone say that this *gringa* (American girl) was teaching about how not to have children. I didn't believe it, because we were good friends, and she had never mentioned it to me. But one day, she said, "This must be enough." I said, "How do you do it . . . what is the best for me, or the correct method?" Because 15 years ago, it was all very new.

It wasn't like people going from door to door, selling chickens. They didn't bring the pills around like that. She told me that I should go to the doctor, and he would examine me, and check my heart, and tell me what the best thing for me was. It was good advice. Then the first one's time came to an end, and another volunteer came to replace her. And this new one went from house to house, telling the women not to have any more children.

It was the first volunteer who helped us form the cooperative in 1967. We came from the village to sell in a tourist hotel, in the town. They would sell the sweaters in the hotel shop and take 10%. People came from all the villages. Then the hotel closed, and we didn't have the shop any more. But the Peace Corps office was nearby, and we knew some of them. So we sold all our things to the volunteers. They said they would give us a volunteer and help us open a shop. There were 10 of us. We had representatives from all the villages — doing knitting, embroidery, wood carving, weaving. We elected a committee, and got together to open a shop.

The biggest problem at the beginning was the money. To start, we had no money, and everyone had to pay something to join — 10 sucres (20p). Some people didn't want to pay. They said they had no money. So we decided to stop asking for money, and we put 15% on the sales. To start, we all had to put a certain number of sweaters in stock. When we sold them, we would get our money back, and 15% went to the cooperative.

We have 97 members now, but no one is very active because we don't have any orders. Everyone used to come to the meetings, and the women would talk, and always have lots of questions . . . even questions that they should have known the answers to.

For example, when I finished being president, a new committee came in, and they didn't know anything about sales or where the money came from . . . nothing. We had lots of sales . . . hundreds of thousands of sucres. They didn't realise that we had to pay all the costs of the shop and the employees. They really thought that it was like a rich boss who had lots of money, that they could have. But they didn't see that once we all took our share, there wasn't much left . . . in short, they didn't see that it was their very own money.

One day a sick woman came in to ask for a loan of 200 sucres (£4) to buy medicine. The committee said, "Let's give her 500". But one of the women on the committee explained to them where the money was coming from . . . that is, from their own pockets, thus lowering the amount of each of their shares. So they decided that the old lady would get nothing. She could have died.

At the beginning the money made a big difference to most of us. We were always selling things, and everyone was earning. You earned according to the work you did. I guess the most you could earn was about 3,000 sucres (£60) per month — for 10 sweaters, but that was working all the time. Sometimes, I would hire people to help me, and I would pay them.

There weren't really any problems with our families, because in the cooperative, we were paying much more for the work than the women had been earning before. Their husbands couldn't say, "No, carry on working for the person who pays you less." They had to agree to their wives being in the cooperative.

In some cases, the women would keep their own money, and in others, they would give it to their husbands. It depended on the couple.

Although, now that I think, I guess we did have some problems. For most of the women, it was all right, because they were earning their own money, and their husbands could see this. This gave the women more strength or courage. But the women from the outlying villages, for example, had to catch the bus to come in to the cooperative. They would pass by the shop to leave their work, then go to the market to buy what they needed and then go back home. Sometimes if there was no bus, they would arrive quite late, and their husbands got angry. They would shout, "Why are you late; where have you been?" Some husbands are quite jealous and they think that their wives should stay home most of the time.

These women suffered. I got angry with some of the men. Word travels faster here if you *tell* someone something, than if you put it on the television or the radio. There was one case where the brother of the husband of one of our women was in the shop. This woman's husband was very jealous, and he gave her a very bad time, but his brother was a more reasonable man. I told the brother in the shop one day, that men should learn how to behave a little better, and not be like children. The word got to this woman's husband very quickly, because he knew that his wife was only fulfilling her obligations. People listen to what I say; they have a lot of respect for me.

The only other big problem we had before was with the quality. We insisted on the highest quality, and had to refuse work that wasn't good enough. None of the members could say to the others that the work wasn't good enough. We used to keep some models as samples which we knew the clients liked. We would use the models to show that they weren't the same, because it is very difficult for one woman to say "no" to another. There is a lot of jealousy.

What is important here . . . it doesn't matter how or where . . . but the women must have work . . . in or out of the house, but they have to be able to work. It is more logical to have work that they could do inside the house. For example, I can clean the house when I want to, and work when I want to. But if I had to leave at a certain time, it would be more difficult. I can look after my husband, the children, wash the clothes, cook . . . and at 10 a.m., I start to knit, and I knit all day until late at night sometimes . . . I only stop to cook the lunch and the supper.

Perhaps it is a little better now, because women do have the chance to work and earn some money, which they didn't have before. Life before was different. In one house, there might have been 10-15 people, but it didn't matter because the land produced enough food, and you didn't have to worry about feeding everyone. There were still poor people. They had to go out and look for work daily. They didn't get paid in money, but rather in food — corn, or whatever, but only when the harvest came.

Now you need money, but there isn't so much land to work now, so there isn't any work to earn money. Now, too, there is no boss, as before, to help a family out now and then. People used to exchange bread for potatoes or corn. You can't do that now. But then because there were no buses, you had to go everywhere on foot, and carry everything you earned. I don't know if it is better or worse, now — just very different. That is why the cooperative was good, because, really, women have to work together to better their own lives. We are much stronger together.

But it is still the man who makes the decisions. Amongst the Indians the wife does only what the husband wants. If he wants to beat her, then he does, and she doesn't say anything. If anyone tries to defend her, the husband says that it is his right to do what he wants. Amongst the *mestizos* (mixed blood, Indian/Spanish), it changes a little. It isn't quite as bad, but it is still the husband who rules.

There aren't many single women here. Most of them get married. It is one of the laws of life. If they don't marry, they stay at home with their parents.

I think everyone gets married, because the body demands it. If you want to have sex relations you have to have a husband. If you don't have a husband, then it is bad, and people talk about you and your parents. If you want to have children without a husband, then you have to stay with your parents. We don't have the custom of leaving your parents' house at a certain age, the way you do in other countries.

Ultimately it is the man who has the freedom to do as he wants. The woman doesn't have much opportunity to do what she wants. I don't think it is fair, but that is the way it is. If the husband dies, then it is the eldest son who becomes the boss. All over Ecuador, it is the same.

THE 16-HOUR DAY

One of the small roads going north from Ibarra led to Cahuasqui, a village high in the mountains. There the road stopped; any further journeys had to be made on foot.

The women of Cahuasqui were also very much concerned with survival. One part of their double day comprised all the usual domestic and agricultural tasks required of peasant women; the second was producing hemp rope and sacking cloth from *cabuya*, the dried inner fibres of a large cactus plant found growing along the roadside.

Working with the *cabuya* was an arduous task. It created a dust that could choke, and the prickly fibres cut and stuck in the skin. Most of the women talked about their long days — difficult with or without husbands.

> *"I get up at 4 a.m. to comb the* cabuya. *My husband doesn't like me to do this, but I have to do it. I spin until about 6 a.m., and then I make the coffee for the family, because they have to go off to work. After they leave, I cook the lunch and take it out to the field. When I return, I spin until it is time to make dinner. I only go out to buy what I need, and I come straight home to do more spinning. That is how I end my day of work, and that is how I will end my life."*
>
> —Luisa

> *"We work approximately 16 hours per day inside and outside the house. Working outside is scarcely four or five hours . . . when you have to take the lunch to your husband in the field. I work with the* cabuya *like a man, combing it, spinning it, and cutting it down. Then I can 'rest'. I do the things that need to be done in the house. That's what they call our 'rest'. We leave one job to do another."*
>
> —Anna

Generally the women spun the *cabuya* and the men wove the cloth from the spun rope. There was a local cooperative which tried to market the sacks produced from the large rolls of cloth turned in by both men and women cooperative members. But they were in financial difficulties, and had gone to the Central Bank of Ecuador to solicit credit. There they became involved with the Foderuma (Marginal Rural Development Project).

Foderuma is the development arm of the Central Bank of Ecuador. It was set up to encourage peasant groups to use the credit facilities of the Bank. *Campesino* groups, and especially women's groups were almost non-existent amongst the Bank's credit users. Thus, Foderuma was established with a field work team, whose job it was to act as community organisers and economic advisors in particular geographical target areas. They had a specific interest in health care, appropriate technology, animal care, agricultural production and small-scale income-generating activities. The women's programme was established as a separate unit within this structure to ensure the participation of peasant women.

Meeting the needs of the women was especially important in Cahuasqui since they were often left behind when the men went to look for work on the coast. As the director of the women's project for Foderuma[1] stated:

> *"In the* sierra, *(Ecuadorean Andes), conditions are very harsh, and the economy is stringent.* Campesino *families try to subsist from tiny parcels of land that will never yield enough to support them. Opportunities for other work are more plentiful on the coast, on the large plantations, and many men migrate from the* sierra *to the coast for up to several months at a time. During that time the woman is left behind as the major provider in the household. When, and if, the husband comes back, he might bring some money, which will then be used for purchases outside of the daily needs. It is common, too, for the men to have two families, one on the coast, and one in the mountains."*

---

1.   The *Foderuma* programme was "reassessed" after the appointment of a new, ultra-conservative
      director of the Central Bank. One of the results of this reassessment was the removal of the director of
      the women's programme. Although no reason was given officially, she had been accused of being a
      communist.

Erlinda did not have to worry about her husband migrating to the coast as she was an unmarried mother. At 28, she had two daughters and an elderly sick father to support. She herself was crippled and had some difficulty in walking.

She earned money by selling her spinning to the cooperative but hadn't become a member because she had so many other demands on her time and energy, that she couldn't be sure of meeting their monthly quota.

She told me about her father's accident which had increased the burden on her to support the whole family.

My father is sick. The burro threw him off some time ago, and he got very sick. The doctor, from here, said that we had to take him to Ibarra because there was no way of curing him here. We took him to Autuntaqui, but there was no help there either. Each day he gets worse, but we can't afford to pay for any more treatment. We have already spent 4,000 sucres (£80).

Until my father dies, I am here with him. If I have to leave here, I have some family in Quito. What am I going to do here, alone?

My father plants on the small bit of land that we have near the house. When we have enough — when God grants us enough — we can sell some of what we grow. But if there isn't enough, we eat everything ourselves. Now he is planting corn and beans . . . but we won't have enough to sell. This corn isn't very good.

With both my father and I working, we just manage. I help him in the fields to harvest or husk the corn — whatever has to be done.

Usually to eat, we have different kinds of beans with rice or potatoes, or corn. We only have meat once a week on Saturdays, when there is money, or I buy milk instead — a half litre daily for the children. And the eggs — whatever I get from the hens.

I have four chickens, and I had pigs, but I had to sell them to pay for the medicine my father needed. We have water and light in the house. The wood for cooking — I have to go and look for it, about once a week. It is about a two hour walk from here, and I have to carry it back.

I am partly crippled — my leg is deformed, and I will always walk with a limp. Something happened to me when I was young and I disconnected my leg. I must have fallen. My father and two brothers took me to the doctor in Ibarra, but he said they should have brought me immediately and I would have been all right. My father had been alone and had to look after all the children, so he didn't take me until two months after I hurt myself.

My mother died when I was four years old. She had a fight with one of my aunts in the street, and my mother fell. She hurt herself when she fell; my aunt ran away, and my mother died a little while later. It has always bothered me, not having a mother. I think that if I had had a mother, I wouldn't be as I am today. I would have had more opportunities, instead of raising myself almost how I wanted.

Since I was eight years old, I have been earning money by spinning *cabuya*. We don't have a loom, so I don't weave the *cabuya* cloth. I only spin the rope. I haven't joined the cooperative, because I don't think I can do enough to turn it in every month. My father needs looking after, and if I were a member of the cooperative, they would expect my work every month.

They pay about 3 sucres (6p) a pound, so I earn about 30 sucres (60p) daily. I get up at four in the morning to brush out the fibres, start to spin, clean the house, make the coffee, and carry on spinning. Then I make lunch and work until about 4 p.m. Then I go to the plaza to get what I need for the food at night. And at 7 or 8, I go to bed. My children are very good. They don't bother me too much, so I can get on with work.

My children — both are girls. One is seven years old, and the other is five. They both have the same father. He is from here. He comes to see the children every now and then. He wants me to marry him, but I don't want to. He doesn't have a very good character and is very irresponsible. He drinks a lot, too, and is always drunk.

Once he shouted at me because I went somewhere alone without asking him. He said why did I go alone, and why didn't I tell him? And he isn't even my husband! Can you imagine how he would be if he were my husband? It wouldn't be worth it.

I told the father of my children to go and marry someone else, but he doesn't want to. I have never wanted to get married to him, nor to anyone else.

I think that a single woman usually has a better life than a married woman. I have heard so many say about me, "poor thing", but I had 27 chickens for my diet and a married neighbour only had two.[2] Her husband works very hard, but he is very miserly and she was jealous of me.

Now that I have children, I expect it will be very difficult for me if I want to get married to someone else. Men don't want women with children if they aren't their own. It would have been better if I had married someone else instead of having this man's children, but it didn't happen that way.

My life has changed so much with the children. Before, I used to do what I wanted. I had my brother and my father who were working . . . and they would leave money for the food. But I hardly ever ate or slept—I was always with my friends having a good time. But that life, I guess I will never have again. Now I am tied to the children.

Of course, I regret having them when they ask me for something, and I can't give it to them. I feel very bitter and angry — instead of feeling peaceful, alone. How I would love to be calm and happy again.

When I had the first baby, my father spoke to me about it — but he didn't say very much. He didn't like it, but he didn't have time to say anything because he went away to work somewhere else. When he came back, I was already pregnant with the second one. He cried, but he didn't say anything to me. I know he wanted to hit me, but he didn't say anything.

People say that I should take care of myself and not have any more children, but they haven't criticised me. Now of course, I am trying to be more careful, but the man must be careful too.

I know a simple remedy — an old man told me. But you must promise never to tell anyone in the village, because it is very dangerous. If you use it, you can never have children again. I haven't done it yet.

I spoke to the father of my children, and he said not to do it because he wanted to marry me and have another child.

What you do is: take a glass of water after it has been sitting for three days. On the third night, you take it at about 7 p.m. and put two limes and the skin of the pip of an avacado cut up. And you let it sit for two mornings, and on

------

2.   In some rural parts of Ecuador, the custom is to eat chickens after giving birth to build up strength. The number of chickens eaten is a sign of wealth and status.

the third morning, you take two mouthfuls. This apparently works every time.[3]

I don't have any confidence in the doctors. Some of them are just thieves. I remember when I was pregnant, I went to Ibarra, because I felt really ill. This doctor said to me, "Don't be silly. You won't have the baby. I can give you some pills so it will abort, but you will have to sleep with me. If you don't want to, it will cost you 100 sucres (£2), but if you want, it won't cost you anything. It is up to you."

Since then, I have hated doctors. I would rather die. Women doctors are all right. I have more confidence in them.

We women help each other when we have babies. The first child I had, I was alone until the baby actually came out, and then finally, a neighbour appeared. The second one — the father helped me, and the neighbours came and washed me and wrapped the baby up. Four days later, I was up cooking and cleaning like before.

What will I tell my children? A cousin of mine died because she took the pills that the doctor gave her to not have children. I will tell my children not to take the pills, and I will tell them about menstruation. I didn't know anything about it . . . it really took me by surprise . . . only my friends told me about it, so I knew what it was.

I don't want my children to have the same kind of life I had. I would like them to marry someone who cares for them and will look after them — and not end up in the disgrace that is my life.

I think that women suffer more — more than men. We have to give birth and then look after the children for the rest of our lives. And the men — all they have is their work. If they are responsible, they are more involved in their families. But if they aren't, they will sometimes wake up in the middle of the road. And you know, nothing will have happened to them.

––––––

3.   Plant remedies suggested by the women have not been tested, to our knowledge.

Señora Blanca, 43, was also very bitter about her experiences with men. She, like so many of her Latin American sisters, had been abandoned by her husband. She too was now the sole supporter of her family.

I went to find Blanca in her house, down a narrow side street. Her children were playing in the doorway. She invited me into the single-roomed house. Although the sun was shining brightly outside, it was dark inside as there were no windows and no lights.

I asked her about her two children, and she explained that she had given birth to seven, but five had died — two had been born dead, and three died before they were two years old.

She began to tell me about her husband.

My husband and I separated about seven years ago. He didn't go suddenly, from one day to the next. He had always been a very good man. He never used to go out at night. He used to treat me very well.

Then he started to leave for two or three days at a time. He would come in at midnight, or at dawn. I didn't like it one bit, because it didn't show any respect for me. Then he left. He was with another woman, and he would come every two or three months to visit, but not to stay.

Once after three months he came to see me full of affection. He gave me a hug, and we were talking about this and that for a long time. Then he said, "I'm going now. I just came to visit you." I got very angry. I pulled his hair and pushed him against the chair. The children got very frightened and started to cry. I was shouting and hitting him. But he never hit me, and he never shouted at me. He never raised his hand. Except once — because I shouted something nasty at his mother, and he hit me. But I hit him back with a stick.

I didn't want him to go, even though I was very nasty to him. I threw his clothes out the door to see what he would say. I thought he would say that I was his wife, and that this was his house and that he wasn't leaving. But he was waiting to go.

He is a radio technician and lives and works in Quito. I have the address where he works, but not where he lives. I know he loves the children, even though he doesn't give us very much. My children miss him so much and need the security of a father.

He loves them very much. He never treats them badly, or hits them, or shouts at them. Of course, you always have to tell them not to do things, but he is very loving with them. But he doesn't give them anything. He loves them, but . . . nothing.

He and the other woman have a little girl . . . but the woman is very cunning. He must put up with a lot from her. She already had three children. She goes with first one man, and then another. I said to him, "None of them are yours"; and he said, "It doesn't matter."

He doesn't want to come back to me. He asked me for a divorce, and I said no. He hasn't bothered me about it since.

I fight alone. I am better off without him. He never was one to work. I used to tell him that he should work at something, but he didn't. We just used to manage with what we had. He used to send me to get money from his mother, and I used to be ashamed to do it.

Frankly, I'm going to tell you why he left me. Well . . . I didn't think marriage was like it was . . . that you had relations all the time — sexual relations. I got pregnant before we were married. I felt very deceived, that the "first time" I ended up being pregnant.

After, I never really wanted to have sexual relations. I was never in the mood; maybe every now and then, once or twice a month, but not every day. I used to be afraid when the night came. I tried to explain that I didn't know it was like this. I would get tired, and I asked him if he never got tired.

Once when I was fighting with him, about the other woman, he said, "Don't you remember that you told me that you were tired?" That is what happened. Nothing else. And how awful it is. You can live without eating, but the love of your husband should fill your life. Everyone says that if your husband can't get what he wants from you, he'll look for another woman.

I blame his mother for part of what happened. She was always wanting him to come to her house to eat. She is a kind of "aunt" to the other woman. She always liked her and never liked me. She used to tell my husband all the time. That is the part that upsets me — because they are an awful family, and the other woman's family too. They can call me what they like, but my parents were good people, and never gave us a bad example.

I support the family by working with the *cabuya*. I used to do washing, but not now. I had a bad reaction to the water. Every now and then, my husband sends me something, to help out.

I spin the *cabuya*, and I pay a worker to weave it into the cloth. I get the food from the shop, and when they pay me in the cooperative for the cloth, I pay for the food. The cooperative gives us the *cabuya* to spin as an advance, and then when I hand in the cloth, they discount the cost of the *cabuya*. Then I have to pay the man who works for me. I pay 1½ sucres (3p) per metre. In one week, the worker can do 150 metres (earning £4.50). He works from 7 a.m. until about 5 in the afternoon, because there is no light after that. I give him breakfast and lunch.

Sometimes I have to do the weaving, because you can't rely on the workers. But to make the warp (for the weaving), I have to pay to have that done. All the dust makes me sick. So I do part and I pay part. The rest is supposed to be what I earn, but then I have to go to the shop to pay for the food, and I am left with nothing.

I get up at 6 a.m. and in half an hour, the children are dressed, and then I give them coffee for breakfast. Then I clean the house and the children go out to play, or to school. At 10 or 11 a.m. I sit down to spin, and then at noon, I have to start cooking lunch, and at 1 o'clock, it is ready.

In the afternoon it is the same. I spin until 5 p.m., and then I have to cook something else. At night, I can't work, because I can't see. But I say to myself, "At least I have my own house, and my children, and we aren't going to die of hunger."

I wash clothes once a week on Mondays. Sometimes I will wash on Sundays to have more time on Mondays to spin. On Saturdays, I spin and make bobbins for the weaver to work with.

I have to pay for everything for the children — food, clothes, shoes, medicine, school. Often I don't have enough to pay the shop, and school costs a lot. Every day, they need something else. If the children get sick and need medicine, I have to borrow, or ask for an advance from the cooperative. Sometimes I take them to the doctor, but when I can't, I cure them myself with plants that we have.

I joined the cooperative when it started, on the first day. I joined because I wanted to know what a cooperative was, not so much for the money. But that's why others joined. One woman went to the meeting thinking that the money was there ready. But we had to form a committee, and organise it well. Now, I think it is good, because we have earned a lot.

The women don't say much in the meetings. They only sit and listen. They are afraid to open their mouths, so you have to guess what they think. Most women have to ask their husbands if they can come to the meetings. But I also heard that some pretend they are going to the meetings, and they go out and get drunk instead.

The cooperative is worthwhile, because it is easier to do things together than on your own. For example, they say that we get the *cabuya* cheaper, because the cooperative has a loan. With the cooperative, I can afford to pay people to help me do the work. It would kill me if I had to do everything alone. And people come to teach us things — people with more experience than us, because we really don't know much.

I went to school here, but only up to the fourth grade. I stayed in fourth grade for two years. There weren't any more grades after that here in the village.

But now both my children go to school here. The 11 year old is in fourth grade, and the eight year old is in second grade. Their father told me that in two years he will send them away to secondary school. Education is much better now. They have work to do every day, and they are learning things that I never learned.

I have never been anything, but I want them to be something. I want them to have a degree or a profession; something so they can live.

I haven't really lived this life, and I don't want them to be like me. If they want to get marrried, that will be up to them. But I know they will look after me until I die. They are good children.

Young girls know so much more these days. Us older women, we used to think — a hug, a kiss, and that was it — pregnant. We were afraid to do more. But now they hear and see everything on the radio or the television. They learn everything bad that there is to learn. All we used to listen to was guitar music.

It isn't like it was before, when no one knew anything. Now there are pills, injections — to take care of yourself, and not have too many children, although I heard that sometimes it can make you sick.

Once my sister found these things that the men use, in the road. Her little girl grabbed it, because she thought it was a balloon. But my sister knew what it was, and took it away from her.

Here some people use birth control and some don't. Most of the people leave it all up to the will of God. When I got married, I didn't hear or see any of these things. I got married when I was 33 years old. When I was younger, I did hear that "bad women" in the cabarets used to use lemons. But it was only talk among married women. It isn't something you talk about in front of girls who aren't married.

In the school recently, there was a film for us about sex education. I think it is important to know. I will tell my daughters . . . that you have to be careful with men; that you can't let them deceive you. I will tell them that I don't want them out on the streets with the boys, the way some girls are now. They can come inside the house to talk.

A man falls once, and he gets up again. A woman falls once, and she is marked for ever. A man can choose what he wants. But women have to get married, and then come the children. Men don't know what it is to be a mother and cry for a child.

"The government has no idea. They live in La Paz and they have everything. They have their own transport, enough to eat, education. They have everything, and they don't want to know about us, the peasants who have nothing."
— Rosa Dominga, Executive Secretary,
National Federation of Campesina Women

BOLIVIA

Bolivia is a landlocked Andean country which lacks the geographical and cultural contrasts between the highlands and the coast found in Peru and Ecuador. It is nevertheless a country of considerable physical diversity. There are three main regions: the river valleys, the eastern lowlands (the *Oriente*) and the *altiplano* or high Andean plain, 16,000 feet above sea level. Three quarters of the population live on the *altiplano*, as it contains most of the major cities.

Like Ecuador and Peru, Bolivia was once part of the Inca empire and today 60% of its population are Indian.

Bolivia is one of the poorest countries in Latin America. Yet in the 16th century, it was one of the richest; Bolivia was the silver capital of the world. Eduardo Galeano vividly described the enslavement of the Indians by the Spanish conquerors and their forced work in the silver mines:[1]

> *"In three centuries Potosi's Cerro Rico (Rich Mountain) consumed eight million lives. The Indians, including women and children were torn from their agricultural communities and driven to the Cerro. Of every 10 who went up into the freezing wilderness, seven never returned."*

—————

1. E. Galeano, *The Open Veins of Latin America*, Monthly Review Press

The silver did not contribute to Bolivia's development. Instead it was shipped to Europe to finance that region's industrialisation process. Once the silver mines were depleted, Bolivia's economy stagnated until another commodity of use to the industrialising world was discovered: tin.

The lives of Bolivia's tin miners, today, do not differ greatly from the appalling conditions of the silver miners centuries earlier. The average life expectancy of a tin miner is 35 years. They are one of the most exploited groups of workers in Latin America but are also amongst the most militant.

Troubled history

All of Bolivia's people have suffered from its particularly troubled history. According to some estimates, by 1981, there had been nearly 190 military coups since independence in 1825.

In 1952, the country experienced a major revolution. The causes of the revolution lay in the extremely unequal distribution of wealth and the country's distorted and backward economy. In 1950, tin mining made up 24.4% of the Gross National Product (GNP) but employed only 3.2% of the labour force, while 72% of the labour force were involved in agriculture which accounted for only 33% of GNP.

The distribution of wealth reflected the general pattern in Latin America; concentration in the hands of a few. Eighty percent of the tin mines were owned by three family firms — the Aramayo, the Hochschild and the Patiño. Their political and economic power was enormous. Agriculture was dominated by the *latifundio* system. According to the 1950 agricultural census, 4% of all land owners owned 95% of all agricultural property, in units of over 1,000 hectares. Two-thirds of the total population existed on 0.2% of the land in units of less than five hectares.

The peasant was a virtual serf, forced to give labour or other services to the land owner in return for his plot. The land owner lived off these free services like a feudal lord, investing very little in his land and resisting all technological innovations. The system was unproductive and unjust.

The 1952 revolution was led by the Nationalist Revolutionary Movement (MNR), a party founded in 1941, in opposition to the tin mine owners. It was the strength of the miners which pushed the revolution beyond the limited reformist objectives of the MNR. The tin mines were nationalised and the army virtually dismantled. The peasants also played a key role in the revolution. Through land occupations in various regions of the country, they ensured the introduction of a radical Agrarian Reform Law in 1953.

By responding to these pressures the MNR gained considerable support amongst the workers and peasants. But because of a deepening economic crisis due to falling world prices for tin, the disruption of agricultural production and the cost of compensating the former tin mine owners, the MNR began to reverse the gains of the revolution by tying itself to the United States and the demands of the International Monetary Fund, (IMF). In return for a loan, the IMF demanded massive cuts in public expenditure, a wage freeze, tax increases and a commitment to rebuild the army. The workers strongly resisted the IMF measures and the MNR began to lose much of its prestige and support.

As disillusionment set in amongst the working class, the effective failure of the agrarian reform also became apparent. Its most tangible achievement was to abolish the service obligations of peasants. By 1963, 4.4 million hectares of land had been redistributed, but this only accounted for 10% of workable land. Most peasants merely became owners of tiny plots and, as little attention was given to credit, technical assistance and machinery, they were unable to improve their land and make it economically viable.

Possession of the land made the peasantry a rather conservative force and in 1964, they supported the coup of General Rene Barrientos. The military assumed power through the Military-Peasant pact of 1964. Apart from a short lived liberal government in 1970-71, Bolivians were to live under right wing military governments until 1978.

The government of Barrientos was supported by the US and he in turn welcomed US capital to the country, particularly to the oil sector which by 1968 supplied 16% of Bolivia's export earnings. Barrientos' government was repressive, particularly towards the militant miners. In June 1967, the army killed more than 100 miners and members of their families in what became known as the "Night of San Juan" massacre.

The dictatorship of Hugo Banzer from 1971 to 1978 was even more brutal. The workers confederation, the COB (Bolivian Workers Centre), was outlawed and many union leaders jailed or exiled. Under Banzer, the peasants increasingly became victims of this repression and many were radicalised during these years.

In the early 1970's Banzer also turned to the IMF for loans and again, Bolivia accepted its demands to cut public expenditure and price subsidies on basic commodities. By January 1974, many prices had doubled and over 100 peasant unions from traditional centres of unrest in the Cochabamba valley blocked all roads to the city of Cochabamba demanding a resumption of subsidies. Banzer ordered a major assault on the peasants and more than 100 were killed in what is now known as the "Massacre of the Valley".

Banzer's power was based on the group of modernising agricultural entrepreneurs around Santa Cruz in the *Oriente*. In the 1960s, cash crop ·production in this region expanded considerably. Between 1962 and 1971, cotton production rose by 809%, coffee by 375% and sugar by 242%. Many poor *minifundistas* of the *altiplano* and the Cochabamba valley migrated to the plantations of the Santa Cruz region in search of seasonal work.

Despite the growth of the agricultural sector, by 1977 the Bolivian economy was in a state of severe crisis. Banzer relied on foreign loans to expand the economy and the country was heavily in debt. There had been little investment in the country and the oil industry was declining. Popular opposition to his rule grew considerably. In 1976, the Bolivian miners went on the longest strike in their history. This was followed by a growing popular movement demanding an amnesty for the country's political prisoners. In 1978, a hunger strike was organised by the prisoners' families and friends. Banzer was forced to call elections in that year.

The following years are amongst the most turbulent in Bolivia's history. Including the 1978 election there were three elections up to 1980 and several coups and countercoups. A centre left coalition won the 1980 election but was prevented from coming to power by another right wing military coup, headed by General Garcia Meza. Meza faced strong opposition from the miners and peasants. At least 500 people were brutally murdered in the first few months of his government. In 1981 Garcia Meza was removed; his corruption and links with the cocaine trade bringing Bolivia into international disrepute. Economic bankruptcy was imminent.

Peasants

Against this background of political turmoil, the Bolivian peasant struggles for daily survival. *Minifundismo* and all that it implies — low productivity, the persistence of traditional farming methods, scarce goods and services — dominated agrarian structure in the *altiplano* and in the valleys.

In the *altiplano*, peasants live in primitive and harsh conditions. The main crops are potatoes and barley, the traditional subsistence crops. The valleys are more fertile and more varied crops such as maize, oats and alfalfa, as well as potatoes are grown. The Cochabamba valley is one of the most densely populated rural regions of Bolivia and pressure on the land is very great. Some commercial agriculture has developed in the Yungas, tropical valleys to the north of La Paz. This is based on coffee and coca, from the leaves of which comes the drug, cocaine. The peasants also grow citrus fruits, bananas and vegetables which they market in La Paz.

Large estates and agri-industry are found mainly in the *Oriente* and it is there that peasants from the other regions go in search of seasonal work on the cotton and sugar plantations. Peasants are recruited by middlemen who come to the villages and offer to transport them, for a fee, to the plantations. The women and children often accompany the men. Work on the plantations is hard, the pay low and the living conditions unhealthy and very overcrowded. Trade unions are rarely allowed.

Role of peasant women

A study of the social participation of rural women in Bolivia in 1978 provides some useful insights into the situation of peasant women in Bolivia.[2] The study was based on research in three areas of Bolivia: the Cochabamba valley, La Paz department and the department of Santa Cruz. Although the position of peasant women varies somewhat according to geographical region, some general conclusions applicable to peasant women in Bolivia as a whole emerge from the study.

One of the main conclusions of the study is that besides playing a central role in production in the rural areas, their participation is greater than men's. The authors include housework as productive work, as it is clearly essential to the survival and reproduction of the family. The study states:

> *"The woman in the agricultural areas is mostly responsible for all the domestic tasks: looking after the children, the home and the husband. Besides this, she participates in all the activities of agricultural production ... Her participation in domestic tasks, which can be considered as family production, represents 19.4% (of her time); in agricultural work, 17.4% and in caring for the animals, 11.6%; this makes a total of 48.4%, a figure much higher than in the case of the men, whose participation in the productive process is only 42%."*

In addition, her role in the marketing of small products is greater at 41.9% than that of the man, at 20%.

But the study concludes that despite the important role of the woman in production and marketing, "the situation of women's participation in goods, power and prestige, is limited and restricted." As is the case with other peasant women in Latin America, there is an inconsistency between their central economic and productive role and their low social status.

The study also points out that the time spent in the home isolates women from community activities and leads to a low level of political

----

2. *La Participacion Social de la Mujer Campesina en Bolivia*, Consorcio de Expertos Consultores, La Paz, 1978

participation in community life. Another research study of women in the Cochabamba valley carried out by the regional office of the National Service of Community Development analysed the variety of domestic and agricultural tasks carried out by peasant women:[3]

TASK	%	TASK	%
Housework	95.5%	Marketing of products	60%
Planting	77.5%	Preparation of the land	60%
Care of animals	73.75%	Crop cultivation/care	25%
Harvesting	68.75%	Weaving	15.5%
Spinning	61.25%		

In contrast only 43% of the women interviewed participated in any organisation or group which worked to develop the community or improve the life of the family. Other data in the 1978 study points to the general lack of education and high illiteracy amongst rural women (53.2% for the countryside as a whole but 72.02% for peasant women).

Another interesting finding in the 1978 study was that while the man values, to a certain extent, the domestic, agricultural, commercial and handicraft work of the women, he is opposed to their taking on leadership roles or positions of authority. The women share the men's opposition to their assumption of such a role, thus not only supporting this form of discrimination against themselves, but also reflecting their low consciousness of this as a factor of their own oppression.

There is a growing women's movement in Bolivia, mainly in the mining areas. In the forefront of this is the *Comite de Amas de Casa* (Housewives Committee), in SigloXX, the country's largest mining town. One of the founder members of the Committee is Domitila de Chungara. Her book, *Let Me Speak,* is a classic testimony of the struggles of women and miners in Bolivia.

The women of the tin mines have experienced the brutality of the army as much as the men, even though the miners have often found it difficult to accept that women should participate in these struggles with them. Through the process of politicisation during these political struggles, many have become more aware of their own oppression as women. An indication of the growing active militancy amongst poor Bolivian women is the fact that in 1972, the first camp for women political detainees in the history of Latin America, was set up just outside La Paz.

----

3.   *Actividades Organizativos de la Mujer Campesina*, Oficine Regional de SNDC, Cochabamba, 1978.

BOLIVIA

The country:
Area: 1,098,581 sq. km.
Main cities:
 Legal Capital: Sucre (pop. 90,000)
 Seat of government: La Paz (pop. 800,000)
 Cochabamba (pop. 150,000)
 Santa Cruz (pop. 131,000)
 Potosi (pop. 97,000)

The people:
Population: 5,790,000 (1979)
 Women: 2,701,000
Rural: 68% (1979)
Annual rate of population growth: 2.6%
Race: 70% Indian, 25% Mestizo, 5% European
Language: Spanish predominates in speech and script in urban areas; Quechua and Aymara in rural areas (both are now official languages)

Social indicators:
Life expectancy at birth: women, 53 years; men, 48 years
Infant mortality rate: 168/1000 live births, 0-1 year
Population without access to clean water: 66%
Adult illiteracy: women, 49%; men, 25%

The government:
Military
Central government expenditure: (1979)
 Education: 27.1% of total budget
 Public health: 8.2%
 Housing: 0.8%

The economy:
Gross National Product: US $2.88 billion (1978)
 GNP per capita: US $510 (1978)
Distribution of Gross Domestic Production: (1978)
 Services: 55%
 Industry: 28%
 Agriculture: 17%
 Manufacturing: 13%
Economically active population (aged 10+): 45.7% (1970)
 Women as % of total labour force: 21% (1980)
 Women employed in agriculture: 22% (1975)

WOMEN ORGANISE

The militancy of the women of the mines has had an impact on the women's movement elsewhere in the country. In January 1980 the first National Congress of Bolivian peasant women was held in La Paz under the auspices of the CSUTC (the main *campesino* workers federation), affiliated to the COB. Over 1000 peasant women attended — 700 more than had been expected, and the Congress proceeded to set up its own Federation to deal specifically with the predicament of the Bolivian peasant woman. A manifesto was produced with 64 points calling for change in the women's political, economic, social, educational and cultural situation.

At the Congress, Rosa Dominga was elected Executive Secretary of the National Federation of Campesina Women. I found Rosa in one of the back courtyards of the office of the Confederation of Peasant Workers of Bolivia. I explained to her and two of her male coleagues, who I was, why I was there, and what I wanted.

For the first time I was actually being made to explain very clearly, by the Indians, themselves, and not development workers who worked with them, what my intentions were. Too often while talking to peasant women, I had the feeling that they didn't really understand what my objectives were, but because I was a *gringa*, no one really wanted to press me or offend me.

But here in the Confederation, being a *gringa* was, if anything, a disadvantage, as I was a representative of all that they were trying to fight and change. The Confederation, in its manifesto, outlined its policies of fighting against the centuries-old oppression and exploitation of Bolivian *campesinos* from both within and outside the country in all aspects of their lives — social, cultural, educational and economic:

> "Let us fight until there is no exploitation, and because, too, as Aymaras, Quechuas, Cambas, Tupiguaranies, we will no longer be oppressed by other systems dominating us. We want to be free as citizens of our own country. The battle isn't only economic. Not only must we put an end to economic exploitation, but also to the oppression of our own heritage and cultural identity."

Rosa Dominga, 31, had two children, both boys. Of her five brothers and two sisters, she was the only one still living in the campo. *The others all had professions, and were living in the city.*

She began fighting for the rights of Bolivian peasant women at an early age. She described how the earlier struggles led to the women's first National Congress.

I went to fifth grade in primary school. In the *campo*, there was a Seventh Day Adventist school and they helped me to pay what it cost. I actually started the sixth grade, but my mother got sick, and I had to leave. There wasn't anyone else to look after my younger brothers and sisters. I wanted to study more but I couldn't. There were nine of us and we didn't have enough money for us all to go to school.

After I left school, I worked as a maid in Cochabamba for three years, and I also worked in a bakery in La Paz for a year. So up until I was 19, I worked selling myself all the time to live. I used to send money to my brothers and sisters so they could buy what they needed for school, and since my mother was still very sick, I used to buy her medicines, too. She didn't have any money and couldn't work.

Then I went back to the *campo*. There was work in the *campo* to grow what we needed, and my grandfather asked me to come back and help in the fields.

Then I got married. (She laughed.) I was 21. My husband is from the *campo* too, near where I lived. We still live there, but we don't always live in the village. We live in one of the outlying areas.

Getting married changed everything. When you are young, you are free to do anything, almost. You just have to ask your father or mother for permission to go out . . . but when you get married, it changes. You have to do everything for yourself then, and if the man doesn't stay, then you have to earn all the money to maintain the children.

I saw my mother's life when I was young. She was the slave to my father. He wasn't a very good man. He wouldn't let her go anywhere — not to meetings, not even to the market. Whatever we needed, he would bring home. When he got sick, my mother didn't know what to do. She wasn't used to going out. So from the beginning, I have always thought that things should be different.

If we could learn to speak in the house, things would be different. My mother could never say anything to my father. He would shout or not listen. From childhood, we women are very submissive and meek. We don't know how to discuss or argue, or say anything. So I knew from the beginning, that we needed an organisation where we could learn to think, speak, and decide for ourselves what we needed and what we wanted to do in the future.

It was the same when I started work as a maid. I had bad luck then too. I worked hard and never received very much money. I used to think that if we, all the *domesticas* (maids), could organise ourselves, we could tell people about the bad treatment that we had from the *señoras* (ladies of the house).

When I was younger, I could see what we needed in the *campo*. There was no one, nobody who was saying to the other women, "Let's do this or that." So I started to work and organise in my community. In my village, I learned . . . that is, the experience taught me. For example, I saw that the women couldn't read or write, so we organised a small group to teach them. I was the only one in the group who knew how to read and write.

When I moved to my husband's community, no one there knew how to read or write either — at least not the women. So we started there with reading and writing. I said to the women, "Let's organise ourselves, and ask for classes in *alfabetizacion* (literacy). After we learn how to read and write, we can educate our children better."

For example, the mothers are always together with their children. There are mothers — lots of women — who don't know how to read and write. When the teachers give the children work to do, we mothers can't say if it is done well or not, and we can't help. When you know how to read and write you can say, "No, you should do it like this or like that." I told the women that, like their children, they could learn . . . they had to learn.

I taught myself to organise. I suffered a lot when I was young, and I don't want my children to suffer as I did. I want my children to have a profession, a house with water and whatever they need.

But women here are afraid. You have to help them slowly. We started with a mothers' club, that someone else had organised, where they used to give them a bit of free food too.[4] We used to have a teacher come and teach us about cooking, and other things. Little by little it all got bigger.

Then we had some money that we saved in the club, and we decided to buy sugar, rice and noodles to make a communal store. At the end of the year, all the women shared in the profits, according to what they spent. In the second year, we bought more things, and had a profit again. The women realised that they had been giving their profit to the shopkeepers. We had a party; people had a good time, and they said it was good to organise.

After organising on the local level, I started to work at the regional level and then nationally. My husband was a member of the union organisation, and some of them gave us some help. My husband started to help me, and gave me and our small group an orientation. That's how I got involved working for the liberation of the *campesina* woman.

It was difficult at the beginning — it still is. It is the first year of the first (national) organisation for *campesina* women. It is hard to get them to understand, and to think about what we are going to do. That is why we set up the organisation.

You know, everyone has been talking about the problems that women have been having for years. But who was going to say to the women that we should organise on such a date and in such a place? But another *compañera* and I — we decided to do it. So we wrote something and sent it to all the groups, and we put it on the radio. The Confederation of Workers helped us. We weren't expecting very many — only about 300 women. But 1000 came to the Congress in January! *Compañera* Domitila came. She spoke to us about their struggles and how women must fight. We read her book — that is one of the things that encouraged me to organise the big meeting.

Women are beginning to discuss, to ask questions, to talk about their needs. If we work well together, maybe we can even make the government listen to us. But if we stay in our houses, we have nothing. No one is going to take any notice of us.

If we are organised, if we can come up with resolutions, we can publish them in the newspapers, on the radio, so everyone will know what we are thinking. Everyone will begin to think about the *campesina* woman. I have seen how

————

4.   This was part of the World Food Programme — the donation of surplus food by the United States to developing countries.

the factory workers and the miners organise, and we are equal. We are producers and workers too. Why shouldn't we have our own organisation to fight for our own needs?

We aren't going to break away or separate from the men. We have to work together. There are meetings, general assemblies, but the women don't know anything about any of them . . . nothing. Our husbands don't allow us to speak. They laugh at us, some of them.

Why? Because we are women, and we don't know how to think. Since childhood we have been like this. Because of our own mothers and fathers, women have been discriminated against. But carry on like that? No, we must change it. To do that, we have to have an organisation where we can talk, where we have a voice and a vote. In this way, we can learn how to fight. Ever since I was young, it has been my dream.

You know, we women are different. The men sell themselves so easily in these organisations. They don't think of the grass-roots. They think in personalities and the politics. But we women aren't like that. With the men — one *compañero* comes, and then another, and they start to buy beer, and drink, and so easily they sell themselves. But the women are different.

In the time of Banzer, when we had so many problems . . . some of the leaders, the men, were exiled to other countries. Four women started a hunger strike, and other women came to join them. They won.

With our organisation we want to support all the women who have been fighting, and we want to wake the others up, to move them forward. We don't want women to be slaves any more — cooks in the kitchen, looking after the children without ever going out. We want to be freer, to think and learn.

Now, if the women say they want to do something, they ask the men to support them. We still need to do this; we are still behind, but at least we are asking now.

The men say, since we are just beginning with our organisation, "What are these women going to do? When did they start to organise all this?" Many have thought about the problems of women, but didn't do anything. Now that we are organising, they will have to do something. Most of them have suffered as slaves to the boss, and we, just like them, want to stop being slaves, and stop the injustices.

Now with the devaluation that the president and the government have given us, we are worse off than before. For example, our potatoes and *chuño* (freeze-dried potatoes) — that is all we have to sell. Now it is impossible to live on what we can each sell them for. So we thought it would be better to organise cooperatives and work together.

What I want is that the President, and the ones who are governing the country, come to the *campo* to see how we live . . . to see that we have nothing, no education, no roads. Many people have to walk for two or three days from the main road to get to their houses, with all their children carrying everything they sell or buy. If we complain about the transport because the price has gone up so much, they just say, "Get off if you don't like it". But if there is no other transport, we have to go with them. We are slaves to them too.

The government has no idea. They live in La Paz and they have everything. They have their own transport, enough to eat, education. They have everything, and they don't want to know about us, the *campesinos* who have nothing.

But we are the workers — the producers. We sacrifice ourselves to produce. If it weren't for the *campesinos*, the workers, I don't know what Bolivia would do. We produce everything — potatoes, vegetables, meat, wool — everything, and at the lowest price, which doesn't allow us to buy anything or look after our families. They say that we are lazy, and that is why we don't have anything. But we are the ones who are doing all the work.

Look at the miners — the poor miner who works for almost nothing to take out the tin and the lead. Even at a young age, they get sick, and all for Bolivia. I want the president to come and see all that. Maybe then they will have some idea of how we all sacrifice ourselves for our country.

The women work three times as hard as the men. The husband goes to work in the *chacra* (small field), and he comes home and what does he do? He lies down to rest. If we have been out working in the field, what do we do? We start to cook; we go for firewood; we wash clothes. Sometimes even at night, we have to wash clothes if there is no other time to do it. *Then* we go to sleep.

In the morning, we get up at 5 a.m., while the men sleep until 6 a.m. at least. When they get up, we have to have the food all prepared to serve to them. After that we go and feed our animals, or take them to pasture. With the children, you have to wash and dress them. This is all work. We are nursemaids, cooks and workers — all at the same time.

We always work with the men in the *campo*. There are very few men who go out to the *chacra* without their women. We take the lunch and we work all day. We work at the planting, and the harvesting, and we look after the animals. The men hardly ever herd the sheep. It is always the women who do that.

If I were president, I would set up nurseries for the children, so that women would have a little time to go to meetings and classes, and learn how to read and write. Because when we have the classes, the women say, "I can't work. The children won't let me study. They grab at the pencils and the notebooks."

So I'd think first about nurseries. Then I would have classes all over the country for the *campesinos*, men and women, to learn how to read and write. Then I'd have a school for the adults so they could learn more still. Nobody here has a good education. It seems to me that there is one education for the people in the cities and another for the country. I think they send all the best teachers to the cities, and the ones who can't teach, or who don't know anything, they send to the country. That is why we are behind.

Most of the men know how to read and write in the regions near La Paz. It is rare to find one who doesn't. But the women don't. In the *haciendas* (large, privately owned farms) the women don't know anything. And it is worse in many of the provinces.

For example, in one of the provinces — where there hasn't been any education, or agrarian reform, neither the men nor the women can read or write. They can't speak Spanish . . . only their own language, Aymara, and in other parts they only speak Quechua. In other zones, at least people understand what "yes" and "no" mean in Spanish. But where there has been no law, no education, people don't even know the name of the president.

I have seen this because I have been all over the 18 provinces for the women's organisation. We are organised all over the country now. Tomorrow, I have to go to Oruru (another town in Bolivia). We have a meeting of all the women in the province tomorrow.

Women need work too. I don't know if they suffer in other countries the way we do here. Perhaps we could see and learn from them.

Or maybe they suffer the same way. In my community, for example, I started a craft project. We made lots of things — knitting small bags. But we didn't know where to sell them. We still have them locked away, because we can't sell them. If we sell them in La Paz, to the shopkeepers, we won't get a good price, and they will get all the profit. We have to buy the alpaca wool, because in our area, we don't have alpacas.

Some people came once from an organisation to help us. They started us making scarves, shawls, sweaters, bags — everything. They were going to sell them for us. But then the woman brought it all back, and said she couldn't sell it. There we have stayed.

Women should be able to decide when they want to have children and how many. Now in the *campo*, the harvest is bad. There are no potatoes or *chuño*. There is nothing for the animals to graze on. How are we going to feed the children? If there was food for the animals, we could sell them, and buy what we need. So we don't have enough to maintain ourselves, let alone the children. We don't know how to read and write. And so we go on, malnourished with no education.

Bolivia goes further and further backward. If we had doctors, lawyers and people who knew how to do things, we could progress. But there is no point in having more people if it is all going to be the same — that the *campesinos* carry on having nothing.

I work with my husband in the *chacra*. We get up at about 5 a.m. We usually do everything together, but he is studying secondary school now. So I have to serve as husband and wife. I am worried about how I am going to maintain him and the children. There isn't anyone to help me.

Children take up all your time. When you don't have any children, life is much more peaceful; you can work more, earn more. But when you have even one or two — it is all different. So he and I talked about it, and because he isn't finished school yet we agreed not to have any more now.

But I don't use any medicine. When I was younger, I went to the church in my village and they taught me about not having any more children according to menstruation. I know which date it is supposed to come, and which days are dangerous.

You have to get your husband to be in agreement. My mother had so many children. She didn't know any of this, and because there were so many, I couldn't go to school. Now, because my husband isn't working, I don't want so many children.

It is a problem for us here. There are two sides. Here in Bolivia, we aren't very many people. There is still a lot of land, and to fight for it, and work, we need more people. But in the time of Banzer there were lots of organisations . . . these groups tried to get everyone to use things so they wouldn't have more children. I went to one of the courses. They told us that we had to have injections, take pills — all this, so we couldn't have more children.

I even heard in this time that there was a new law. I never knew about it exactly. I only heard that Banzer tried to bring foreigners to our country to try to change the race — to change the people. We thought in our meetings, why should he want to change the race, if we all have been here since the beginning? So I decided not to use anything not to have more children. Then all those organisations stopped working because all the people became very angry.

Other women have asked me, "Tell me what you use not to have any more children. You must have used some sort of medicine." I don't tell them anything. I just say, "It's just my luck. I don't use anything."

It isn't easy to talk about these things. If I say something — how to look after yourself, or how to mark the dates to know about the dangerous days —their husbands for sure will come to ask me what I told their wives. With some women I have confidence, and I have told a few how to mark the dates, but I have to be careful.

Like I said, we need people here in Bolivia to fight for our country, and our rights. But to have children and not be able to educate or feed them — what is the point of having them?

If I have a lot of children, I can't send them to school, or give them a good life. With just two children, I can manage. I can sacrifice myself until whenever, so that they learn, so that they have a profession. Then they can look after themselves. My husband and I can be happy. But if you can't study, you have nothing. Your children will be the same as you — working in the fields for the rest of their lives. So I don't think people should have so many children, but I don't know. We need people too. I don't know what is right. I don't have the answer.

I'M DIFFERENT, BUT I'M STILL THE SAME

"They think that someone different, from another place, like you, is more important than the people from here. So they don't take any notice — men or women. They say, 'That woman is just like us . . . she doesn't know anything'.

"And that is a real problem, if they think that a local person, or someone like me, who is really the same as them, can't teach them anything. They are always saying that they want someone from somewhere else to teach them new things . . . that foreigners are the only ones who know anything."
—Maria-Luisa, a Bolivian peasant woman, a community worker.

Maria-Luisa was another Bolivian peasant woman committed to working for change in the lives of *campesina* women.

She worked for a cooperative located almost at the Bolivian/Chilean border. The journey from La Paz had taken nine hours by jeep with the last three hours of the journey made over open fields; no road had yet been built.

The cooperative was attempting to better its production and marketing of llama and alpaca fleece[5], as well as introduce new forms of technology to the area, such as solar heating, hot house vegetable gardening and underground irrigation. The project received technical assistance and financial support from two American organisations. Within the larger cooperative, there was a women's project, making specific attempts to promote women's educational and income-generating activities.

Members of the cooperative lived at great distances from each other, and came to the central office only once a month for meetings. For some, this meant two to three days walking or bicycling over the vast *altiplano*, as there were no roads or other transport.

Before my interview with Maria-Luisa, I had the chance to talk briefly with a few women involved in the project. *Señora* Felipa was the elected president. She told me why the women had been singled out for special consideration.

"We wanted to do something for women, because before there was

---

5.   Llamas and alpacas are animals bred on the *altiplano*. Both are bred for wool; the llama also serves as a pack animal.

nothing. All we ever did was look after the house and our children and the animals. That was it . . . nothing more.

"There was never enough food to feed the children. The husbands would say, 'Well, go and find something.' What could we do — steal? No, we had to create some work, so we could earn money.

"So we set up a little shop here because there are no markets, and the women bring in the fleece from the animals and sell it. Then they buy what they need — flour, sugar, oil. We manage the shop ourselves.

"The men used to say, 'Ah, women . . . you don't know anything; you aren't worth anything.' They used to do all the buying and selling in La Paz. None of us could do it. We didn't know the city, or how things were, or where to sell the wool . . . so we could have been robbed or cheated. Now two of us always go with the men, and we are learning.

"Many of the women are very shy. They won't even speak in Aymara. They are frightened. They never used to leave the house except to look after the animals, so it is no wonder they are scared. They can't even think.

"But I'm not afraid. I've always liked to talk to people. I lived in Chile for two years. We went there to find work; and the Chileans talk a lot, all the time. So I got used to it."

Maria Luisa had two unique characteristics. First, she was a peasant woman paid to work with other peasant women. Generally those jobs went to women with urban backgrounds. Second, she was still single at 39.

She explained the opportunity she had been given 16 years earlier to move away from the traditional future of a young peasant girl, and the problems she had encountered initially with her family.

Because of the work I was doing where I lived, the community asked me if I wanted to go on a special course — a pilot programme for voluntary workers — to learn about leadership and other things. There were 60 of us . . . no, about 50 . . . 25 men and 25 women — all young.

I went for 12 days. It was a short time, but they taught us a lot in that time — improving the home, knitting, embroidery, nutrition, health, leadership in groups, raising animals, setting up cooperatives — everything. I listened to everything the teachers said, and I learned everything they taught us. I haven't forgotten it yet, and I will never forget it.

They told us that when we went back to our villages we had to report to our communities about all that we had learned. There were Peace Corps volunteers in our village too, and they helped me. We had to form groups, to do what we had learned — the same as now, forming groups of women, organising so they can learn about making their homes better.

Before, there wasn't anything for women in the village. I didn't even know how to hold the *pelota* (ball). I had never even touched one, but in the course, I learned sports — how to play volleyball.

I started a small club for women to do sports. We organised teams and went to play teams in other communities. People used to come to visit the communities, to see the work we were doing. They were the supervisors, but I didn't know that at the time. They used to arrive and talk about the work I was doing in the community.

I was still a volunteer then. We did lots of different things in the group — knitting, embroidery, weaving cloth. We made and sold a lot of things. We used to have discussions about agriculture.

My mother used to get angry. "Why are you doing all this?" she asked. "What are they going to pay you? Nothing. They won't pay you anything."

She thought I was wasting time. But I always wanted to help my sisters — the other women in the community. I had something inside that made me want to do it, no matter what. I believe that we are equal and that we should all help each other. Before, I had nothing that was really important to me.

I used to help the *gringa* from the Peace Corps. My boss, the one who organised all the projects, would come sometimes too. The *gringa* didn't speak our language — Aymara. She used to take me with her to translate from Spanish to Aymara so she could talk to people. I did that for a year.

After that year, they sent me to a course in Cochabamba for development workers in the community. It was for three months, and out of the 25 people, only two were women. They said they were going to give us a salary for the work we were doing. We each had to speak to our families, and it was all right. They accepted me onto the course. I went, and I never returned home after that, at least not in the way I had been living there.

I have been working here in the cooperative for two years, and I don't think we have been that successful. In the first year, we didn't have any transport, and we had to walk a lot. We lost a lot of time. We weren't doing many things, because we spent most of our time travelling to the different villages. The women don't have time to stay here at the centre. They have to be with their animals. Once a month, we have a meeting here.

We have courses, but we haven't had much success with those either. We are always having problems with the men. When the teachers come to give the courses, the men don't want their women to go. They don't make it easy for them. Even for our own meetings of women, the men say that the women should stay in the house to look after the children. But whenever there is a course, or a meeting, the men are all here. They don't have a problem in getting away.

As a result of some of the work we are doing here, the women are beginning to get involved in the affairs of the community. Little by little, as in everything, we are gradually overcoming the problems. We have separate meetings. The women meet together and the men meet together. The men never let the women talk when the meetings are mixed. It is very difficult, but gradually, the women are getting used to saying what they think, and the men are getting used to it too. Soon we will start to have mixed meetings. But in other communities, it is still like it used to be. They haven't had this kind of training.

We should have about 60 women at our meetings, but as I said, they don't all come. Usually 20 or 30 appear . . . sometimes as many as 50. They have to come from a very long way. It takes at least two days walking for some of them to get here.

The change is very slow. I would say that most of them aren't changing very much. We are trying to work with some younger women now. They are afraid too, and sometimes don't come to the meetings. Or they say that they have other things to do — their parents want them to help at home. But I still have faith that we will achieve something in the end.

Already there are two women who participate quite actively. We had a meeting here for all the animal owners and these two women participated actively in all the discussions. They weren't afraid of speaking up. They know how to take the floor now. When there are courses and meetings, we are always saying that the women should come and participate, or at least listen. And little by little, some are coming and saying the occasional thing.

In Bolivia, our biggest problem is the lack of education. The women have never received an education, and as a result, they are frightened. They say, "I can't express myself very well." Most of them are illiterate, although the younger ones can read now. But they are still afraid ɔ speak ɩp and say what they think.

I think that we have to carry on having meetings with just women until they all become less timid. Otherwise, they will just sit there, and let the men talk.

Each *ayllu* (community) has 60-90 people living in it. We have been thinking recently of trying to develop leaders in each area — to teach about animals, human relations, socio-drama — the women like that. If they are only among women — sisters — they lose their fear and start to make jokes, play games and say what they feel. It is very good for them.

We also want to develop the production and sale of the things the women make — the handicrafts and the clothes. The women spin alpaca. They sell it by the pound in the market. Sometimes they will contract to make a sweater. One of them made this sweater for me.

It is mainly the women who go to the markets, but those are the markets that are close by. If the market is far away, the men will go to do the buying and selling.

When they sell their wool, they use the money right away to buy what they need. They don't keep it because they always need to buy something. For example, today they will bring all their wool, and sell it to the project. Immediately after, they will buy bread or rice for the whole week.

Life is very difficult for the women here. They have never been able to study, and they have a lot of work to do, especially looking after the children.

In this area, people tend to have about five children. In other regions they have slightly larger families — about seven children.

They don't really know about anything that will prevent them from having children. There are some nurses — they work in the Ministry of Health. But that is not enough. They don't know anything about the lives of these women. All they know is how to give injections, and nothing else. The women here — no one helps them, not even to give birth. Sometimes their husbands will help, or a neighbour, or someone in the family.

I don't know anything about contraceptives. Some women from other areas told me that you can buy pills and take them, and that will stop you having children. But the women here aren't interested. I think they know that these pills exist, but they also say that they aren't good for you. They want to have bigger families . . . well, some want big families, and some don't. They are worried about how they are going to feed so many. If you have many children, you usually can't afford to send them all to school.

But I think it is important to know about these things. Unfortunately, the women are afraid to ask questions. The young ones that have been to school, know a little about it, and aren't so afraid. But the older ones are either afraid, or they don't think it is important. I didn't know anything at all about any of that. When I went on this course years ago, it was all a surprise to me, what I learned there about health, and my body. My parents, my mother, didn't teach me anything.

You know, without that course that I went on — the very first one — I would have a husband, my babies — the whole thing — an established home and family. I'm sure it would be that way, because that is what has happened to all the girls from the village. They have all done that.

They say to me, "Why don't you get married?" And I say, "If I get married, then I will have to serve my husband, and work for him. I wouldn't be able to carry on working as I do now."

I know many women who have been on some of the courses with me . . . they have married . . . some to teachers, or engineers, or they just stayed in the country. But they have all stopped the work that they were doing. I think I would have to do the same, if I got married.

Other young girls — before they get married — they go to find work somewhere else because there is no work here. They go to La Paz, or the Yungas. They go to work as servants in other people's houses, or they might have a bit of land in the Yungas. Sometimes they stay away permanently, and sometimes they come back. But there are always problems when young girls from the mountains go to the cities. So many of them end up as single mothers. They don't know how to look after themselves, and people, men and women, take advantage of them. But the reason that they leave in the first place, is that there is no money here, and no work.

We have to keep working towards making people aware. It has to be done through courses and discussions . . . as much for the men as for the women. They could have mixed classes. In other places, closer to the city, the women are much more active, and participate more, because they are always coming and going to and from the city. Different people always come to visit the village . . . volunteers from other countries, and people from the department of agricultural extension. There are good roads.

Here there isn't even a road, so we are totally ignored and isolated. If people had a chance to see other ways of life, then they would gradually change, too. The women know they have to study to move forward — the same as men.

But there are some problems. We always say to the women, "When you go back home, you don't have to be the one in charge. You should be a support to your husband." But some people have said that we are teaching women in the groups to order their husbands around. I think it was some of the men who said that. (She laughed.) I think they must be afraid. So they say the opposite of the truth . . . that we are teaching women, and encouraging them to take the reins from their husbands.

"You know why there are so many poor people in Peru? It's because the rich people want it that way. We think it should be more equal, but the rich want us to be at the bottom and them to be at the top. They say that one day it will happen that everyone will be the same, or at least more equal. But I don't believe it. It's a lie."
— woman working in an artesan cooperative.

PERU

Peru, the third largest country in South America, is a land of great regional contrasts. Its 16.4 million people live mainly on the Pacific coast or in the *Sierra* (Andes mountains). The tropical forest and jungle in the east cover 62% of the country's area, but hold only 8% of the population.

From pre-Conquest times to the early 19th century, Peru was one of the cultural and economic centres of South America. The capital of the Inca empire was Cuzco, in southern Peru. Today, Indian descendants of that empire, now living mainly in the *Sierra*, make up 50% of the Peruvian population.

The Spanish formed the Viceroyalty of Alto Peru from Peru and Bolivia, and established Lima as its capital. It has survived as Peru's capital to the present day.

Economic resources

The region's wealth was based on silver. In addition, large quantities of mercury, used in silver refining, were discovered around Huancavelica, an Andean town. Many thousands of Indians who were forced to work in the mercury mine died from mercury poisoning. It has been estimated that two-thirds of the Indian population died from disease and overwork during the first 50 years of the Spanish occupation.

Since its independence in 1852 Peru's economy has been based on the exploitation and export of vast natural resources. Like the rest of Latin America, Peru's periods of prosperity and depression have been dependent on the fortunes or misfortunes of the world commodity market.

In the mid-19th century, after a prolonged period of economic stagnation, the economy revived due to an increased demand for fertilisers in Europe. Peru had the world's richest supply of an important fertiliser component — bird droppings rich in nitrogen (*guana*).

Mineral nitrates were Peru's other major resource. In 1875, Peru and Bolivia went to war with Chile over control of the nitrate area. Peru lost the war and the nitrates; Bolivia lost its exit to the sea — and a depression set in.

After the first World War, growing world demand stimulated sugar production on the coastal plantations. Until the 1950s, sugar and cotton were the country's leading exports together with minerals such as lead, zinc and copper. By 1967, export agriculture had been surpassed by fishmeal and mining as the country's main export earners, and industrial production replaced agriculture as the main contributor to national output.

In the 1950s and 1960s, the structure of the Peruvian economy began to change with the growth of foreign investment. The sugar and cotton plantations of the northern coast were still owned mainly by Peruvians who were members of the country's traditional elite. But by 1968, foreign interests, mainly US and other multinational companies, controlled three-quarters of the mining capital in Peru, two-thirds of the sugar refining industry, half the cotton and wool processing plant, half the fishing industry, half the commercial banking sector and about one-third of the manufacturing industry.

Political developments

Until the 1950s, Peruvian politics were dominated by the hostility between the American Popular Revolutionary Alliance (APRA) and the army and wealthy elite. APRA was founded in 1924 by Victor Haya de la Torre. Although its main support came from plantation workers, the party also tried to establish a power base amongst the middle class.

Its considerable broad based support and strong stand against the concentration of wealth and power in the hands of a small elite made it a frequent victim of government repression. The army regularly intervened whenever it appeared that APRA might win an election.

In the 1950s, new political movements developed as the urban population grew with the migration of peasants to the cities in search of work. The migrants, non-unionised workers and the urban and rural middle class formed the basis of a new party, the Popular Action (AP). Led by Fernando Belaunde Terry, it pressed for moderate reforms. Simultaneously, there was a growth in parties of the left, and in particular in organised peasant struggles.

Land ownership and agrarian reform

The French writer, Marcel Niedergang wrote in 1962:[1]

> *"One wonders in fact how much longer Peru can continue to progress while its 5½ million people along the coastal strip live in the 20th century and its six or seven million Indians in the Sierra remain in the 16th century."*

At that time, 3% of the land owners held 88% of the land, while 74% of land holders struggled with a meagre 4% of the land. Only 1000 individuals owned 60% of the country's farm land.

In the coastal regions, the land owners had turned their estates into profitable and relatively technically advanced enterprises. But in the highlands, agriculture slumped. The land owners with large estates in the highlands had little interest in the land except as a source of political power and rent. The Indians remained tied to the land owner by the service relations common in other Andean countries.

In Peru, the Indian who worked for the land owner in return for a small plot of subsistence land was called a *colono*. There were also village communities, (*comunidades*), which were the main social and economic unit in the high Andes. The village communities had anywhere from 100 to 1000 individual members — *comuneros*.

Historically, the *comunidades* derived from the *ayllu*, the agricultural commune which predated even the Incas. Within the *comunidad*, each family owned or cultivated its own small plot which provided basic subsistence. The peasants were collectively responsible for land which was held and cultivated by the community members.

In the late 1950s, peasant unrest grew and *comuneros* took over large estates throughout the country. In the southern province of Cuzco, Hugo Blanco, a Trotskyist leader, organised the *colonos* into a regional uprising which was violently suppressed by the army during 1961-63.

––––––

1.   *The Twenty Latin Americas*, Vol. 2, Penguin, Harmondsworth, 1971.

In 1968, Belaunde's right of centre government was overthrown by the nationalist, reformist general, Juan Velasco Alvarado. He nationalised the International Petroleum Corporation and two US mining corporations, Cerro de Pasco and Marcona. The military government took control of major natural resource exports, nationalised the fishmeal industry, and took charge of developing heavy industry. In 1969, it declared an agrarian reform.

By the end of 1979 approximately five million hectares of land had been expropriated — nearly 47% of the arable land. Although this was a significant amount of land, little more than a quarter of the agricultural sector benefitted from the reform. The majority of *minifundistas*, landless seasonal labourers and *comuneros* living outside large estates were not affected.

Only about 5% of the expropriated land was divided into individual plots. The rest was handed over to cooperatives set up by the government with the aim of creating profitable and productive commercial enterprises.

The cooperative system was more suited to the coastal regions where large efficient farms had existed for some time. However, in the Andean region, the cooperative structure was inappropriate and ultimately a failure for the peasants. The *comunidades* would have been the most suitable basis for the agrarian reform, but the government refused to recognise the *comunidades'* titles to their lands, which often dated back to the 1500s.

The cooperatives in the *Sierra* began with a considerable burden. Former land owners withdrew all their moveable wealth from their estates before moving out. The compensation they received was subsequently invested in other sectors of the economy such as industry. This left the cooperatives without capital, machinery or management experience. They had to borrow money to cover the cost of the land and machinery and, as long as they were in debt, the state reserved the right to intervene at will.

The state also had an important say in the appointment of managers to the cooperatives, and rarely did the peasants effectively run the co-operatives themselves. Lack of capital and technical skills made it difficult for the peasants to increase production. Most peasants found they were no better off working in the cooperatives than before..

The secretary general of the Confederation of Peruvian Peasants described the situation in an interview:[2]

> *"For us the State became the new land owners and maintained not only the same forms of exploitations, but above all maintained the same methods of production."*

—————

2.   *The Guardian*, "Land Cheat on the Sierra", February 5, 1981

By 1975 the Peruvian economy as a whole was in deep crisis and the reformist period of military rule was coming to a close. Velasco's programme had required massive state expenditure and heavy foreign borrowing. Velasco had not attempted to shift agricultural production away from export crops and large amounts of food still had to be imported. Food prices rose steadily. In 1974-75 the drop in world commodity prices and the failure of the fishmeal industry triggered a major crisis. Militancy amongst the working class grew as prices rose and the government tried to cut public expenditure. In 1975 Velasco was overthrown by General Morales Bermudez, and the country moved to the right.

By 1977 the country was in deep depression. The International Monetary Fund demanded an austerity programme in return for financial help. This involved a devaluation, further cuts in public expenditure, the selling off of state owned firms to the private sector, fuel and food price rises, and wage increases far below the rate of inflation.

The programme sparked off massive protests. Three general strikes were held between 1977 and 1978. The military were forced to retreat, and announced elections for a Constituent Assembly in 1978 with a return to civilian government in 1980. The election, the first in 17 years, was won by Belaunde and his centre right AP party.

In the 1980s, rising world prices for Peru's copper, oil and other exports have led to a partial recovery of the economy. The country, however, is still beset with enormous socio-economic problems. The military hover at the edge of the political arena ready to suppress any real challenge to the ruling order.

The poor bear the burden

The austerity programme has hit hardest at the poor, particularly rural peasants. Studies show that instances of malnutrition, disease and infant mortality have been rising. Vitamin deficiency and diseases like glaucoma and rickets are widespread.

In southern Peru, 60% of the rural population are without access to health services. Three-quarters of rural children who start school do not even finish the primary years. Services such as clean water and electricity are available only to people living close to the urban centres, and even then, only to those who can afford it. In fact, 83% of the rural population are without clean water; 98% have no sanitation facilities.

Illiteracy is high amongst the peasants, higher still amongst the women. The Indians speak Quechua or Aymara to each other, using Spanish only when they themselves have to go to town or when an outsider comes to the village. Very few women in the remote areas speak Spanish.

The struggle for daily survival on tiny plots of land continues. The staple crops are maize and potatoes, with perhaps some wheat, beans, *quinua* and *tarwi* (two local varieties of pigweed yielding a high protein grain). What they need and cannot grow, they must buy. Cash comes from selling part of their subsistence crop or raising and selling small animals such as guinea pigs, hens, or pigs. Wealthier families will invest any surplus in a cow, llamas or alpacas.

The other source of cash is for the adults and young people to hire themselves out as labourers — the parents working for local small land holders or the local cooperative, the young people, usually the girls, working as maids in the nearest large town, or in Lima. Women add to the family income through the sale of craft work, such as weaving. Men will migrate seasonally to the coastal plantations, leaving the women in charge of all domestic and agricultural responsibilities.

Both men and women are expected to contribute their labour to the *faena*, the village work party on communal land or communal facilities. Although the work is unpaid, *chicha* (corn beer) and *coca* are available. The chewing of *coca* leaves is a custom long practised by the Indians in Peru and Bolivia. Landlords used to make sure that the peasants had an ample supply of *coca* as it provides an effective sudden rush of energy and numbs the sensations of hunger and pain.

As in other Latin American peasant societies, the women are active agricultural producers and are responsible for all aspects of domestic life. But their role in public life is discreet and passive. Most are excluded from the political life of the community. The men, and the women themselves, justify this exclusion by the women's illiteracy, inability to speak Spanish, general isolation in the house and fields and their resulting fear, shyness and timidity. When the women do attempt to participate, they are laughed at or criticised. This effectively keeps them quiet.

There is an embryonic women's movement developing in Peru, with several groups such as ALIMUPER, the Flora Tristan Association, Peru-Mujer — all working to establish the specific rights of women. Most of these groups have an urban, middle class base, although some are now actively working in the shanty towns of Lima running leadership training and community development programmes specifically for women. Unfortunately, this activity has not yet been broadly extended to the rural areas, although several organisations working with peasants are now turning their attentions to peasant women.

An illustration of the failure to involve women occurred at a conference in a rural government training centre, where a dozen field workers, women and men, were talking about working with rural women. The workers were all clear as to what they thought the "problem" was, and what the solutions should be. Someone then asked what the rural women, themselves thought. There was silence. *Not one worker had ever spent any time in any of the communities talking to the local women about either the particular difficulties of that village as a whole, or the situation of the women living in it.* Although these workers were in the field every day, in the villages, developing and giving training courses, they always dealt with the men. It was clear that without a specific effort to involve the women, they were virtually excluded from any activities outside their traditional domestic and agricultural roles.

Within these traditional areas, there is some work going on with women, most of it dealing with crafts, health, nutrition and hygiene. But even where there are active women's projects, there are still problems. As one Indian woman said:

> *"None of the women have been to school. They are afraid to speak up because people will laugh at them. We need someone to come and help us and teach us what we don't know. There have been a few people who came out to talk about health and food, but they never stay. They come for one or two visits and then they go away. They should stay longer until the women understand. If you have never been to school, it takes a long time to learn things. And the women don't learn in one or two visits."*

PERU

The country:
Area: 1,280,219 sq. km.
Main cities:
    Capital: Lima (pop. 3,500,000)
    Trujillo (pop. 400,000)
    Arequipa (pop. 355,000)
    Cuzco (pop. 143,000)

The people:
Population: 17,625,000 (1980)
    Women: 8.8 million
Rural: 37%
Annual rate of population growth:
    2.9%
Race: 50% (approx.) Quechua and
    Aymara Indians, remainder are
    Spanish and mestizo, plus black,
    Chinese, Japanese and European
    immigrants
Language: Spanish, also Quechua and
    some Aymara

Social indicators:
Life expectancy at birth: women, 58
    years; men, 55 years
Infant mortality rate: 92/1000 live
    births, 0-1 year
**Population without access to clean
    water:** rural, 83%; urban, 23%
Population without sanitation: rural,
    98%; urban, 49%
Adult illiteracy: women, 38%; men, 27%

The government:
Civilian constitutional rule
Central government expenditure: (1978)
    Education: 17% of total budget
    Public health: 5%
    Housing: 1%

The economy:
Gross National Product: US $12.4 billion
    GNP per capita: US $740
Distribution of Gross Domestic Production:
    (1978)
    Services: 50%
    Industry: 36%
    Agriculture: 14%
Economically active population (aged 15+):
    49.8% (1970)
    Women as % of total labour force: 23% (1980)
    Women employed in agriculture: 16% (1975)

Ecuador

Peru

Lima

Cuzco

Bolivia

Arequipa

WITH US, NOT AGAINST US

In one village in southern Peru, positive attempts were being made to offer women a programme designed to support and increase their participation in the community at all levels, not just within the home.

Andrea, one of the women in the village, said:

> *"We have finally realised that the woman is very exploited. She does everything. Why is it that she comes loaded down, carrying her bundle, her children . . . and he walks in front, with hands empty?*
>
> *"Some of us are saying now, 'Why can't the man do something to help? Really, he could carry his own children.' We want them to help us, and we want to be united with them."*

In response to sentiments like these, the men of the village, through their general assembly, invited a team from the local government CENCICAP, (Campesino Education and Research Centre) to work with women in the community. For a couple of months, two women community workers visited the village, talking to the women both in groups and individually.

I arrived on the last day of a three-day training course which had developed out of these informal talks. Over the three days, many women had been meeting to talk about their own needs and the needs of the community. In the evenings, they watched slides and films. One of the films, showing peasant women from another village organising a protest against the military, had stimulated a lot of excitement and discussion.

The next night, slides on health and nutrition were shown. The discussion started well, but gradually, the women began to stop talking, and the meeting was soon dominated by one or two men. The films and slide show had been shown in the open air and everyone in the village had come to see them.

Apparently the men doing the talking had been drinking, and were not known to be sympathetic to the cause of women in the village. They proceeded to dominate the meeting, and were ably assisted by a number of other men who took the opportunity to make short speeches on a wide variety of subjects, none of which related to the issues at hand.

The next day, the women decided to hold that evening's meeting in a less open area, and restrict it to men and women who were interested in the issue of women's development and participation.

Señora Andrea was a young, pretty girl who looked older than her 18 years. She was an active member of el Frente Femenino *(the women's project). We sat and talked in the yard of her house, surrounded by chickens and baby chicks. She was peeling potatoes and cleaning corn, and would occasionally take her six month old baby from the thin, unhealthy looking girl who was taking care of the child.*

I got married about a year ago, when I was 17. I finished secondary school, and wanted to study more, but here ... people ... everyone talks about you, saying you have done things. I was just friends with Ricardo, but someone went to my father to say that he was my ... that we had been together ... lots of things, they said. Even though none of it was true, my father made us get married.

I didn't want to get married. I wanted to keep studying and working. I had been working a little bit as a teacher. When you finish secondary school, you can be a replacement teacher. That is what I wanted to do.

I am very happy now. My husband is a good man, and we have a very good understanding between us. That is the most important thing.

Right now, Ricardo and I live with my family. We are building a house, and we are going to put a little shop in it, over there, at the side of the road. Until then we have to live with my parents.

Ricardo is working on a commission that is dismantling the agricultural cooperative. They are redistributing all the land, the animals and the equipment to all the *campesino* communities.

The people who were running the cooperative from the government were very corrupt. My father had to work like everyone else, earning very little. But those running the cooperative were earning a lot of money. They never went out to the fields. The *campesinos* were very exploited. Even now, the members who worked, and suffered there, haven't gained any advantages ... they have no future. Those that were in charge ... they have their houses, their cars ... everything.

The commission that Ricardo is working on — they don't pay him for his work. I think he is doing it until the beginning of next month. He was appointed by the government in Lima, and he is obligated to do it. Sometimes, I say to him, "Why do you have to do this, without a salary . . . for nothing?" But I still have a little bit of money that I earned from teaching, and that has to last us.

I have to give him money every day for his transport. If you knew what it cost . . . 50 soles (10p) each way. Luckily I have a relative in the town where Ricardo works who cooks his food, if I send the potatoes and beans.

After this commission finishes, he will have to find other work. Someone in one of the organisations here, one of the Dutch people, said that they might have some work for him with the Ministry of Agriculture, but with a salary. Now Ricardo has a family, he has to find work. But he says we shouldn't have any more children because we can't afford it. We want our daughter to be better than us, and better than the people in the village.

They told us in school that to take care of yourself, that is, not to have children, you have to go to a doctor, a specialist. They taught this to all the women in school. Before, it was prohibited to talk of these things, but now . . . no. They explained how you could take care of yourself without using anything, just knowing your body.

I know there are others who use the pills. But here in the *campo*, they say . . . I heard . . . (she started to whisper) that the pills can do the same as one of the plants here. There are some girls who have been pregnant, and they take this plant with milk, and they have an abortion. It is true. I have heard a number of people say that. These plants and the pills are bad for your body. But there are still women using them — more the young ones, who don't want children.

The last time, when I went to the hospital, they said to me, "How old is your baby?" I told them, and they told me about this pill and the *espiral*. They said the pills were free. Now I am thinking of going to see a doctor — a specialist.

The men . . . at least, my husband is in agreement that we don't have any more children. But the others . . . here in the *campo*, the women . . . oooh . . . when we get together to work, we talk. They say, "Wouldn't it be wonderful to have a *señorita*, a teacher, who could tell us more about these things? Because year after year we have children." They say that they want someone to explain it to them in Quechua, because they don't understand

Spanish. They say they can't look after so many children . . . can't feed or dress or educate them. They say their husbands think the same way.

The day before yesterday, in one of our meetings, when we were talking, I said to Dolores (the community worker), "How good it would be to have someone come, or could we ask that someone comes to talk to the women."

I was a little shy, and ashamed to ask. But I decided to overcome my shame, and try and be as frank as I could, and I asked her.

As you know, most of the women don't speak Spanish. Most of them never went to school. Their fathers never gave them an education . . . young women too. Some of them didn't go for economic reasons. Their fathers only have a little bit of land, and from that they only manage to get enough to eat — sometimes not even that. Some didn't go because there is still this idea of not sending the girls to school. They send the boys but they say, "Why should I send my daughters to school; so they can learn to write letters to their boy friends?" There are fathers who still think like that.

The other day, we were here, just talking with one of the fathers of a family in the village. I said, "Look, why don't you send your daughter to school? She should go and learn something." And he said, "No, I will send her to the end of primary school, but after that she can start to work. Why should I send her to school so she can find a boyfriend?" Even today, there are men who think like this. I was surprised.

That is why we need *el frente femenino* . . . it is for the women in the village. We are really very backward, here, much more than the men. There is an *asamblea* (meeting) . . . if the women go, they have to sit quietly. We don't have a voice or a vote. The women are very timid. We asked for training for the women, so that at least we could talk in the meeting. Most women don't even come. So the first thing we have to do is convince the women and the men that the women should come and listen.

They don't go . . . I don't know . . . there are some fathers of families who think in a different way. They say, "What are you going to go for? What do you have to do there? What will you have to say?" If someone talked to the women, and explained to them why they should go, I know they would go. But some of them are afraid to speak. That is why we wanted Dolores to come and teach us.

The women are enjoying what we are doing now — seeing the films. The day before yesterday, we saw a film from another village. It was about the seizing of the land, that the women organised with the men. The women here said, "We are women too. We should be united with the men to fight for our rights." The film showed that the women had gone to fight — men and women and children — to get the land back. It was very exciting, and beautiful. The women here said that they could fight too.

Here the women suffer more than in other areas. They are more exploited. The woman has to take care of the house, look after the animals, cook, and wash. The husband only works in the *chacra*, and doesn't do anything else.

We have to talk, have meetings and prepare the women. We have been having courses, and now there are a few women who speak up. Why couldn't a woman be president, or a member of the council? The first woman in this region to be on the council is from the next village. Only recently do you hear of a woman doing this at the regional level. We are asking the same thing about our village. Why couldn't it happen here?

We are inviting women to come to the course and register. Mothers can learn to knit, embroider, cook . . . well, most of them know how to cook, but they don't know which are the best foods to use. We have lots of vegetables, but we don't know how to cook them. We also want classes in reading and writing. We have only just begun, but there are already lots of women who are enthusiastic to learn.

The woman's life is difficult, here, because she has to ask her husband for money. If not, she would have nothing to maintain her family. Most of the women aren't professionals. They can't earn money, except in the *chacra*, and the greater part of the harvest is to eat, and the rest is to sell. With that money, you have to pay 50 soles (10p) to the people who worked there with you. But most families don't have enough land to hire other *campesinos*. In fact, they usually have to work for other people. Life is difficult here. There are some people who don't even eat breakfast before they go to work.

There really isn't any other alternative for women. Only one or two of us have worked outside the village. It would be better if there were a source of work for women. They would be more independent. But now, the young girls are realising . . . that women here don't even have shoes or dress well.

The girls are thinking and saying that they have to do something else with their lives. "I have to go and get an education, and find work," they say. They tell their mothers, "Mama, I am going to Lima." And their mothers ask them,.

"What are you going to do? How will you manage?" And the girls say, "I will have to work during the day, and study at night." Then they come back with shoes, and good clothes. And people say, "Look, there is the *señorita* Chalca who has come to the village. She isn't a *cholita* (insulting term for an Indian who has moved to the city from the country). No, she is the distinguished *señorita*."

I have a *muchacha* (young girl/maid) helping me with the baby and in the house. She comes from a very poor family in the mountains, and to help them out, I will send her to school. She is just going to start this year. Some places are very backward. They don't have any schools. She is 13 years old, and has never been to school. She should be in a secondary school by now. She doesn't even speak Spanish. I know her father, who is a very poor man. I asked him to find me a *muchacha* to help me and my father in the house. He brought me his daughter, on the condition that I look after her as a younger sister, so that she doesn't suffer.

I used to work in Lima, as a maid for a very rich Italian family. There were only two children, a boy and a girl. What I want to know is why didn't they have a bigger family? Did the women have a special treatment not to have children? I have seen in various rich families — millionaires, that they have only one or two children. The poor people have so many. I don't really understand why.

In another family, the daughter of the *señora* was married for seven years, and didn't have even one child yet. One day, when I was cleaning the kitchen, I asked her if she didn't want a little baby to look after, and she laughed, and looked a little embarrassed. Then I made a joke to the *señor*, and said that the *señora* had told me she was pregnant. The gentleman was so happy. I think he really wanted a child.

I think the rich people should have children, because they can afford to look after them. If you are alone, you should have a child, and then you won't be alone any more. Your child can look after you when you are old.

But looking at those rich families makes me wonder why there are rich and poor people in the world. The rich people have everything, and no children; the poor people have nothing, and so many children. The poor people, the *campesinos*, are always afraid. For example, they would like to invite you to eat with them, but they know that what they have is not very good. They are embarrassed, that someone will criticise them. They aren't bad people . . . they — we — have no confidence.

Señora Herrarda was also involved in el frente femenino.
*She owned her own small shop, and provided the community
workers with accommodation when they came to the village.*

*She was 17 when she married and moved to the village
from another town. Although she had given birth to eight
children, three had died. At 58, she lived alone since her
husband had died nine years earlier.*

*She had strong thoughts about how important the project
was for the women in the village. At the same time, she spoke
about how difficult it was to try to introduce something new,
especially to the women.*

Recently a couple of young women started to come out to the village to visit
and talk and explain about different things. Before, everybody was in their
own house or their own fields. You had your own things to do. We weren't
united in any way.

I don't know who invited the *señoritas* (the community workers). Possibly
they might have been sent from Lima, or even another country. They go
from house to house to talk to the women, during the day.

The problem is that the young women they send don't speak Quechua. The
women who live here might understand a little Spanish, but they can't
answer. They aren't used to strangers, or having contact with other people.
They are a little shy and a little afraid.

If the *señoritas* spoke Quechua, they could speak to the women like sisters,
with confidence. And the women here would be able to talk about their lives.
You could tell each other things. But since they can't speak each other's
language, they can't do that and there is no confidence. To send people who
can't speak Quechua is a real burden . . . because we understand, but we
can't answer. If we had women who could come and talk to us in our own
language . . . then we could get together and each woman could say one by
one, what she thinks. That is what we want.

The women don't want to talk when their husbands are around either. If
they do, when they get back home, their husbands will say, "What did you
say that for? You said something wrong. You shouldn't speak — you should

keep quiet." Sometimes, too, other people will talk to you and say, "Well, *señora* so and so said this . . . "

Recently, women have begun to speak up a little bit in the meetings. They will ask to speak and say what they think about things. Every Sunday there is a village meeting. We all go. They call for both men and women to come to the meetings. It is mainly the men who talk. If they attack the women, or say something about us, we will speak up for ourselves. Otherwise we don't have much to say.

The committee members are all men. Sometimes you might get a woman as treasurer. But if you are on the committee you have to travel — to Cuzco and to different meetings. A lot of women can't leave the village because of their families, and most of them can't read or write, so they can't do anything on the committee.

Before, young girls only went to school until the second year of primary school. I went to third year, but my mother and father died, so I couldn't carry on. There was no one to help me — to buy me notebooks or pencils. I wanted to go on in school — very badly. Without education, you can't even open your mouth to speak.

Now quite a few young girls are going on until the fifth year. Those with better possibilities even go to college in Cuzco. A lot of them will leave the village to try to earn money to support themselves in college, because their parents can't afford to pay for it all.

I think the boys have much more chance than the girls. They can go out to play or to the *campo*, but the girls have to stay in the house with their mothers. The boys go out, look for their friends, go horseback riding. Then they go to college. That is how they get used to the way they will live as men when they are married.

That's why I think all these classes and films are very important for the younger women. I'm old already, but if the younger ones get enthusiastic, they can learn lots of things. They want to learn how to sew and knit. It's cheaper if you can make things for yourself, and you can sell sweaters and scarves. Until now, we haven't had sewing machines to do that sort of thing. People haven't been able to afford to buy those kinds of things.

We have always had films here, about land and the animals. They made the films here and then showed them back to us. Once there was a film from

Chile — showing how the women live. In this film, all the women were working. It was beautiful. You didn't see any men at all in the film. The women — young ones, old ones — they did everything in the house, in the *chacra*, in the factories — in everything. We were all saying how wonderful it was, and how could we manage to do the same things? It was very exciting to see it.

In the Agrarian Reform, in 1972, they came to give us classes then too. In the morning, the women went to the classes in the school, and the men went in the afternoon. They said there weren't going to be any more private farms — that everything was going to change. But it is all the same. In fact, it is a little worse.

Other women came and taught us to cook and make cakes. They brought wool and taught us to knit. They even told us which colours to use. One woman took the things away to sell. I don't know where she took them, but she brought us the money. She was going to bring more wool, but we never saw her again.

And now it's worse . . . life, that is. The situation is terrible. Everything is so expensive. Before, I used to go and buy sugar from the shop. Now I can't even buy it. You have to have a special card from the Ministry to sell sugar. And because I'm alone, I don't have time to go to the offices and fill in all the papers and forms. So I don't have any sugar to sell in the shop. Before I'd just go to the wholesalers, buy a couple of bags . . . everything was fine. We sold it at a low price . . . but not any more.

The women here need a way of earning money. I never had any problems with my husband about money. When we came here, I realised that there was no shop. We had a little bit of money, so we built this house. We would both decide what we needed, but we only had just enough to manage. Maybe when people earn more, then they have problems and arguments about how to spend it.

A LEADER

"There is no better experience, no better school than you get in the factory or in the fields. That is where you truly learn what the reality is."

—Aida Hernandez

Aida Hernandez was one of the several hundred members of the cooperative *Los Laboreles* (the oliander trees). Both the cooperative and Aida were well known throughout the country.

The cooperative had been created when, under the slogan "land or death", the local peasants had fought a pitched battle to seize the land in the late 1960s. Located on the coast, about an hour from Lima, the former *hacienda* (land owner's mansion) now served the cooperative as an office and meeting place. Behind a grand entrance gate, and amidst lovely gardens complete with miniature water falls and bridges, the white stone walls of the buildings were covered with revolutionary murals and slogans. The cooperative was recognised for its high yield orange crop and dairy production.

Aida Hernandez had achieved national recognition as a strong leader of both women and men. She began her political life with the strikes and battles to form the co-operative in 1968. She went on to become President of the cooperative and a member of the executive committee of the Peruvian National Federation of Campesinos. For a peasant woman, 39 years old, with four children, she had moved far beyond the woman's traditional role.

I found her in one of the rooms at the back of the hacienda *talking with a few of her* compañeros, *and putting up large production graphs on the wall. She had about an hour before a meeting was to start, and we went into the garden to talk.*

Listening to what she had to say was a lesson in itself about the situation of peasant women and the role leaders must play in stimulating change from the "bottom up" rather than the "top down".

I have always worked here in the fields, when there was a *hacienda* before the cooperative — before the Agrarian Reform. In 1968, when we had all the problems, I began to see the strikes, and the stoppages. At the beginning, even though I was a member of the union, I didn't think it was that important. I didn't understand. Then, each day, I saw more and more, and I began to realise what it meant for each of us to belong to the fight . . . and I had a clearer vision of what the union could do, and what each of us could do if we participated.

The women, especially, shouldn't have been quietly at home, washing, cooking, looking after children. No . . . we should have been fighting and participating equal with the men. We could have responsibility, the same as men.

Amongst all the women, I was the only one who began to participate more, in an open way . . . not because I thought I was special, or because I wanted to be a personality, but because I believed it had to be done. My *compañeras*, good women they are, but at the end of it all, they seemed to want to stay where they were. Maybe because of their children, or their husbands, they couldn't do anything else. Who knows?

The battle for the land began in 1968. My husband and I separated then. He was already a member of the union, but our problem had nothing to do with that. It was completely independent. He got an attack of "hot headedness", and went off with another woman.

But I went on. I left my children with my mother and father, and I carried on with the struggle. I became a union leader, and then a delegate to the valley federation. I carried on struggling and finally became president of the union, but because of certain political ideas and problems, I was removed.

Some members of our group didn't agree with my ideas, denounced me, and with help from the government, had me removed. Then they got really angry, because I went on to become a leader in the National Federation of *Campesinos* — for all Peru. I carried on fighting . . . always fighting.

Before . . . I was the same as all the other women . . . I didn't really think about things. Then I began to see the problems more clearly, and learned a bit about politics . . .Although I'm not in any political group, I understand a little about what different people say. I realised that if we stay in our ignorance, we will never change anything. I asked some of the *compañeros*, and they explained things to me. I have always gone to many different parts of Peru, and each time I talk to the *compañeros*, I learn. I tell the women they must come out, and talk, and see, and above all, participate without fear.

Before women can change, they have to get rid of the prejudice that they have had for a long time . . . for years . . . since they were born . . . about women and men . . . and all the social prejudices, too. We aren't going to be free that quickly.

There is a long, hard job to do so that women, not only here, but all over Peru, learn how to feel differently about themselves, and what they can do . . . not just to be able to do more work, but also to take on responsibilities and participate in their communities like equal human beings.

The problem, as I see it, is that women are not organised, and don't have an awareness of the fact that they have the same rights as the men. Women need to organise so they can change. They need to prepare themselves politically. Because until women have a political awareness, we won't be able to do anything. That is true of anyone . . . woman or man.

The problem for women has a number of aspects. One is that many times, the women can't go out to do things, because they are completely tied to the house — washing, cooking and looking after their families.

Another problem is the lack of understanding amongst many of the husbands. "I am a man," they say. "I can go out, but you can't." Of course, the men do some things . . . going out drinking, staying out all night . . . we aren't going to do those things. We are women; we aren't going to wake up at dawn in a canteen. But participation . . . being leaders, and assuming responsibilities . . . that we can and should do, equally with the men.

Women are not accustomed to doing this. From the time they are born, in school, in the house, women are taught to be submissive. They are taught to dedicate themselves to the wishes of their fathers and husbands.

The problem is also with the women themselves. They say, "No, because of my husband . . . no, my children . . . no, how can I . . . no, because the men are there . . . " They actually believe that we, the women, are inferior beings . . . that the men are superior. I am always saying that women have equal rights with the men. We have our papers, our voting cards . . . everything to prove we are equal.

The women here do come to the meetings, and they have their vote. It is the place where most of them participate. After that there aren't many who have any responsibility . . . one woman is on the control committee, and another woman is on the administration committee, but that's all . . . only two women out of the whole cooperative — about 600 people. The problem is not only that the men don't want to give them responsibility, but also that the women don't want to take it.

The women here also earn less than the men. Some women do earn more than the men, but that is because for some work, the pay is more. For example, my brother works in the section where they fumigate the plants, and I work in the children's nursery. I earn more with the overtime that I get, than he gets working the basic hours. But in the basic wage, for example, packing oranges, the men earn 10 soles (2p) per hour more than the women.

In one of our meetings, I suggested that the women should earn the same as the men. "We do the work equally," I said. "The only thing we can't do is drive the lorries." But they said, "No, how can we pay the women the same as the men? The men are worth more. The men have to be paid better than the women." So we have those basic inequalities. If the women can't get paid the same as the men for equal work, they will never feel equal.

We also have a discrimination that I think is wrong between the full workers, and the casual workers, whether they are men or women. The full members get more. So even there, we have men exploiting men. That didn't change with the Agrarian Reform. The cooperative, like the "boss" before it, carries on exploiting the poor workers.

I believe that as a woman, I have the same rights as a man, and whatever a man can do, I can do as well. I don't feel inferior to any man, not in work, or in anything. A man works to maintain his house and family . . . but so do I have to earn the money to feed my children.

Because I am a member of the cooperative, I am able to earn. It makes you stronger, if you have paid work. I think you are more "full of life", and you learn more . . . even more than the work you are doing. You feel more able to do other things, and you have more experience.

Every day, you can talk to the other workers . . . in the office or in the fields about many different things — about what is happening in the work. Your understanding of things can change, because other people have different opinions. The person who is in the house all day, who doesn't have any other work, never leaves . . . never has an understanding of what is happening in the world. Many women never leave their houses. Reality frightens them.

A woman doesn't really have what you could call "independence". She must always do whatever her father, her husband, or her mother tells her. And she doesn't try to do anything to educate herself . . . to find her own liberation. I talk with the women, and they say there is nothing they can do . . . that's the way it is. They feel even weaker because of that. The men work six days a week; on Sundays, they go out, to a movie or to get drunk. But the women work all the time and can't go out. I ask, "Why can't you say that you are going to visit your mother? Why can't you say that you are going out?"

Unfortunately, they can't. They say to me, "If I say I am going out, my husband gets annoyed, and then the problems start." But I have always said I was going . . . and I went. When I was with my first *compañero*, I would say I was going to visit my mother. And he would say, "You aren't going there, because your mother has a canteen, and you will come back drunk."

I would say, "Look, I said I was going to visit my mother and I am going! She is my mother, and you aren't going to stop me from seeing her." And I went. He said, "If you go, you will have to find somewhere else to live." But why should I find somewhere else to live . . . it was my house. So I went to see her. He wouldn't talk to me for a couple of days, but I didn't care. I hadn't said or done anything wrong.

Then one Saturday, I said I was going to the movies, and he shouted, "No, you aren't going to the movies." I said, "You go to the movies. Why can't I go? There is nothing wrong with going to the movies. You aren't going to have me under your thumb like a slave . . . working all day, at night, looking after the children, and at the weekends, washing and cooking." And I went.

Now I am alone, and I work. I was with another man for a while. I have a three year old child by him. He is a good man, and all that, but being with him just really didn't suit me, or him. So I said that it would be better if we went our different ways — me on my path of what I have to do, and he on his — much better than staying together so that I would have more children.

It is better to be alone. There is no one to tell me, "No, what for; where are you going; why are you going; when are you coming back?" It is better to live alone, than live with someone in a bad situation. My children are quite old now, except for the little one. The others are bigger than me.

I have four children . . . and now that they are bigger, they help me. My daughter helps me in the house. When they were small, they were all in school. In the holidays they would help me. It used to be difficult, but I would say to myself, "I can do it; I have to do it."

I believe that you can manage anything if you really want to . . . *querer es poder* (to want to is to be able to). That is what I used to tell my children. I would say to them, "We are going to do this, but I need your support. If you help me we can build a wall." Now we are fixing our house, in spite of the fact that I am a woman, without a man to do it for me. We are fixing the roof, and painting, doing everything that has to be done.

I think a good number for a family is four . . . four children. I had three, but I wanted to have four . . . that is why I had the last one. If you have any more, when it comes time for them to go to school, you can't afford the shoes, uniforms, and the other things they need. The land that we have won't support so many people. The men also feel this way . . . it is very hard for them if they have six or seven children.

In reality, people here don't want to have big families . . . for economic reasons. They can't maintain or educate them. Another reason is that there isn't enough work here for all the young people, and a lot of them leave.

Some women use contraceptives . . . pills and injections. Others have their own methods of looking after themselves. The husband and wife have to be in agreement, whatever they use. I think that with some families, yes, it is a good idea, because the women who are working . . . if they have children, year after year, they can't work. It is better if they have some kind of control. Because if not, the children suffer. Here, the mothers can leave their children in the nursery, but in other places there is nowhere to leave them.

Once, a while ago, someone came to explain birth control to us. They came from Lima, and told us about injections and pills. They explained why it isn't good for women to have children year after year, because they get very weak, and sick.

We talk about it sometimes, and someone will say that she doesn't want to have so many children. Someone who is pregnant will say that she hadn't taken good care ... that she was careless and she is pregnant again. But there are some women who are concerned only with their work, and looking after their children ... they hardly have time to talk about anything. That's why the women will always be behind. We need some kind of orientation ... someone to explain things to us. There are so many things that the women know nothing about.

I only know what I know because I have left the village so many times to go other places, and I always have the opportunity to talk to people and learn. All my experience hasn't come from just here ... from my village. It comes from all over Peru ... from everyone I've met in the mountains, in the jungles, on the coast, in all the places I've been. It has all been at the level of the workers themselves ... living with the workers, sharing their suffering, and their misery. We all are exploited in the same way, especially the women, who are more isolated. So all this experience has taught me what I know. Whatever I know comes from them ... my *compañeros*.

The women here ... they have fought ... we have been dedicated to the fight together, but now, they don't want to continue. They started and finished with the first battle. I don't know why they have stopped and gone back to their kitchens. I guess some of them have problems with their children, and others, with their husbands, or their *compañeros*.

The men are very jealous, and they think that if a woman spends time with other *compañeros*, it must be for personal reasons. They don't believe there is such a thing as *compañerismo* between a man and a woman ... a loyal friendship based on the organisation, and the work they have to do. No, they think in quite a different way, and it is a big mistake.

For example, if I am with four or five men — *compañeros* — it isn't for what these other men might think. These prejudices ... social and bourgeois prejudices . . . don't bother me. I am free of all that; I don't believe in it. I could go somewhere with 20 men, and we could all sleep in the same room, and there wouldn't be any problems. We go because we have work to do together. They have a lot of respect for me. How many times have I gone with groups of men, and nothing has happened? But here in the union, amongst *compañeros* and *compañeras*, things have happened, but not with me. The other women listen to their husbands, when they say that a woman shouldn't go with other men that way.

It is important to me that my children respect me. But the rest . . . I don't care what they say. There are some who say I am crazy . . . that I am with the men all the time. I just turn my back on what they say. It isn't something to worry about and spend time on.

They can say what they like, but I will always do what I think is right, and important. I never get involved in gossip. I don't really like being talked about, and I don't like talking about other people. As long as I believe in what I am doing, I can lead a life of peace. My conscience is the best judge, for me, of what I do.

My children, even they say, "Don't go . . . don't leave." But I say to them, "Look, I have to go to this meeting in Lima, for my work. I will leave Saturday and come back Sunday." I tell my oldest child, my daughter that she is in charge of cooking and looking after the others. I tell her to keep the door closed, and not let the others wander all over the place, and that I will be back on Sunday. And I go, and they are all right.

They have their duties and their independence. I don't want them to be dependent on me. One day I'll die, and I won't be coming back. They have to learn to be independent, to know their own worth, and to manage for themselves. Even though they are young, they have to learn.

For a woman to be a mother . . . she has to learn to understand, learn to know her children, and give them an education . . . teach them about life. Because children are like plants, and the woman who doesn't look after them, and worry about them, and provide them with what they need to grow, is not a good mother. To have children . . . just to have them . . . it would be better not to have them if you aren't going to look after them.

I had a hard time with my children, but we carried on. I wouldn't say that they are perfect, but people who know them congratulate me for having children that many mothers would like to have. So many fathers say, "My children are lazy, or rude", or "they drink". But my children work hard, and are very respectful.

For example, my daughter . . . I want her to go out. Every time she goes somewhere, she comes and tells me that she is going out, and where she is going. Sometimes, we will go together to the movies, or she will go out with her brothers.

But my son, the third one . . . he doesn't say anything to anybody. He just goes, and sometimes he will tell me where he has been. And I tell him, "I'm not going to tell you not to go, but I just don't want to worry about where you are. So tell me when you are going out." But he is very independent.

The other one, the second one is very different. Even though he is older, he doesn't have the strength of character that the younger one has. The younger one is more like me . . . he makes people respect him.

I hope my oldest daughter doesn't get married until she is older . . . until she is about 25. And I hope she marries a good man, who respects her, and who, above all, is political . . . who realises that there must be an understanding between the husband and wife, and who believes that the wife must participate and be strong. The most important thing is that he must be a worker. His family . . . they should have four . . . no more and no less. Because if you only have two, and one dies, you are left with only one. Three is an unlucky number . . . I don't know . . . I think it is a bad number. All the time I had only three children, bad luck followed me. I don't really know where I got the idea that three is a bad number, but I feel that it is.

I have always wanted to see and learn. I am not afraid of life . . . I have never been afraid . . . not even in front of my father when I was a little girl.

My mother was always raised at the point of a fist, or a blow. She has had a very sad life, and has been very oppressed. She was an orphan when she was nine years old. She always tried to raise us in an old-fashioned way . . . or the way she was raised, but I have always shown a certain kind of independence. She never used to like it, but she couldn't change me. I'll probably die this way. I won't change.

I used to talk to my mother, but we never talked like two good friends. I would never tell her that I was in love . . . we didn't have that kind of confidence. The person I did talk to was my stepfather. I would tell him everything, and he would advise me. My real father left us when I was 11, but my stepfather was the one I called "papa".

He always advised me . . . and my brothers and sisters, too. He would talk to us about the way things were. He didn't know very much, really, but it was always very important . . . his advice. It was like gold. Thanks to him, we were raised in a good environment, and we haven't made a lot of mistakes.

I have talked to my daughter . . . I have explained everything I know to her . . . about how things are between men and women. I don't want her to be deceived by anyone. I want her to live with a different mentality than the one I grew up with. She must understand what the reality of life is, but also, how she must fight within that.

Last year, I thought of stopping all my work here . . . all my political work. I was so tired of hearing my name everywhere, and everyone always calling for "Aida Hernandez here . . . and Aida Hernandez there". But last month I was elected to work on the electoral committee of the cooperative. So I have special permission to do this, and leave the other work. When I finish this committee, I will go back to my regular work. I have never done this before, and I wanted to learn about it. That is why I accepted again to do something. Because you know, without the experience of being a leader, and president, even for the little time I did it, I wouldn't have learned anything.

The time they denounced me . . . it was done by a small minority of people here. They said a lot of bad things about me . . . which weren't true, and they had me removed from being president. Then they had me removed from my work. For 2½ years, I didn't do much here. They said I was with people who had "infiltrated" the cooperative. I couldn't even talk to some people.

But, you know, when you are a leader, you always have that inside of you, even though you say that you don't. You carry it with you in your blood. I remember one of the battles, here, when the police were after us, and we were throwing bombs, and they were beating us . . . there was no way to say, "No, I won't carry on." As a woman, I had to carry on. I have always tried to represent the women — the *campesina* women — wherever I went.

But I think you should stop, after you have been a leader for a while. If you are always a leader, doing the work of a leader . . . you need a rest. More important, you get to expect certain things, or you get used to working on a certain level. You should stop, go back to the earth . . . to the people, because you forget what it is like. You should give other people a chance, and you should start again from the bottom, just so you don't forget what it is like . . . what you are fighting for.

NO REVOLUTION FOR THE WOMEN

As in other parts of the country, land reform also bypassed the small village near Cuzco in southern Peru. Because his sons were well-placed in the military, the local land owner had managed to avoid the Agrarian Reform laws. But in 1977, the peasants from two communities banded together, seizing the land from the land owner. Several people were killed in the struggle, but the peasants won.

Three years later, the cooperative was a financial success, and had also been instrumental in organising a federation of several other local co-operatives to share resources, develop new products and establish a unified marketing system for their produce.

The 210 full members of the cooperative were all men, except for five widows. It was an unwritten rule that the only women who could be full members were widows. All other women worked in the fields, the office, the kitchen or the knitting workshop, on a full or part time employed basis, but not as members in their own right. It seemed that the revolutionary spirit had not affected the women's struggle in any significant way, as a conversation with one woman showed:

"The CENCICAP organises courses for the men in agriculture, but not for the women. There are few women who go to the meetings of the cooperative. The ones who have gone to school — the younger ones — go. But there are no women on the committee. The men think that the women can't manage responsibilities like that.

"The men think that the women are incapable of carrying out any kind of official duties for the cooperative. And so most of the women have this kind of complex. They feel inferior. They think that whatever they are going to say will be wrong. Or they think that people, especially the men, will make fun of them. Women live in isolation, here. And it is worse for those who don't speak Spanish. They only speak Quechua, and so, they can't even to go the health centre to tell the doctor what is wrong with their children.

"What do the men think? They think that you should be in the house, in the kitchen — washing, cooking, looking after the children."

Señora Mathilde worked in the accounting office of the cooperative. Married to one of the two men who organised the peasant uprising, she was very active within the co-operative, trying to better the situation of the peasant women.

On the day we spoke, she was at home, very busy preparing lunch for a number of officials from various development agencies who were coming to speak to her husband. We talked in the kitchen while we prepared the food. To my surprise, some of the men came in to help, including her husband. But when the meal was ready, all the men went out to the patio to eat. I stayed with Mathilde. We ate in the kitchen. Mathilde is 27, and has two children.

Religion isn't as important now as it used to be. It used to keep the peasants at a certain level. The priests before always used to . . . well . . . they were always with the land owners in the *fiestas* (festival day or holiday) — and always giving their mass in the *fiesta*. In the middle of the mass, the nuns would always say, "You must respect the land owner as you do God — for he represents another god — he gives you food."

It is changing with the cooperative. Now the priests hardly ever come around, because they really believe that we are all communists, and that nobody believes in God any more. So they don't come.

I have always talked to the other women, to tell them that all the *chicha* and alcohol at the *fiestas* suits the "bosses". If the peasants are drunk all the time — then the bosses can treat them very badly and the *campesinos* don't care.

I talk to them about many things . . . about family planning for example. I tell them that they shouldn't have so many children — that with life the way it is today — they can't even buy bread for their children. What do they think they are going to give them?

They say to me, "God has given me all these children. I must have whatever God gives me". Others say, "I work in the *chacra* and I need help from my children. The more children I have, the more help I will have."

Some understand . . . the younger ones . . . they don't want more than two, because they want them to go to school and have a good life. Now we have hired a nurse to teach the women about health, and their bodies. She will also tell them about family planning, and help them with it. It is a first step.

Many men think that women were made only to have children and look after their family and husbands, to prepare the food and work in the house. There are so many women who are so conditioned to this way of thinking, that they agree, and say that that is the way it should be. They say that women don't have the same abilities as the men; that the women can't work as hard; that we can't lift a tree trunk, or even a rock as well as the man.

I don't agree. We can, and we do most of the work in the fields that they do, and with the same speed and force. I have seen women stripping the leaves off the corn in the fields — and the work is equal.

I have said many times in the cooperative meetings that the women should earn the same as the men because they are doing the same work . . . putting down fertiliser, weeding with machetes, clearing the corn . . . all the same but we earn less.[4]

"No, *compañera*," the men say, "you can't ask for equal pay, because women don't work as fast as men, and don't do as much in a day." But that is wrong . . . there are times when women do even more work than men.

We have the work in the house as well. I say to the women, "*Compañeras*, why should we let the men say these things to us . . . that we work less than them, that our only purpose is to cook and raise children? We shouldn't have to stay in the house all the time. Why can't they stay in the house one day to look after the children, and we will go out to work?"

In fact, there isn't much specifically for women in the cooperative. We want to have more things that they could learn about. We have started a knitting workshop, and we want to have a sewing workshop too. But the husbands say, "Those things are for women who have time — who never do anything in their houses. That is why they can go to classes."

Many women don't come to the classes when we have them, so we have been thinking that on the days when the husbands aren't working, the women could

---

3.   Women working in the fields earn 250 soles (50p) per day. The men earn 450 soles (90p) per day.

come out and the husbands could stay in the house. But there are still so many women who think it is a waste of time.

The younger ones are more aware and try to explain to their husbands. But the older women and the mothers of these young women . . . say that they shouldn't go . . . that it is a waste of time . . . and they should stay home and cook, and mend clothes, and look after their families.

We need someone to come and work only with the women, to try to change the way they think — so they can explain it to their husbands. I say these things to the women, but I can't spend all my time doing it. It will take a long time to change the way people think . . . and for women to stop being slaves.

The women lack contact with other people, and other ways of thinking. Now they don't know anything. They could stay in their houses for the rest of their lives, devoted to looking after their children, and their animals — nothing more — and drinking too. The women get drunk just the way their husbands do — and then the children don't have anything to eat.

I suppose I have always thought in a slightly different way to most women here — that it is wrong the way things are, and that they should change. But nothing special has happened to me — I have always thought this way. I did go to university. My parents were poor — and for that reason, I was different from a lot of students at university. My parents made sacrifices to educate us. I have four sisters and four brothers. Some of us have stayed in the country, while the others are professionals and live in the city.

Even my own brothers and sisters are different. We think in completely opposite ways. They don't agree when I say that whether we are illiterate or professional, we are all equal and we must treat each other as equals. They think I am a communist. They say to me, "Why don't you go and live in the country with the peasants who think like you?"

I hope that with the cooperative, we will be able to change things here. For example, before you never even noticed what colour clothes the women were wearing. They always wore the same clothes as when they were working in the fields. But now with the cooperative, they get paid a fair salary and they have been able to buy other clothes.

If their way of thinking ever changes — things will be much better. Up to now, the cooperative hasn't been able to change that. They think as they did before — that they have to work for the "boss". To them the cooperative is just another form of "boss". They still work with suspicion. It will be years before everyone is participating and sharing all the responsibilities.

FEAR AS A BARRIER TO HEALTH

We had been sitting together all morning in the first session of a two-day health course for women, listening to a young, male doctor explain, in Spanish, various aspects of women's anatomy and the reproductive process. This was with the aid of a video tape, also in Spanish, and a male community worker who did some translating.

Except for one or two younger women, the 15 women in the group spoke almost no Spanish. They spoke Aymara, the language of most of the indigenous population living on the *altiplano* around Puno, in southern Peru. And all morning, the women had said nothing . . . no questions . . . no answers.

At lunchtime, I went outside with the one or two who spoke a little Spanish, and we started to talk. We were joined shortly, by the rest of the women, and soon we were huddled together on the grass. The younger ones translated for the rest of us, as I could speak no Aymara.

Most of them said that their husbands had sent them on the course. They were all working in a local agricultural cooperative, and the management committee had set the course up for the women. The husbands had been more or less directed to send their wives.

Towards the end of our half hour together, one of them asked me if I could explain to them "how not to have children". I suggested that it would be better to ask the doctor . . . silence from the group. Finally someone said that that was why they had come to the course . . . to find this out, but they were afraid to ask.

Could I ask him, please, to explain it to them? I checked with the rest of the group . . . and, indeed, that was why they had all come, but understandably not one woman was able to overcome her terror of raising such a subject in public, let alone in front of men, and in a language that hardly any of them spoke.

*At another health course, a couple of hundred miles away, I
had a similar experience. This course had been set up by the
Department of Health for leaders of village health committees
and local health promoters. There were about 25 people on
the course, nine of whom were women.*

*I arrived on the last day of the four-day programme which
had covered hygiene, sanitation, nutrition and communicative
diseases. I spoke to Soyla, a 33-year old woman, married,
with three children.*

*She lived in a village about ten kilometres away. She told
me that her husband had sent her on the course.*

My husband is at home with the children. He said to me, "Go to the course.
They'll explain things to you, and you'll learn something. And then you can
tell people here in the village." He also said they might talk about how not to
have any more children. We have three and we don't really want any more. I
think three is enough. In my village, some women have 12 children. They
will help in the house or in the fields, or their parents might give them away
to other people who don't have any children.

I've been here in this course since Monday, but they haven't explained
anything about controlling birth. They've only talked about looking after
children, or the actual birth. I have heard about the pills, but I also heard
that they are very bad for you. Other people have also told me about a
special injection that stops you from having children for three months. But I
wonder what might happen after the three months. I might get sick or
pregnant. I don't want to take any of those things.

I thought about asking the doctor, on the course, but I haven't dared to do it.
And there hasn't really been time because we've been talking about other
things — about being careful and not carrying heavy loads if you are
pregnant. All the women in the village — we always did our work as usual
even if we were pregnant. So I have learned now that it shouldn't be like
that.

I never knew about things like that before. I've never been to school, and no
one has ever explained it to me. It is the first time I've ever been out of the

village to a course like this. All my life, I've been in the mountains. We are all very poor. My husband and I don't have any land . . . just a very small piece that I have from my mother. And in the village there isn't anything. There is no bus, except on Sundays, market day; so we have to walk everywhere. We don't have water or electricity. You can't even sell *chicha*. It's not like here.

Most of the women in the village don't read or write, or speak Spanish. I am a little different, or at least more open because I learned to speak Spanish when I worked as a maid in Lima. I can read, but I can't write. I would like to learn, but the baby won't let me. We started a little bit in the course on Monday, but the baby was always bothering me. It was a waste of time to try.

Many of the women on this course haven't understood anything. It's as if they weren't here. The one who was knitting, and the young girl, for example, are completely ignorant. They have never been to school. They only speak Quechua, and even though it is translated after, it isn't the same. The teachers start talking in Spanish, and that scares the women, because they don't understand. And if you are afraid, that stops you from learning.

But since Monday, I have learned things that I can take back. If someone has a problem that I learned about this week, I can do what they taught us. I'd like to come back and learn more. It is the only way that the women in the village will learn.

But even I am afraid to ask the doctors about birth control. I don't know — I think they might say, "Why do you want to know?" Or they might not tell me. So I am afraid to ask.

At a similar course for village health promoters, I met Señora Valentina, 40, with two children, who were 20 and 14 years old. She was not attending the course, but had come to see the doctors with a different kind of problem.

She had left her village in the middle of the night, and walked for eight hours to get to the health centre in the morning, in the hope that the doctors could help her. She had recently remarried, and wanted more children by her second husband. At least, he wanted her to have more children.

My first husband died. He was the father of my two children, and my second husband wants to have lots of children. He says without children, there is nothing to work hard for. If he has no children, we have no one to leave the land to. He wants me to have children very badly.

He said I should come here to the health centre, so that I could talk to the other *señoritas*, the other "virgins" like me, to see whether I could still have children. I have seen women older than me still have children. He thinks that there might be some kind of injection or pills, or another method so I could have children. I think he is afraid that people will think he is sterile, or that it is his fault that we can't have children.

I have to do whatever I can so I can have a child. If I am not able to have one, I don't know what his reaction will be. I suppose he might leave me. I don't know. But I have to do something — there must be some way.

I haven't told any one in the village about this. It isn't fair for them to know. The women do talk together about things like this, but mainly about not having children. The only thing I heard was that you can go to Cuzco, to the pharmacy, and consult with them about not having children. I think they can give you something.

(She was watching the other señoras nearby who appeared interested in what we were talking about. She changed the subject.)

There really isn't anything for women in the village . . . only what we have to do every day. I suppose what the women do need is some kind of work where they will be paid. The men are paid when they work as labourers in the fields, but they don't pay the women, or at least not in money.

The men get paid 300-400 soles (60-80p) daily, but they pay the women in kind. You get paid in food from the community's shop. They say it is a fund for the community . . . so you go there, and they will give you rice or corn for your day's work. You work and get paid in food, but I don't believe that the money is going to the community. I think it is going to the ones who are in charge of the shop. And there is nothing we can do. The only women who get paid are the widows. They say that it is a law that we don't get paid in money.

But the women never get together to talk about these things. Usually you are in your house on your own, and you go to the hills. But each one goes separately. You don't really have the chance to meet anyone else, much less talk to them. By chance maybe you will see someone and say hello. But everyone is preoccupied by the animals and keeping them all together.

When we get together for the *faenas*, then we talk, but we don't talk about other people — not really. We will make jokes together. "How are you? Has your husband gone to Lima yet? Do you want to borrow my husband while yours is away?"

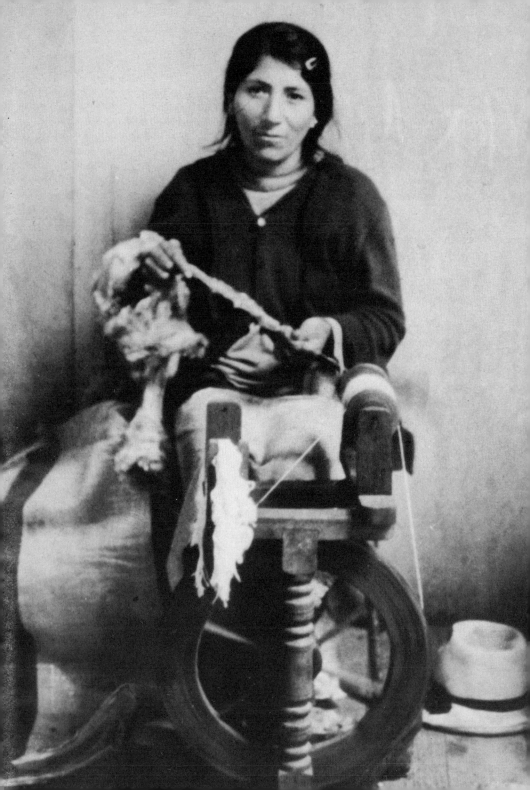

EQUAL PAY, BUT NO VOTE

"I would like to see the women more united with the men. The men should really change their ways of thinking about this. It is machismo... egoismo. The men don't want the women to be equal, to give their opinions, or have their own ideas. And the women have to fight for this.

"We should all have the same rights — men and women. For example, a woman has never been elected to any office in the cooperative. It is always the men who have the responsibility. We women have to have our own meeting to say that we don't want to be left on the sidelines."

—Women working in an artesan cooperative in San Pedro de Pirca

The hundred mile journey from Lima north to Pirca, a small mountain village, takes seven hours or four hours, depending upon whether you are travelling up or down the mountain. The road stops at Pirca, and the 200 families living there are often completely cut off by landslides on the road. The village has no electricity or water system.

Pirca is a traditional *comunidad campesina* — a village community with common lands. It also has a sheep ranch with 4,000 head of sheep. The affairs of the community are managed through community meetings, and by members of the village — men, elected each year at the general assembly. Women are not allowed into these meetings.

"I think the men are afraid to let us into the community meetings. I don't know why. It isn't the custom... women have never been involved. But we do talk and think in the meetings of the cooperatives... sometimes better than the men, I think.

—Nilda, 28 years old, four children

In late 1977, two development workers, both foreigners, were invited into the village by the community to help re-establish weaving as a local activity. Weaving had been the work of the men in the village over 100 years earlier.

The cooperative, now with a mixed membership of about 30 people, produces textiles, spun, dyed and woven by hand. A major part of the project, after establishing technical expertise, was to train cooperative and community members in financial management, marketing and the general running of the entire cooperative.

This was the only cooperative I visited where men and women were paid equal wages for the same work.

Rosita, Flor and Estrella are spinners in the cooperative. They also work together as a team making mattresses for sale in the village. Rosita is 26 years old, and has one child. Maria is 35 with five children. Estrella is 43 and has seven children. All three women are married.

ROSITA: We have all been members here in the cooperative from the beginning — about two and a half years ago. Before the cooperative, we worked in the *chacra* — all of us. We didn't earn very much, and it was very hard work. We only earned about 100 soles (20p) a day. That wasn't all the time; it was only from time to time. Our husbands still work in the fields, while we work here.

ESTRELLA: I wanted to work here to have a steady income because when you work in the fields, you don't always get money. Sometimes you have it, and others not. So I thought it would be much better to work here for that.

The cooperative is a big success for us — we earn a lot, and it is always going up. You earn 520 soles (£1) a day, depending on how much you produce. The one who is in charge of the spinning weighs up the wool in the morning and gives us each some. At the end of the day, you give back to her what you have spun, and she weighs it, and that is how you know how much you have earned.

A lot of women work in their houses. They spin there, and bring the wool in. They aren't members, but they can still work and earn money.

They say they have too much to do, or too many children to look after, so they can't be away from their houses, and they don't want to come to the meetings.

Some of their husbands might be very jealous, and think bad things if women and men are working together. I don't know what they think, but that is why they won't let the women leave the house and come to work in the cooperative.

ROSITA: I don't have any problems with my husband. he is a good man.

FLOR: I had terrible problems with my husband, and I had to overcome them.

"Don't go to work there. You must stay here," he said to me. But I said, "I have to go; even threat of death wouldn't keep me away, because I know that from this work, I will be able to feed my children." I knew I had to go, and that he couldn't stop me. I had to convince him.

He had other ideas. My husband is someone who has never had any kind of training or development at all. He doesn't understand things. Everything seems bad to him. Now he is all right and calm. I convinced him.

Before we used to be much poorer. Now he realises that I am earning money, and we can eat better. Little by little he has realised and changed his ideas.

ESTRELLA: We are all learning things — how to spin on the spinning wheel, and how to make mattresses. When you stay in the house all day — that is a completely different way of life to working here. Now we are aware of many new things. You come here and you know; you can talk to people; you can learn and you can change.

We three work together making mattresses, and we have a lot of fun when we are together. It is much better than working at home alone.

ROSITA: When we go to the meetings — every Tuesday we have meetings — and each person gives their opinion about whatever we have to decide. Before, and at the beginning, when I first came here, I couldn't do that — we were afraid of John (one of the organisers). Whenever he would ask us anything, we didn't know what to say . . . and so we said nothing. But now, we aren't afraid. We were afraid of Anita (the other organiser) at the beginning too — because we didn't know her.

FLOR: We were all afraid because we didn't know them — so we were very shy. But now we all know each other, and we work together and we understand each other.

The men weren't afraid to speak, or at least not like us anyway, but we have never been used to speaking like that with the men, or with anyone. We don't go to the village meetings, so we never get a chance. That is why we have always lived disunited — the women and the men — not working together. They have their meetings; they talk about things and know. We, on the other hand, stay at home. We don't know anything about all of that.

ROSITA: I would like to have a meeting of all the women, to see what all their ideas were, and to talk about how we could solve our problems — how we could do it together.

We need to have people come here, who know more than we do, to teach us new things. For example, how women should change and be a different class of person. Because sometimes, you don't know. You don't know how you can progress either; how you can change anything. We need someone to come and lead us. Without someone like that, we will never know anything, and we will never learn anything.

ESTRELLA: For example, I would like to learn how to knit — someone could come here and teach us that, or, for example, how to raise and look after a baby — or about the health of our children or about food. They could give us a talk so we would know about things like that.

ROSITA: There is nothing here. When you get sick, if you are poor, you just wait for death. The few that have money, go to Lima or Huaral (a town on the coast). But we don't have medicine here.

Many of the children die here. I had two children but the little girl died. She got measles, and then terrible convulsions and cough.

ESTRELLA: I had one who died. From one moment to the other — it was so sudden. He got a fever — he was nine years old. We didn't have any medicine here — nothing and just as we were going to take him down the mountain to the town, there was a landslide and you couldn't get through the road. In April — there was no traffic; nothing could move. My little boy was very sick for five days, and then he died.

A lot of children here die of measles. Since last December, there have been 15 babies who died. Almost every other day one died. There was no one here to help us.

We want to learn about these things, but no one ever comes here. We don't want to carry on as we have been, in this situation. We have to learn, and our husbands have to learn too. There are some who won't listen to anything, but there are others who are more understanding.

ROSITA: Some of us would like to know about . . . birth control. There is nothing like that here. The custom is just to have children when they come to you. We don't have a doctor or a nurse, so we don't know anything about things like that. That is why all of us have so many children, year after year.

There is no one to ask about it. There are quite a few who say that God rules our lives, and we have to receive whatever He wants to give us. But year after year after year — I don't think so.

FLOR: There are some women who have 12 or even 14 children.

Life would be so much easier without so many children. Having one or two is all right, or even up to four — that would be better, but to have 15, you just can't manage.

Children do help in the work. For most women, it is their older children who help at home. They cook and look after the children. When we come home, the lunch is all ready. That is the only reason that we can work here all day.

ROSITA: I have a woman who cooks.

ESTRELLA: (laughing) It is her mother-in-law who does it.

I want my children's lives to be different. Above all, they should be a different class of person than me. The same as me — never. I want them to study in Lima so they can all be professionals.

FLOR: I don't want them to be the same as me either. If it weren't for the cooperative, we would have nothing —no money, no new things to learn. Now we can see that our children, too, should learn new things, and think in a different kind of way.

ROSITA: Things are much better now than before . . . we didn't have a school here. Our mothers didn't know anything except working in the *chacra* and living with the animals. My mother didn't even know one letter of reading and writing. She never spent even one day in a school. Now we know a little more.

ESTRELLA: We have the full primary school, and now there is a secondary school as well. The children can study without having to leave the village. When I finished primary, I wanted to study more, but my parents were poor, and they couldn't afford to send me away. They needed me to work with them as well.

I did go for one year to study in secondary school, away from the village, but I had to come back and help because my father had no money. My sisters couldn't carry on studying either.

You know, if your parents had money and died, they would leave it to you as an inheritance. So the rich children stay rich, and the poor people like us carry on being poor, without anything. Poor people also have so many children and the rich ones only have two or three. So it is much easier for them.

Hopefully, our children will have more freedom with their lives than we have had. We are tied to the village because of the children. On the other hand, the men can go wherever they want to learn things. They can go to Lima or Huaral to learn to drive — and then they can earn their living that way. But the women have to stay at home to look after everything. The choices are always for the men. You have more freedom if you don't get married.

ROSITA: Yes, single women have more freedom. When you have children, you can't choose to do anything for yourself. If I hadn't had children, then, maybe I would be alone, and could do something I wanted to do. With my children, I can't think that way.

FLOR: I had an arranged marriage. I was working in Lima, not here. My husband went to ask for my hand from my mother and father. My mother went to Lima and brought me back here to get married. So it was all arranged by my parents. That is why in my house, my husband and I have so many problems. We didn't know each other at all. When two people get married who don't know each other — and there is no understanding, well, they shouldn't get married. With my husband, there was no understanding at all between us. Gradually we got used to each other, and it was really only for love of the children that we have carried on.

Before, the marriages were always something arranged only by the parents. It isn't like that now with young people. Now they fall in love and get to know each other, and they get married. But before, the majority of the parents made their children — or the daughters — get married. I think it is better now that it is changing.

ROSITA: It is much better now. How can you live with someone you don't even know? You can't form a happy house or family. If you know each other, that is different.

There are times when marriage is all suffering. If they aren't good men, they can beat you a lot. If you try to do anything, they beat you more. They are stronger. What can we do? There is nothing we can do if they don't understand.

*Ramosa, 29, and Francisca, 19, were both single and
members of the cooperative. Ramosa had a nine year old son,
although she did not mention him in the discussion. Each of
the women explained to me how their obligations as daughters
— the only single daughters in their families — had
constrained plans for their own futures.*

RAMOSA: I joined the cooperative so that I would be able to help out in our
house, and do something good for the village. We have tried to make things a
little better for the people here. At the beginning, it was difficult and a
number of people left the cooperative.

Before I joined the cooperative, I worked in the house and helped in the
chacra. Before that I was in Lima studying business, but my father died, and
my mother was left alone. She didn't want to come to Lima, so I had to come
back here. There wasn't anyone else to look after her. It was an obligation
. . . it wasn't something I could even think of not doing. She can't maintain
herself . . . she can't work on the land, or look after the animals.

I have brothers, but they are all married. A single daughter has the
responsibility of looking after her mother because the married children
already have their families.

She couldn't live with any of my sisters, because she is quite old now, and
she doesn't have any patience with little children. When all the children
come to the house, they sometimes bother her. It isn't like before when she
had children. She is 68 now.

FRANCISCA: I was studying here in the village. I was in the first year of
secondary school. I wanted to go on studying, but my mother became ill, and
then I had to stay at home cooking for my father, and looking after my
younger brother who is still in school.

My mother got better after a month, but I didn't want to go back, because I
had missed so much time. My friends were all ahead of me. I was very
embarrassed to carry on one year behind everyone else. So I lost the year,
and never went back. I am quite a coward.

There are eight in my family — five girls and three boys. I was the only one who could look after my parents, because the others were all married, except for my younger brother. I have two brothers living here, and the others all live in Lima. They all have their professions, or are still studying. Because I am the last daughter, I have to stay home to look after my parents. It is bad luck, but there is nothing I can do.

The cooperative, of course, is a help for the women in the village. There are women with families, single mothers and single girls all working here. It is good for the development of the village — for the economy of all the families here. We are learning new things and we are earning money at the same time. We each earn 500 soles (£1) daily. It has been going up little by little. We began earning 150 (30p) per day, and then up to 180, and then 200, 350, 450, and now it is up to 500 soles.

RAMOSA: Last year, we went to an exhibition. There were three men and two women elected to go from the cooperative. They elected us to go as the two women. We won the prize for the best work in the fair. It was the first time that the cooperative had entered, and we hadn't seriously been thinking of going until the last minute.

FRANCISCA: Before I started work here in the cooperative, I was very shy — very cowardly; and, furthermore, I didn't really know anything. I didn't know how to spin or weave. Now I am learning, and I am aware of much more . . . and I know that I can learn, and that I can do things.

For example, I would never have come to talk to you. I would have been too afraid, and I wouldn't have known what to say.

RAMOSA: You see, we aren't that clever. When you have lived here in the village all your life, you become very timid and shy in yourself. You don't have the ability to talk to everyone, and say what you think. When you leave here, you begin to take steps to change, and you see the way other people are and the way they live.

As they say here, "The home forms you", or rather shyness forms you when you are in the house all the time. It shouldn't be that way, but we are very afraid to speak to people — strangers to the village.

Often it is because that is actually the way your parents taught you. They taught you, strangely enough, to be a little afraid and shy . . . "You shouldn't talk to that person," they would say. What did we know? Who else could we talk to about that? I think they did that so that we would be unlikely to talk back to our husbands. That is the only reason I can think of. It is different now for young people. They are much more awake and aware of how things should be.

FRANCISCA: It's true. The girls of today know much more than we ever did at their age.

RAMOSA: I left the village about 12 years ago — I have lived away more than I have lived here. So in my youth I learned about other ways of life, about talking with people — even foreigners. In fact, I think foreigners are more interesting — but you must always remember where your roots are.

FRANCISCA: I am not like Ramosa. I have always been very shy . . . and I have never really left the village properly. From time to time, I've gone to visit my family in Lima, but I have never left on my own. I am not used to talking to strangers like this.

My mother — her work is the same every day, and has been the same — every day of her life. She works in the house, in the *chacra*, and looking after her animals. She says she got married at 16. She had a lot of brothers and sisters — a big family, but she is alone now . . . her father and mother died, and all her brothers and sisters moved away.

RAMOSA: Girls get married very young here — at about 15. They have to, although it isn't like before when the parents made them get married. For example, my older sister got married to someone from the village . . . she didn't know him. She had never even spoken to the man.

He came to ask for her hand from my parents. His father came to talk to my father, and said he had seen my sister, and his son would like to marry her. My father and mother said she had to marry him. "You must marry him," they said over and over and over. My sister didn't want to but they said she had to do it, and she got married at 16. She is still with the same man. She has eight children and is pregnant with the ninth, and she is only 34.

Now, thank goodness, the custom has changed. Now young people know each other first, fall in love, start a romance, and get married, although some don't wait long enough before they get married. The custom of arranged marriages only stopped about five or six years ago. (They laughed at their luck in escaping.)

FRANCISCA: I don't want to get married yet. Before I never wanted to, and my father has never said anything to me. I know that I will get married, and I would like to have children — but only one or two. I have a boy friend, but I haven't known him for long. Who knows what kind of luck will come to me?

RAMOSA: I had a very special romance — one of these blows that life gives you. I had a boy friend in Lima. He was from somewhere in the Amazon area — very far from here — and not like the mountains. He didn't like the mountains, and I don't like the jungle. So we separated seven years ago. Who knows what will happen now? Sometimes it works out that you get married, and other times it doesn't. It depends on the fate that comes to you. If my life doesn't work out so that I get married, I will stay single.

I have a cousin and she got married at 36. When she was 37 she had her first child. Now she has three and says, "No more, no more." She got married to a younger man. He was 30, and I guess that is why they had children so quickly. Usually here, women marry men older than themselves.

I think we really should try to live our lives a little differently — have the same idea that you and that my cousin had. That is, to try to secure your future — to study and work so that you can take care of yourself — whether you get married or not. Because if you can't maintain yourself, then you have to get married, and have a man to support you. Most girls don't think about anything other than getting married. Very few remain single.

FRANCISCA: For example, of all the girls that were my age, almost all of them are married. I think that there are only two or three who are single. Most of the girls younger than me are all married, or going to be married.

RAMOSA: It is the environment. I think it happens in school. You know that the schools are mixed here. In the later years, they teach them about sex — I think that because of this, the young people wake up to this much earlier than we used to . . . and some of them are already married when they leave secondary school. The girl is in first year, the boy is in second or third, and they get married. Then immediately the children start to come, and the girl has to leave school.

We don't know about . . . we don't use any kind of control. They say that there are these things, and that you should take care of yourself that way.

Even though I only want two children, I haven't really thought about it. I guess when I get married, I could end up having more than two. It will be difficult to have only two, if I don't know anything else.

It isn't something that is really talked about. That requires an understanding between the man and the woman, and if there isn't that, then they can't talk about it. I am always saying to my sister, who has six children, "That's enough now. You shouldn't have any more". Another of my sisters has eight children. She says, "What can I do . . . my husband, when he is drunk . . . there is nothing I can do to say no." That is the way it is for a lot of women. If the women say no, or say they don't want any more children, the men can get very nasty. They say terrible things to you or they beat you.

FRANCISCA: The men think that if you don't want to have more children, then you must be with another man...or want to be with another man. The poor wives have to accept that this is the way their husbands think.

RAMOSA: Before, the women used to use plants not to have any children. Once, my mother told me that one of her sisters had taken this plant, and the baby died inside her. It was like an abortion. I said to my mother that I thought that was bad advice. I would never do that.

She thought that when she took the plant the baby would die and be aborted, but she had to carry it for the nine months and then it was born dead . . . my sister was very sick . . . she couldn't eat or drink anything . . . so she was very weak, and that is why the baby died.

FRANCISCA: There is no doctor here, and no health centre — there isn't anything. If we get sick, or don't feel well, we will make some tea from plants . . . before we knew exactly which plants were good for which things. So all you would do would be to find the plant. When that remedy stopped working or stopped having the effect to make you better, you would die — that's all.

Now people are using medicine more, or they will go to the coast and look for a doctor and buy medicine. If they don't have any money to do that, they just stay here and die. This village is so far, it is abandoned by everything.

RAMOSA: I would like to see progress — and see us live and work together in a more united fashion . . . we would have to really think about the position of the woman here. We all have different ideas, and for things to change — for progress to happen — there are certain things here in the village that we would have to change.

For example, in the village, we have meetings — but they are only for the men. The women can't go. But I have said, because I am like the father of the family, "I am going to the meetings." And they say, "Go ahead, and say what you think at the meeting." But when you go, they say that they don't want women in the meeting; women should be in the house with the family, and not in the men's meeting. It is complete selfishness.

FRANCISCA: It is *machismo*. They want to be the only ones making decisions, and they don't want to know what we think about anything.

I say that many times there are things that the women should be talking about both amongst themselves, and with the men — giving their opinion, and having a dialogue. That is how it should be. We should all agree about things in the community.

RAMOSA: We all have to give our opinions in the cooperative. We have meetings every Tuesday for everyone working in the project. Everyone — women and men — has to say what they think about all the decisions. The men will say something, and we women will say what we think. It is important that everyone understands and that all the issues be explained, so that people have time to think and make up their minds.

FRANCISCA: For most women — their husbands go to the meetings. If their husbands say, "No, the meetings are only for men," then, the women won't go. They are afraid that their husbands will come home and beat them for disobeying in public.

I think that quite a lot of women would like to go to the meetings, especially if their husbands don't go, or don't tell them what happened. Because often the women don't know what is happening in the village.

RAMOSA: The men think that women don't have anything worthwhile to say. They always have a "guard" at the door — a few men who won't let certain people in — that is, the women. I know because they use a stick so you can't get in. (She laughed.)

For example, there was a meeting in January — there was a problem with the cooperative. It was being discussed at the meeting, and we wanted to go and support Anita and John. They wouldn't let us in! We had to stay outside, or go home. What could we do when they stopped us like that, and wouldn't even open the door — just because we were women? They are the authorities . . . you can't force your way in.

We were very excited at the thought of going in — but there were only six of us. If we had organised all the women in the village, it would have been different. They would have had to let us in. But with six of us, what can you do? They can stop six women, but they couldn't stop a whole village of women. They say that we have nothing to say, but I think they are afraid of us, and that is why they won't let us in.

They say that the woman is made to be in the house — in the kitchen, cooking, cleaning. What kind of woman would be in the streets? The men are the only ones who have the freedom to be in the streets. That is the way it is.

That isn't going to change. For example, my parents — my mother isn't going to say to me, when I get home, "Why don't you go out in the streets and see what is happening?" (She laughed again.) No, I get home and I have things to do in the house — cook, weave, or mend clothes. That is the woman's life . . . we are very domestic and home-loving.

For some women that means they can't even come here to work every day. Some women have a lot of work in their houses. We have a lot of work too . . . but, for example, in my house, my mother does a lot of work, so I can come here. Other women who don't have that kind of help, have to stay at home. Quite a few women had to leave the cooperative, because there was no one to give lunch to their family — and the children have to go to school — and then there is no one to look after them when they come home. Some of them had problems with their husbands who didn't want them out of the house all day.

FRANCISCA: Not only does the woman have to cope with the family . . . and house work . . . but when her husband gets drunk, she has to come up with some way of buying food for the children. Here in Peru they drink a lot. Foreigners don't seem to drink as much . . . but here if the men have money in their pockets, you can find them in the canteen.

Money is a problem . . . different people do it different ways. I asked my cousin, "What do you do with your money? Do you give it to your husband?" And she said, "No, I keep it so I can buy food for the children. If I give it to my husband, he hangs on to it, and then he will use it for drink. What am I supposed to buy the food with?" When there is no understanding, the husband and wife argue about these kind of things all the time . . . lots of fighting. That doesn't happen if they can talk to each other.

RAMOSA: I also think . . . I have said to my mother . . . that the daughter must be one with the mother. The mother must be able to talk to her, advise her about the way life is . . . so that she can be another class of woman . . . so she knows how to look after herself.

Often, because the mother is so shy, they don't want to talk to their daughters about such things . . . about taking care, and not having children.

That is why so many young people have problems. When young girls menstruate, for example, the mothers should explain what it is, and say that you must take care, and not be with men at certain times. But they don't . . . they don't say anything . . . They keep it a big secret. They don't tell you anything. So what happens is that the young girl, not knowing anything, goes with a man, or her boyfriend, and she ends up pregnant. Instead of talking and advising their children, they just hit them, or shout at them. If they talked to each other it wouldn't be like that.

FRANCISCA: I feel the same way. If I have a daughter, I want her to be a better person than I am, so that she isn't like everyone else — working in the *chacra*, or working here in the workshop. You don't earn very much here. In Lima, you can work and have a profession. You earn more than here, and it appears to me, that people and life are better there than here.

RAMOSA: When I came back here, I had to start my life over again. I had to leave my friends, my studies, and everything I had established there. If I have a daughter, I want her to be educated — so she has a profession, so she can take care of herself. I want her to have a more socialist way of thinking, so she might actually be able to change the way she lives . . . not the way I have lived here in the village. I don't want her to follow in my footsteps.

FRANCISCA: If I had been a boy instead of a girl, I would have been able to go on studying — but here I am. I would like to be in Lima, because all my brothers are in Lima. I had the chance to go, but I stayed. Because, you see, I am the last daughter in the house, and my parents didn't want me to leave. They wanted me to stay here and learn something in the cooperative.

RAMOSA: Be a man instead of a woman? Of course, I would have preferred that because . . . as they say, "whenever a man falls, he lands on his feet". Nothing happens to a man . . . A man doesn't have to worry about not having children, for example. A man is educated; has a profession; looks after his family; and has more liberty and freedom to do what he wants.

Women from other countries are different from here. They are more aware and more socialist in their thinking. Why do you think that is? Because they have been raised in a different way. We are tied to the way that our parents were raised, and they have tried to raise us in the same way.

People who are rich are different, too. It is another environment altogether. They are more aware, from the time they are children.

*Señora Teodora was a weaver in the cooperative. She was
39, married and had given birth to five children, although
two had died.*

*For Teodora, the cooperative was a way of earning a
steady income and therefore, the chance to give her children
an education. She was especially concerned that her
daughter's life be different from her own.*

I think that the only way for us and other women to live better lives, is to
learn and study . . . to know more than we do now. If I were a teacher, my life
would be much happier and more peaceful. I know that I would have a
regular income each month, and then with some of what I had earned I could
look for a *muchacha.*

Unfortunately, that isn't the way we live. All we think about is doing the
same thing every day . . . especially the women . . . staying in the house is the
only idea we have. We can't advance at all. We lack education — that's why,
all my life, I have wanted my daughter to have more education than me.

I want her to study. I will do whatever I can so that she can study. And I want
her to be happy. I tell her to go out, but she doesn't want to. She doesn't even
like dancing. She is a very good girl . . . but she has her problems. All young
girls have problems at that age.

I would like her to have a profession. After that she has to be a mother. I am
not going to live forever, and if she stays single all her life . . . of course if I
were immortal (she laughed), perhaps then she could stay single . . . but no
one is free of death. She has to get married, so she will have someone after I
die. But above all, I want her to study. Last year, I had the idea of putting her
in some kind of academy so she would learn . . . at least she would learn to
speak properly and take care of herself.

There are lots of girls . . . I don't know. I can't even analyse what their ideas
are. Who understands how or why it is that they grow up so early and why
they behave like they do? Many of them get into trouble very quickly — as
young girls . . . they get married, or they have babies without husbands.

They promise themselves to someone without knowing anything. The
parents can't advise them. How many young girls leave school to get married?

That is what worries me at night . . . I can't even sleep for worrying about it. My husband says that I worry too much about it . . . there is lots of time yet . . . and lots of things could happen.

My sisters are all still single. They say they don't want to get married, and have the same problems that I have had. I think sometimes they miss having children . . . but generally, I think it is better if they don't get married. They can do what they want. If they want to leave the village to work they can. I know that they will have a more peaceful life than the one I have had.

There are some good marriages, but others . . . once you are married, you don't go out. You stop doing everything you used to do. It is very difficult to have fun, or to go out in the streets, or to have a conversation with friends, the way we are talking now.

But the man — no — the man is free, independent. He has the right to do only one job in the day, and then he is finished. But for a woman, it is very different. It is all right for me now, because I do my work here — I arrive, and I don't have anything else to do here, but the work. But if I were in the house, first I would have to cook, clean up, then wash, then make more food. Then, if I had animals, I would have to take them out to pasture. And there might be other animals in the house that I would have to look after. So I would have to go out and find food for them, carry it back, feed the pig . . . and finally, at the end of the day, at night, I might have to sew or mend the children's clothes. And my husband would arrive, and I would have to have his food ready. There is a lot to do . . . but the woman does it, not the man.

And if I want to go out, I have to ask for permission. That is the way it is in my house. Others might be different. As they say, "everyone has their own way of ordering their house." Maybe there are some women that don't pay attention to their husbands, but if I want a peaceful life, I have to listen and do what my husband says. If I want to go out, I tell him that I am going to such and such a place, and when I am going to be back. If he agrees, he says, "Fine, go ahead". But if he doesn't want me to go, he says, "No, no you can't go out . . . because there isn't time . . . we are going here . . . " or "you have to do this, so you aren't going to be able to go."

I got married when I was 18. Now I can't complain. But, at the beginning, I thought it was . . . something quite difficult. I always had to battle to carry on. At the beginning we had nothing . . . really absolutely nothing. But after the first child, it got a little easier, and in the later years we were able to manage better. And now I think we do understand each other.

I met my husband in Lima by chance. My mother took me to Lima when I was 17 to work in the house of a woman who looked after children and babies while their mothers went to work . . . like a nursery. It wasn't bad . . . it could have been a good job. There were three of us who worked for her, and we were always chatting to each other about different things.

But I suffered quite a lot when I was in Lima . . . I was going to leave and work somewhere else . . . in a house where they paid a little more. I had learned all about looking after babies, in two months, but I wanted to learn about cooking and washing, too. And a friend of mine told me about a woman who was looking for a maid. So I decided to go there.

My friend was waiting for me there. I was in that house for four – six months, I think. They were very good to me. It was a woman and her daughter. She taught me how to cook and clean, everything that you have to do in a house. Her daughter went out to work, and the *señora* stayed at home. And sometimes they would even take me out with them.

My husband was working on a house nearby, and he came out to buy something in the shop. I met him by accident on the corner. I was so happy to meet someone from my village. We stopped and talked for a while.

When I returned, the *señora* asked me what I had been doing for so long. I told her that I had met a *paisano* (a countryman) and that we had been talking for a while. She shouted at me, "I don't want this to happen again".

After two or three days, we met again. It was a Sunday, my time to have off . . . and with my luck . . . we had just been talking for a few minutes . . . we hadn't done anything, and my father arrived, and found the two of us. What bad luck! And the way my father thinks . . . even though we had only met each other recently . . . My father said that we had been meeting each other for a long time. He was very angry with me.

That very day, he brought me back here to the village with him. He said that he couldn't leave me there to get into trouble. He went to the *señora* and told her that he found me in the street . . . he went on and on.

The *señora*, very pleased with herself, said how sorry she was, and that after a month, I must come back to work again. I left my clothes and my shoes there. I only had time to bring a few things with me.

We got back here, and I felt like a real martyr. Why had my father caused me all these problems when I was learning something? I could have helped the family and my brothers and sisters. I was the oldest.

I was bitter, and I wanted another adventure. Then all of a sudden, my husband — the *paisano* appeared. Not even a month had gone by, and he appeared in the village. And so we started to meet here.

That is the custom. The men look for the women; they court them; and they become engaged for a year, or sometimes only months . . . depending on how they feel. Sometimes they get married right away . . . the men rob the girls from the parents.

After we were married we went back to Lima to live for a while . . . I had two children there. We lived there for four years. My husband worked in a shoe maker's shop. He used to do very good work. Really beautiful it was . . . all for export. But we didn't have much money for him to establish himself.

I really enjoyed living in Lima. For me . . . I wasn't stuck in the house. I always enjoyed working, or on other days, I would meet people in the street. Because I had worked there before, I knew a few *señoras* who were very good to me. I would always go to them when I had no money.

And I said, "*Señora*, please — do you have any clothes that need washing?" And they said, through the intercom, "Who am I speaking to?" "To Teodora," I said. "What a surprise . . . come in . . . where have you been . . . how are you?" they would all say. I would tell them what I was doing, and about all my problems. And they would say, "Of course, you can do some washing . . . today and tomorrow". "But *Señora*," I said, "I don't even have enough money for the bus." "Don't worry," she said, "I will give you money for fares, and something more, too." And she did give me the money, and I spent the day happily washing. And the other *muchacha* who worked there all the time, gave me lunch. And then, at the end of the day, I went home with my money — and I could buy things for the children — fruit, milk . . .

I was going to start to study sewing, so I could make clothes for the children, and earn some money that way too. I was just about to pay the tuition fee — just ready — and my husband got sick, and then we just didn't have enough money. We couldn't manage with him being sick if I went to school. There was no one to look after the children, and no one to cook for my husband. So even though he got better, it looked like it wasn't going to be possible.

When my husband got sick, he went to the doctor to have some tests, and the doctor said he should go back to the mountains to get some rest. And that was our failure there. If only things had been different.

I would have liked to have stayed there, but we couldn't. At least my children are getting an education here . . . but when the children have to continue in their studies, we will have to buy a small house in Huaral and find work there. I will do whatever I have to, whether it means washing clothes, or working as a maid . . . whatever is necessary for them to study.

I want them to leave the village eventually, because we don't have anything here. Some families . . . their parents had land, houses, but we don't. We are from poor families . . . and that is why I don't want the children to stay here. We can't give them opportunities here for anything. It is all right for us . . . but not for the children.

There isn't even a health centre in the village. It is easier to die here than to live. Now I have a kind of haemorrhage. I started to menstruate, but very heavily. I couldn't stand it. It had never been like that before.

The day it happened, I was fine at first . . . I came to work at my loom, but by 12 noon, I had to go to bed. But it wasn't a bed; it was a pool of blood. What could I do? There was no one to help. I was like that the whole day and night, and I thought, I am going to die. I cried for my children. Who was going to look after them? I couldn't stop crying. My husband said we should go down the mountain to find a doctor . . . but there was no transport.

Luckily there was someone here — one of the teachers who gave me an injection to stop the blood, and the next week I was a little better. But I was still afraid to travel because with the movement of the bus, the blood could have started again.

After a while, I decided to take the chance, and we went to Lima. They did some tests, and they said, it was a form of anaemia, and they gave me some vitamin capsules . . . and six injections — three here, and three here. It was all pure vitamins. And since then, I started to get a little better.

All this happened only last month. I don't know what the reason was. I have to go again for another checkup. The blood came twice this month. Why would that be? I want to go and find out why. But since we don't have any money now . . . the blood test costs money — 3,500 soles (£7) and then the medicine costs on top of that. So that is why I have to come to work, even though I don't feel well. I have to earn the money, so I can go to the doctor.

My husband doesn't really earn in the way that I do. We live from my salary and my work. He has gone up the mountain to look after the cattle. Before we lived only from the *chacra*, and from the sale of the animals. We used to sell the rams for 3,000 soles (£6) or 2,500 soles (£5). That was money . . . but now you can't buy anything for 2,000 soles.

Right now it is very difficult. It has been a holiday month for the whole workshop, so we weren't earning. I had to come to work. My husband said I shouldn't go . . . it would be better to rest. I said, "I am going to work, even if I die working. I don't want my children to be without food . , . I'll work".

The problem is that the work we have in the *chacra* and the money we get is only seasonal — nothing more. Now is the time to plant beans and corn. For example, in September, we will have a little money. In October, November and December, we won't see any money. What will we do to support ourselves without anything?

And the animals. I just bought them recently, so they are still small. If I sell them now, they won't bring a good price, but if I wait, I might not be able to sell them if people have no money.

One day or two days of work in the fields — and they pay you the miserable sum of 200 or 300 soles (50p) per day . . . or they might pay 500 (£1) on one day. And then there is no more work. What can you do?

I joined the cooperative at the beginning, to be able to earn some money. Nothing more than that. And it is a big help. Even though you don't earn much, at least it is 500 soles more every day.

If you want to move forward, there is more work you can do. The maximum you could earn here is about 600-700 soles (£1.30) a day. For the women, it is a way of being a help in the house.

My husband is pleased that I work here, because he knows that I am helping . . . and we need the money. He is also very worried, because our children are going to go into college soon. The oldest girl is in second year of secondary school; the boy is going into second year of primary, and the little one . . . will start primary soon. We need uniforms, shoes, schoolbooks — without the cooperative, we couldn't pay for it all.

It does mean more work for me, though. I arrange all the clothes and the food for the children before I leave.

If I have a lot to do, I will get up at 6 a.m. If there is nothing much to do, I will get up at 7:30 a.m. so that I can get to the workshop by 8 a.m. My daughter is old enough ... she makes the breakfast and lunch. Before she was old enough to do it, I suffered a lot. It was very hard. I had to get up very early so I would be able to do everything. But now, she helps me a lot.

I think all the women in the cooperative have definitely learned something. Because in the house, you don't talk to anyone; you don't learn anything. But here — we are all alike — and we have meetings, and we discuss many things. You have to learn something doing that. You hear other ideas, and you have your own ideas. In the meetings, you listen to what other people have to say, and you decide whether you agree or not.

The men still talk more than the women. It must be because they know more, and have more ideas about how things should be. But when we have meetings it is important for everyone to give their opinions.

There is one problem though. Sometimes when you speak a lot or say what you think, people think badly of you ... that you talk too much ... that you put yourself in everything. Many times I have thought that it would be better to keep quiet than say what I think. If I say something, they think ... they say that I never shut my mouth ... that I always have something to say, and why can't I keep quiet. They always say things like that here.

I used to speak more than I do now. I don't say very much but I am still listening. (She chuckled.) And sometimes, if I say something, someone else will get up, and disagree, and we will have a big argument. So to avoid that, it is better to keep quiet. That is the way I think.

But we, the women, aren't allowed into the community meetings. The nun is allowed in ... she goes in with the priest. She is always asking them to allow the women in, but not so far.

In any case, we don't have time. When the men are in the meeting, we are already off for the day to do our work — to the *chacra* — to hoe, or weed, or harvest the potatoes. There are so many things to do, that we probably wouldn't have time, even if we were allowed in.

And there are a lot of husbands who have strange ways of thinking. They have already said lots of things. They say that it is bad for women and men to work together in the same place. I don't know ... they have always had those kinds of criticisms. And they say that the women have too many things to do in the house, so they shouldn't be doing those things anyway.

MARRIAGE? — I DON'T THINK SO

The themes of marriage and independence ran through all the conversations I had with women near Huancayo, a town several hours south of Lima. It is an area rich in craftwork, produced mainly in the outlying villages of the region. Most of the women I talked to were members of small cooperatives or associations, affiliated to *Kamak Maki*,[4] a federation of about 20 different craft groups. The federation was created to provide a more reliable market for a number of groups which had been struggling on their own.

It also resulted in a new impetus for various women to come together in groups instead of trying to market their spinning and weaving on an individual basis. Most of the women were therefore able to count on a more or less steady source of cash for their work. This may have been why some of them showed more independence in terms of deciding who they would marry and when. Earning her own money meant a young girl could initially resist the pressure from her parents to get married:

> *"My mother wants me to get married but I want to wait for at least two years, because once you get married, you are under your husband's thumb completely. You can't go where you want or do what you want.*
>
> *"One boy here asked me to marry him but I said I wanted to wait. I think he will marry someone else now. And then another one asked me, but he has no work.*
>
> *"You have to be careful who you choose. My sister is married to a man who hardly every works and she has to do everything, and support the family. They have two small babies, and she is only 22.*
>
> *"So now I wish I'd married the first one because my mother and father want me to get married, but the second one isn't a good man."*
> —Paulina, 18 years old

---

4.   *Kamak Maki* is a Quechua word meaning "creative hand".

Lucinda is 33, a single mother with three children, aged 15, 11 and six. She had been an employee in a small semi-commercial weaving workshop. When the workshop closed, she and several other women, with the encouragement and help of their employer, organised themselves into an independent cooperative, and joined the federation.

Lucinda had learned a lot from her experiences in the cooperative, and explained how the women participated in the meetings in spite of being outnumbered by the men.

She also took great delight in telling me exactly how and why she was better off as a single mother than a married woman.

I see a lot of women with husbands, who live much worse lives than I do. They complain all the time that they have no money, that their husbands beat them, that they fight. (She burst into laughter.) They are always having to punish their children — the fathers sometimes treat them badly.

I have seen quite a few women who have been married for 10 or 20 years, and then their husbands leave them with eight, nine or 10 children. I think it is better to live alone from the beginning.

It isn't everyone who has bad luck . . . some women have good lives. But for me, it is much more peaceful to live on my own, with my children.

I say to my daughters, "Well, if God sends you husbands, I suppose you will get married . . . but let them be good men and good husbands. They have to be responsible, and take care of their home and family. There are some who get married, and you never see them. They expect their wives to look after everything in the house and the children."

Many women say that without their husbands, they couldn't live; that there wouldn't be any life without them. I don't understand that, because I live very well, in fact, better without a husband. I have a free life. I can go where I want in peace. Married women can't, because if they go out, their husbands get angry and often beat them when they get back. You have to ask permission from your husband before you can go out.

I don't know why women get married. I think it is an illusion for them. Maybe their mothers told them it was the best thing to do, but since I never had my mother at my side, and my godmother didn't have a husband — I don't know. I just never wanted to get married.

People do talk about me though, but I don't pay any attention. I know some of them are just jealous. One of the single women in the group always says to me that I have my children to help me, and she doesn't have anyone. I say to her, "Why are you being so silly? Why don't you have a child, too?" She just gets bitter. She always complains that she has no one to help her, and she has to look after her sick mother all the time. I have to look after three other people, and she only has to look after one. Then she says that her mother doesn't help the way my children do . . . and so it goes on . . . we argue.

I have always lived alone as a single mother, and supported myself and my children. It has been difficult at times. When I had the children I had to have social security because I couldn't work. That helped me.

When I was 20, I started in the weaving workshop. Before I was working for this other shop, sewing clothes. A friend of mine worked for the *señorita* (the owner of the weaving workshop), and she said I would earn more with the *señorita*. I wasn't earning very much in the other shop. She said she would recommend me to the *señorita*, even though I didn't know how to weave. So when I started at the weaving workshop, at first, I made bobbins, ironed, sewed, cleaned — everything that had to be done. After a while, I said to the *señorita* that I wanted to learn how to weave.

I had been watching the weavers for five years — as I ironed, and inspected the weaving; I saw how some of it was done. It was making the designs and patterns that was difficult for me, but I learned.

It was a good salary. When I started there, they were paying us 210 soles (40p) weekly. At the end we were earning about 1000 or 1100 (£2) a week. It was enough to live on.

I enjoyed my work, but at the end there were lots of arguments. At the beginning, we were all very happy working together, having our meetings. Then the women began to fight. Some were getting paid more because they were working faster, and others less if they arrived late.

From all the different discussions we had, I learned how to think and give my opinion but it took me a long time. At first, I was afraid to speak. We had a committee but I was never elected to it.

Then one day, the *señorita* told us she was going to close the workshop. Before we never thought that that would happen. Saturday would come, and we would be paid, and that was all. We never worried about the administration, and the money. Now we have to do all the things that the *señorita* used to do.

She told us two years beforehand that she was going to close the workshop. We talked to her and thought about forming our own group — to weave and carry on taking the orders that she used to have. She said she would recommend us to all her customers. For most of us, the only way we can earn money is to weave. So as soon as the workshop closed, we began to weave for ourselves. There are nine of us in the group; and I think we are better off now, because we all work for ourselves, but we are working together too.

The accounting is a little difficult. The other day, we almost lost money because we couldn't add up the invoice very well. We were losing money, because we didn't know any better. We can't afford to give it away to other people. In fact, I have been thinking of studying book keeping. I don't know yet, but as the group's representative, I have to collect the money, and share it out, and figure out all the different amounts to give everyone. We have to give a percentage to the shop, too.

Today, we had to go and collect some money and share it out, and put some of it in the bank. We can do this when it suits us, and we can weave at the hour that is good for us. We don't have to be in the workshop at a certain time like before.

A couple of us have been thinking of going to Lima with the *señorita*, to meet the people who we send orders to. Then we could send them directly without bothering the *señorita*. She is trying to teach us all the things you have to know. She helps us to learn . . . it is important to her that we learn everything.

We didn't even know how to send parcels. We used to give everything to *Kamak Maki* and they would do it. Now, the *señor* in Lima wants us to send to him directly, and he won't have to pay the percentage for *Kamak Maki*.

We are learning a lot — about money and administration. I go to the meetings, of the federation, and they explain different things to us — about how it should be in business, and about things you have to do.

I think it is important for women to get together and work together, because when you speak to other people, and listen to them, you change your ideas and you give them your thoughts too. I have changed what I think by talking to other women.

Now in the group we have — it is very different from before. Because we each work in our houses, and we each do as much as we can. We get paid for the weaving that we do. It is a good group. We have a president and a delegate who go to the meetings of *Kamak Maki.*

There are meetings of all the delegates from the different cooperative groups in the federation. Both women and men go — but we all speak as equals. When I first started in the workshop, I didn't say anything. At the beginning, in the federation, the men spoke more than the women — but little by little, we began to speak up. There are four women in all, and the rest are men — 25 men. I am the delegate from our group, and I go to all the meetings. Sometimes we argue with the men. Before, at the beginning, I was afraid, but not now — little by little you get used to it.

Some women in the group don't come to the meetings, because they have problems at home. If their children are sick, they can't come. For example, the last time we had a meeting two women couldn't come. One of them had just given birth to another baby, and the other — I think her husband had just gone back into prison. In our group, there are two women who are married; the rest of us are single women or single mothers.

We have meetings here, too, in the village, about the community. Mainly it is the men who go to the meetings. Almost always, I am the only woman in the meeting. I lost the fear I used to have and I'm not afraid of anything now. (She laughed.) But the other women are still afraid. If they do come they never speak. It must be because they don't have much contact with different associations and meetings. Many of them say they can't come because they have to cook and look after the house. Their husbands go, they say, so they don't have to go.

I don't think women should be afraid to speak up. We have to tell them not to be afraid. In the meetings in the village, we talk about all sorts of things that have to do with the village — water, or money or who is doing different things. Now we are building a cemetery. We bought a piece of land . . . it is interesting to go to the meetings to know what is going on, to listen to other people. For one thing, it gives me a rest from weaving. I am here at the loom every day, weaving all the time. There are times when you need a change or need to talk to someone.

Rosa used to be the delegate before, but she never went to the meetings. She said she lost too much time if she went, and she also thought she was better than everybody. She used to say, "Who wants to go and meet with those Indians who come from the mountains". Well, I think that no matter where they come from, the mountains or not, we are all people. She thinks it makes a difference — she doesn't want to be with poor people because she thinks she is too good for them.

I think it is good to work in groups like in the cooperative, because we do help each other. One person alone couldn't do all the orders that we have, but if we work together we can manage.

I helped another group here in the village. All the women who spin have formed their own group. I helped them set it up. Now they say it is my fault that they have so much work to do. (She laughed.) But now they have something. Before they all used to complain that they never had any money, that their husbands never gave them any money. They used to say that I should get them some work.

Then *Kamak Maki* opened the shop, and I told all the women about it. So they all started spinning. But in October there was no money in the shop to pay anyone — for two weeks or a month, I think. All the women got very angry, and said it was all my fault. (She laughed again.)

I think it is much better if women have their own money. For example, one young girl who is married and has two babies . . . her husband never has any work, and she supports the whole family from her spinning. What does he do? Wash the nappies and cook? (She practically fell off the chair with laughter.) Scrub the wool; look after the children? No, nothing. His wife has to do all that, and earn the money, too.

It is important that women have work, or a profession so they can earn money. If you don't have money, life is suffering. If you don't have some kind of education, you can't do anything.

It is very important for children to go to school. You can't live without knowing. Of course, I want my daughters to have a profession. Now they are all in school. I want them to study until they all have professions — the ones that they want. I want my son to be a doctor. He says he is going to be president of the country. Well, I will wait until he's president or a doctor. (She and her son both laughed.)

Victoria was an active member of another small cooperative in the same region, well-known for its naturally dyed, handspun alpaca textiles. We discussed the problems of the cooperative, but we spoke more about her own life, and her recent marriage to one of the organisers of the cooperative.

They were both older, he in his 30s and she in her late 20s when they married. Victoria seemed to feel that perhaps they were each "too independent" to make a successful marriage. At least she, as a woman, was not able to behave in the accepted submissive way.

I was born here, but I went to school in Huancayo. There were seven children, and we all went to school. We were lucky, because so many children can't study. In most families, where there are a lot of children, the parents can't afford to educate them all. But my father went to work in the mines. He earned more money there, so he could give us an education.

My mother died when I was nine. Before that she used to rule our house. When she died, my father did everything. He washed the clothes, and cooked for us. We were all very small. As we grew, he taught us how to do it. He never got married again. He's 70 years old now.

After finishing secondary school, I worked in Cerro de Pasco (a mining centre), as a third grade teacher. I was living right up at the top where the snow is on the mountain. I worked there for two or three years, but then I decided I didn't like it. It was so cold. They were paying us very little as teachers, and it wasn't worth it. I came back here and started to weave and spin. I wasn't planning to get married, but suddenly I fell in love.

We don't have any children yet. We are planning to have only two. It is too expensive these days to have more than two, because you can't feed or educate them. My husband agrees. We are being careful now. I don't take anything. I know when the dangerous times are, according to my "period". We went to a doctor, and he explained it to us. We bought some books too.

The pill, the *espiral* . . . I think they always cause problems in the end. When you are older, and arrive at the critical age, there are terrible consequences.

Sometimes the women go crazy, and one of the doctors told me that most women get fat and have headaches, and are in a bad mood all the time.

Most women here don't know anything about all that. There is a health centre, but the nurse doesn't really explain things very well. Some of the women talk to each other. I explain it to the ones who ask me, but I don't think they believe me. They think I don't have any experience.

I think there should be courses for both women and men, so they would understand. Some men, not all, actually think that if their wives use something, they will go off with other men. They get jealous, and hit them.

My husband is a good man, but we have had our problems too. We had to get used to each other. He didn't understand me. He was very jealous and didn't like it if I dressed up. "Why are you getting dressed up?" he would say. "I am your husband." I explained that just because we were married, I wasn't going to stop looking after myself. Now he doesn't say anything.

We also had a terrible problem at first because he didn't understand why I didn't want children right away. I said, "We don't even have a house. If we have a baby, I can't work like before, and we would need even more money." I also said if you have a baby, it sometimes means the husband gets less attention. With the books we bought, he is beginning to understand.

If I do have children, I want them to have a better life. We have suffered a lot, especially my sister and I. My father went to the mines and we stayed here. My older sister got pregnant. When my father realised what had happened, he came and took us all back to the mine with him. I had to stop studying to look after the younger children, and the animals we had. Later I went back to school. My sister is still a single mother. Her 15 year old daughter lives here, and my sister works in Lima as a cosmetician, but doesn't earn much.

I have been a member of the association (cooperative) for four years. Before, I used to spin and weave, and sell my work to tourists, or shop keepers. Now it is a little better, because we get a better price from the cooperative. I earn about 300 soles (60p) per day. But sometimes there is no money in the association, and we have to wait to be paid.

On the other hand, the shop keepers pay less, but they always have money to pay you right away. I would still rather work for the association because we receive the profits, and other benefits.

It is better too, because we are all working together. If a big order comes in, say for 20 kilos of wool, we can fill it. One woman working on her own couldn't do it. Every Saturday, all the women from the outlying villages bring their wool here . . . it is about 60-80 kilos in total.

We have meetings at the end of each month, and all the members are supposed to come. If they don't come, they are fined 500 soles (£1). Most of the members are women. There are probably about 10 men. Many of the women won't speak in the meetings. They just sit there silently. They are afraid that if they say something against the president, or anyone else, it will be noticed, and when they bring their wool, it won't be accepted. That is the way they think. They don't have much education. Others of us talk, no matter what. I don't care who notices. I want people to know what I think.

Some people talk about me, though, saying that I should be more timid, more under the rule of my husband. Most of the women, the younger ones too, go along with the way things are.

The woman has all the responsibility of the home and the *chacra*. Sometimes the men are just like your oldest children, that is, you have to tell them what to do. Not all of them, but some.

The men have all the freedom. They sleep, eat, go out onto the streets, come back, eat some more, and sleep. They don't worry about the children or the house. You go to the market, and you can see. They walk like this (freely swinging her arms), without carrying anything. The women are carrying the children, a bundle on top of that, more children at their side, and they are pregnant too. I tell the women, "Why don't you tell him to carry something, or to help you?" But is there a man who would do this? Not most of them.

It is better when you earn your own money. Because if you have to wait for him to give you money, you can't say anything about anything. "But," the women say, "if I earn my money, it is my money, and I have the right to speak because I am bringing money into the house too."

I keep my money and try to save it. As we were just married, we need so many things. We share all the money we have, my husband and I. At the beginning, he said to me, "This is my money". But I said to him, "If this is your money, I'll go and live in a separate house . . . me with my money, and you can stay here with your money." He changed his mind, and now, what is his is mine, and vice versa.

At least now, there is always work, because of the cooperative, but we don't have any special activities for the women. My sister is president of the education committee. She organised classes for the women who can't read and write. We had a teacher come to give classes in the afternoons from 6 to 7 p.m., but the women didn't come. Of the 15 that should have been there, only two or three came. The teacher had asked them when they wanted the classes. They had all said that time. Either they didn't have any interest, or they were afraid. The teacher was much younger than all of them. I think they probably didn't like that.

We have problems with the meetings too. They say they will start at noon, but they sometimes don't start until 4 p.m., and don't finish until 7 or 8 at night. The husbands only give permission for the women to be out for two hours. Sometimes the men come and take their wives back home, because they are so late.

If I were in charge, I would also give the women classes about taking care of their homes and children better. I would tell them about not having so many children. It is important, because there are some women who have so many children, that they can't feed them. They don't want so many; they just don't know how to look after themselves, and the men don't care what happens.

Women don't talk amongst themselves much, especially about sexual relations. Sometimes I speak with a few friends that I have, but I think they make fun of me. I don't think they want to talk about it. They are ashamed to discuss such things. They will listen to what I have to say, but they won't say what they feel.

It really is the fault of the parents. They should treat both boys and girls the same. But they teach the girls to be weaker than the boys. If you treat them the same, and buy the same kind of toys the boys have . . . planes, guns, cars . . . the girls will have more character too. That is the way I am going to treat my children. I want one of each, in about a year, but you never know. For as much as you take care, suddenly there they are.

I think that women must stop being timid. In whatever meeting or discussion you must speak. It doesn't matter what other people say, and it doesn't matter if you say something wrong, or bad. Little by little you will learn. You think that what you are going to say is all right, but it comes out badly, and everyone laughs. For that, none of the women will speak.

We have meetings of the village, and the majority say nothing. Not one woman has ever been elected to anything in the village ... not secretary ... nothing. One of the girls protested in one of the meetings. She said, "Why can't a woman be elected as mayor?" Most people said no, because women have to look after the house and the *chacra*.

I guess the rich women always have more chance in the world. They have money, and can go wherever they want, well-dressed. Everyone accepts them. But if you go like this, like a poor person, you get stopped at the door, and they don't let you in. I think everyone should be equal, but people need an education for that.

I am lucky because I went to school, and I have the experience of being in other places, and talking to people. There are girls here who have no experience outside the village. For example, I like going to the movies to see ... I would like to ask you something ... how can two people be happier together ... have better sexual relations if they are married? Because people say that you can be quite happy together, but I don't know.

I think that when you are single, you should have sexual relations with the man you are going to marry, to see if you will be happy together, because if not, it could be a total failure. But if you do, people talk about you, and you are "marked". The men make fun of girls who do that. They won't be seen with someone like that. I think the men need some kind of orientation. They are just like animals. The only thing important to them is that they enjoy themselves. It doesn't matter if the women are happy or not.

At the beginning, my husband was like all the rest of them. It still is a little difficult. How can I tell him that I'm not happy? I don't know what to say.

I wasn't going to get married until I was 35, because I thought that it was better to be single. Then I thought it would be better to get married. I had no experience, and no one told me, and now I have changed my mind. I have only been married for six months, and I wish I were single again.

He got married very late, too, and he is used to doing what he wants. And so am I. So there are lots of fights. Maybe I should be like the other women who don't say anything. But why should I ... just because it is the custom?

THE WOMEN'S COMMITTEE

The agricultural cooperative, Simon Bolivar, located two hours north of Lima had taken a step towards changing the traditional role of peasant women. It was the only agrarian cooperative in the region with a women's committee. The cooperative had about 320 members, 60 of whom were women. They earned about £1.50 for an eight-hour day, working in the fields. Most had to leave their children at home alone, or in the care of other members of the family.

The committee and an education programme of literacy classes had been set up to enable the women to participate more actively in the running of the cooperative and to help develop their own personal resources.

As one of the women on the committee told me:

"That's why we formed the committee — so there would be something — some work for women in the cooperative. It is just over a year old. We wanted to be able to teach the women different things, like sewing. So far we haven't done that. There are a lot of things that we wanted to do that we haven't been able to yet. But this year we started the guinea pig farm. The cooperative used to run the guinea pig farm, but they stopped it three years ago. So we decided to start it up again. And we also work on our other project — the cafe — as well as on the land belonging to the cooperative.

"We still owe the cooperative for the loan we took out. We are all still very worried about the debt that we have taken out from the cooperative. Once that is paid, and that worry is gone, we will all be much happier, and able to do more things. When the guinea pig project begins to yield profits, we can either begin to pay back the loan, or set up another project, like a sewing workshop."

Gloria, 35 and single, was in charge of the literacy programme and worked with the women's committee. She had been educated in a convent, and had worked in Lima for 11 years. She saw the cooperative, and in particular, the women's project, as an opportunity for the women to overcome their fear of expressing themselves and the chance to take on new responsibilities.

I left the convent in 1973, and went to study to be a literacy teacher. I already had some experience because in my town, I had worked with the peasants, the miners and with prisoners, too.

When I finished my course, I worked for the Department of Education for a while teaching literacy, and then after two years, I came directly to the cooperative and presented my papers. They already knew me, and they agreed to take me on to do this work here. I am employed by them now; I'm not a member.

The women's committee was formed in 1976 — through a rule passed by the cooperative. The committee exists within the cooperative, and they support us in our projects.

The idea came from the women themselves. They wanted to work together and participate in the cooperative. They had always worked within the larger group, but didn't really participate, because they were very timid in front of the men, so they formed their own committee and, since then, they have really developed. They discuss things in their meetings and give their opinions. Before, it was very different, because in the time of the land owner, before the cooperative was formed, the women never participated in anything. They were not permitted to speak, and they never went to meetings. So the idea was to give the women a chance to develop, and promote their own activities.

The guinea pig farm was the women's idea. They all gave guinea pigs to start it. The other project we started was the cafe. The management committee of the cooperative realised that many of the workers came in the morning without breakfast, so we decided to start a cafe. The cooperative gave us 800 soles (£1.60), and helped with the construction. At first they said no, but then they extended their hand to us. They want to give facilities to the workers. The workers eat on credit for two weeks, and when they get paid, they pay us. Then we can buy what we need for the next two weeks.

It will take a year or so for it to get well established. We decided not to share out the profit we make from these two projects, but to reinvest it in setting up a nursery. The women don't have anyone or anywhere to leave their children. They take them with them or leave them alone in the house. So we need a nursery.

If it weren't for the committee, it would be the same now as it was before. There wouldn't be any involvement amongst the women. They aren't used to giving their opinions. Before, the boss would tell them everything they had to do, and there was no discussion. They had to obey quietly. It was the same for the men in that sense. There was no participation for anyone.

At the same time we have literacy so they can learn to read and write. It is important for the women to learn to read and write — so they can learn not to be cheated by other people. We also talk about the rights of women and men, saying that they all have the same rights, that women are worth as much as the men and that as workers they have the same rights from the state, and they should learn what those are. They have to learn to do mathematics so that when they go to the market to buy and sell, no one can cheat them and take money from them.

They have to learn to express themselves so that if they have to go to the doctor for themselves or their children, they can explain what the illness is. So many women are afraid to talk to the doctor, partly because they never know what to say.

The young ones can read and write now, but the older women who started at the same time, have had difficulty learning. Only a little bit has stayed with them. Most of them can write their names now, and add up a few numbers, but not much more. We will be stopping the classes for a while, and they will forget a lot of what they have learned. It is like anyone who is learning — like children — if you don't practise what you have learned you forget it.

We have two women members of the cooperative who are studying somewhere else to be leaders within their areas of work. They have been away for two months now.

One of them is a single woman, and the other is a widow with three children.

What they are learning won't only influence them, it will influence all their friends, in the home, and at work. Everything they have learned they will tell their friends ... "This shouldn't be this way. We can change this, or we discussed that." They both work in the fields, and when they talk to their friends or their family, they will transmit what they have learned, what they have talked about, what they have done. Each of them will be like a seed ... and little by little, they will influence other women and men in their groups. When the women come back, we are going to have a meeting of all the women, so these two can tell us all about the courses and discussions they have had.

In our sessions, we don't just talk about work. We talk about how things should be in the family, and relations between wife and husband, and parents and children ... that people should treat each other with love and respect. We talk about hygiene in the home, and many other things like that.

We have just finished a whole series of meetings about the health of the women ... how your body works from when you are young to when you are an adult and have children. But none of them have made any comments about it ... not that I have heard anyway. They are still a little shy. (She lowered her voice, even though there was no one in the room, and the door was closed.)

The women don't want so many children, but the men ... well ... they can't say no to the men. What really needs to happen is that we explain group group — to men and women so they both understand and agree.

I haven't spoken to many men about it ... but I have explained to quite a few of the women. They are still a little suspicious. They are afraid that it won't be good for their bodies ... but I say it is wrong to have so many children if you can't look after them properly.

My older sister is married and has three children. I don't think she wants any more — but I think she uses a natural method. After they have relations, she washes herself with boiled water and a little bit of lemon. That is all she has to do. She has been doing that for six years. A lot of women do that. Another natural method is when you have relations, you mustn't let the man's liquid come into the vagina. The man has to pull himself out, and it goes somewhere else ... onto the bed, or wherever, but not into the vagina. Men here are very demanding. They don't have anything to distract themselves with. The men masturbate a lot, but we women have a relief, because we menstruate.

Some women go to the doctor, and get pills or injections, but I don't know much about that or who uses it or not. In some cases the men know more about it, and want their wives to do something. They go to a doctor in another town, and the wives have a treatment. Since the women are malnourished, they conceive more easily.[5] Women who eat better, have more protection.

Another big problem is that many men have more than one women — they even have children with other women. The wives know, but what can they do? How could they support their family? How would their children eat?

The men often abandon the women with two, three or four children. They just leave them and go off. The women don't do anything except suffer.

To try and change all this . . . it must happen all over Peru. It will be a very long, slow job. But we have to begin, because if we don't, it is going to go from bad to worse.

There are two kinds of men — those who aren't interested in what we are doing, or think it is a waste of time, and those who give a lot of support. Actually, we have overcome a lot of the problems with the men.

But we still need training for both men and women, even though the women need it more. The women have to be in the house, have to educate the children, and manage no matter what happens. But the men also need to realise that they must give more time and support to their families . . . many men don't do anything with their children. They leave it all to the women. The work in the house must be shared by both of them.

From the moment that she wakes up, until the moment that she goes to sleep, the Peruvian woman is working, and looking after her husband, her children, and the house. If she works in the *chacra*, she must do that too. If she is tired, or sick, it doesn't matter. She has to fulfill her duties. There isn't anyone else who is going to do all these things for her. The man can't do it, or doesn't want to. He doesn't have the instinct to see what has to be done. The only thing he can see is the chair, and he sits on top of it. He doesn't sense or feel things the way a woman does. We have that instinct.

Women here are used to that way of life — the way things are. But I have lived with people from Germany, Mexico and America. Foreigners are different.

----

5.   Although this statement is incorrect, it has not been altered as it represents a belief on the part of the woman speaking.

They both share the work in the house. A family I know from Belgium . . . they both made dinner, washed the dishes, and looked after the children.

But here, if a child is sick, the men carry on sleeping. They just turn over the other way when a child is crying. Women here, because they have never seen how other people live, can't say that this shouldn't be the way it is. So they live a closed life here. If they had, or could see the way that others live, and relate to each other, they would think differently here too.

I suppose the men would all be very angry at the beginning, but gradually they would understand, and they would change too.

Without the training that we are giving in the cooperative, it would only be a source of work for the women, and nothing more. It has other advantages, other benefits, like help with medicine. If they need to borrow money to buy notebooks, or uniforms for school, the cooperative will loan members money, and they pay it back over a long period of time. They get a share of the profit at the end of the year. At the time of the *fiestas* they get a little extra money to spend on things for themselves or their children . . . or to send to their parents.

The most important thing now is that the cooperative is giving the women a chance to learn and become involved, and develop their own abilities. When a woman is in the house, she is trapped. But when she leaves, to go out and work, she talks to other people — as a human being who is also growing. Her energies, her thoughts . . . when you work somewhere outside the home, you have to use your intelligence and your initiative — it is a challenge to you as a person. Then when you go back to your home as a mother, you are still the same woman who is growing, and you will be different as a mother and wife too.

Women should have work. Especially widows, and single mothers who just barely survive . . . buying food, clothes. They just barely earn enough money to eat.

So women must really prepare themselves, in case their husbands abandon them. They must know how to survive — what they can do. Because if not . . . if all they have are their small animals and nothing more, they will just go off with another man, and it will be the same thing all over again. They will just look for someone who can support them, instead of surviving on their own.

Really, I think we should be working with the children. It is very hard to try to change people when they are adults. So for women and men to have a different future, or a different understanding, you should start now with the young ones — before they go the way of their parents. They should all study so they could have some kind of profession — a way to earn money — so they won't be abandoned without being able to look after themselves.

They shouldn't get married so young. They get married at 15 or 16 years old; and then they have a lot of children. These young girls who haven't been educated themselves, can't educate their children. They haven't had any preparation, and they can't set any kind of example for their children, except for the one they got from their parents. That is what we are trying to break.

You still have to work with the adults too, because they are still teaching young ones. The parents have to understand what the young ones are trying to change, otherwise there will be only battles in the home, and nothing will change.

When girls get married, that is the end of any liberty they might have had. They are under the thumb of the husband to do whatever he says and whatever he wants. The men think that the women belong to them, and if a woman has any liberty, it is because a man gives it to her. Before they get married, they don't think; they don't discuss; they don't plan or communicate.

She has to ask her husband for anything she wants to do, and without his permission, she can't do anything. But if you are a woman, and you have a profession, it is different, even though this sort of thing happens amongst professionals, too. I have seen it amongst my friends — the men order their wives around; they always dominate.

I don't think all the work has been in vain. I can see a change. Now the women come together and talk and question, and say what they think. When I first came in 1972, there was nothing like that. In 1974, there was a little bit. But now, in 1980, you can see a big difference. The first committee we formed wasn't very strong; the second did a little more. The third is more involved than the first two. It has been a slow process — very slow —but now you can actually see some progress. They have taken some steps forward.

"The Salvadorean man is like the government. He doesn't want to share or give up his power, or his arms. And that is why there is no change. The one who is in charge, stays in charge."
— Isabel, 43, a health promoter

EL SALVADOR

El Salvador is the smallest and most densely populated country in Central America. Its population density of 500 people per square mile is five times the average for Central America. A central east-west chain of volcanoes, with valleys in between, forms the structural backbone of the country. On the Pacific side of the country, there is a narrow coastal plain.

The lack of physical land barriers facilitated the Spanish colonisation of the country at an early date. Intermarriage and a rapid assimilation, together with wars, enslavement and disease reduced the Indian population. By the end of the 19th century, most of the population was classified as *ladino* although Indian culture and customs had by no means totally disappeared. Today only about 10% of the population are of pure Indian ancestry.

As in the rest of Central America, unequal ownership and control of the land is the root cause of the political crisis which today has brought El Salvador to a state of civil war. The early Spanish settlers introduced cattle raising into the lowland valley regions while the indigenous Salvadoreans cultivated subsistence crops, primarily maize, in the highlands.

In the late 19th century, coffee planting was introduced into the highlands. Rising world demand for coffee and easy access to the coast made this a competitively profitable crop. This encouraged the wealthy classes to seek ways of gaining control of the Indian's communally owned land.

In 1881, the government abolished all communal forms of land tenure, paving the way for the unofficially sanctioned expulsion of the Indians from their land. In return for their labour, the Indians who had been evicted from their lands received a small plot from the coffee plantation owner. These labourers became known as *colonos*. From then on, land was to be concentrated in the hands of a small, conservative clique of wealthy families: *los catorce* — the "14 families". Today, 92% of the 4.8 million population owns only 22% of the land, while the richest 2% owns 60%.

During the 20th century, wage labour gradually replaced these traditional landlord-peasant relations. The introduction of new cash crops, such as cotton and sugar cane, and the need for more land, accelerated the eviction of many *colonos* from their land. *Colono* plots declined from 55,000 in 1961 to 17,000 in 1971. Not every evicted *colono* was able to rent the little of the poor quality land that was available and the number of landless peasants increased from 11.8% of the rural population in 1961 to 65% in 1980.

But work opportunities for the landless and seasonal labourers are in minimal supply compared to demand. All work in the rural areas is seasonal, and the cotton and coffee crops have the same seasons. Between February and October, underemployment in the rural areas generally affects over 50% and sometimes as much as 80% of the population. The number of permanently unemployed has also risen steadily as land owners have modernised their plantations by introducing labour saving machinery.

Industrialisation

In the 1960s, El Salvador embarked on a process of industrialisation with the formation of the Central American Common Market (CACM). It was the aim of the CACM to create a market out of the consumer elite of five Central American republics.

The new industries employed little labour and those who migrated to the cities in search of work inevitably ended up in the service sector, living in the sprawling shanty towns at the edge of the cities.

By the 1970s, survival for the poor, especially the rural poor who form 60% of the population, had become increasingly precarious. El Salvador was one of the few Latin American countries on the UN's "hunger" list. Salvadoreans had the lowest calorie intake in Latin America; 73% of children under five were malnourished; the infant mortality rate was one of the highest in Central America.

The resistance of the country's elite to any social change was intense. They had been severely shaken by a peasant uprising in 1932. The rebellion was suppressed by a massacre of an estimated 30,000 peasants. Peasant leaders were hung in the town squares; people with Indian features were lined up in groups of 50 and shot down by firing squads. It was estimated that

4% of the entire population was killed. Since then the elite has ruled through the army, and until the 1960s, they faced no serious challenge.

But with the process of industrialisation, new social groups emerged: a small working class and a professional middle class. They began to challenge the power of the elite. In the 1960s new political parties were formed seeking economic reforms and a greater, more broadly based, political participation. In 1972 they formed a united front to fight the elections, and were only deprived of victory by a fraud.

Terror was also used to suppress all peasant organisation. In 1968 a rural vigilante organisation called ORDEN was set up. It had members in almost every village charged with identifying the "subversives", who would then be systematically eliminated. According to a recent publication by the Latin American Bureau,[1] there is reliable evidence that ORDEN was set up with the assistance of the United States.

Faced with the impossibility of bringing about social change through the electoral process, radical movements began to grow, bypassing the process altogether. In the early 1970s, a number of guerrilla movements emerged. These were followed by the formation of mass political movements. Links were later established with the guerrilla groups; both attracted widespread support. The response of the elite and the military was to escalate repression. Death squads appeared in the mid-1970s and suspected members of popular organisations were kidnapped, tortured and killed.

Role of the United States

The US has traditionally played a central role in the political and economic development of El Salvador. Its policy has always been aimed at preserving its own economic and security interests. With the increasing growth and strength of popular organisations and guerilla groups, the US began to fear that unless certain reforms were introduced, the country would succumb to the revolutionary forces as happened in Nicaragua in 1979.

In October 1979, the US backed a military coup which purported to stand for agrarian reform and other progressive measures. The new civilian-military Junta included members of the traditional opposition parties. But it became clear that the Junta's commitment to reform was very slight indeed, and that the army was more intent on repressing the popular movement. The progressive parties resigned. Only the most conservative

––––––

1.   Jenny Pearce, *Under the Eagle*, Latin American Bureau, London, 1981.

sector of the Christian Democrat party, led by Jose Napoleon Duarte could be persuaded to join the replacement Junta. There is no doubt, however, that power has remained with the army.

The bloodshed which has been unleashed since the 1979 coup is staggering. An estimated 13,000 people were killed in 1980 and another 10,000 in the first six months of 1981. The Salvadorean army has continued to receive US arms and training. In addition the United States has sent a team of military advisors into the country.

A land reform was announced in March 1980, and some of the largest estates were taken over. But the main beneficiaries were the "loyal" peasants such as the members of ORDEN. More important is the fact that the reform has been used to allow the army to go into the villages, under the guise of carrying out the reform only to shoot those peasants suspected of involvement in the guerrilla movement.

A NACLA report on El Salvador illustrates this point:[2]

> *"The troops came and told the workers the land was theirs now. They could elect their own leaders and run it themselves. The peasants couldn't believe their ears, but they held elections that very night. The next morning the troops came back, and they shot every one of the elected leaders."*

The Catholic Church has been a major force in supporting the people's struggle for liberation. In March 1980, Archibishop Romero was assassinated. He had been the Church's strongest and most vocal critic of the government, and of the support, both overt and covert, that it received from the US.

In October 1980, the Farabundo Marti Liberation Front (FMLN) was formed to provide a unified command of all the guerrilla organisations. In spite of government repression, torture and mass murder, the guerrilla movement has grown in strength. Unlike the army, it has support from the peasants which gives it more mobility. Although it has not been able to take the major cities it controls considerable parts of the countryside and will not be easily defeated. Many people fear that the US will be tempted to intervene directly in order to rescue its allies, and analogies are being drawn by many US citizens to the role the US government played in Vietnam.

Peasant women

In this polarised situation, the particular problem of peasant women remains

---

2.   North American Congress on Latin America, *Women in Latin America*, Vol. CIV, No.4, p 17

hidden, but no less real. Salvadorean peasant women suffer in their attempts to support large families on their *minifundios* or through seasonal migration from one plantation to another. Miriam Galdemez, a member of the Revolutionary Democratic Front in a recent interview described the life of peasant women:[3]

> *"The day starts very early . . . even before the sun has risen. (The woman has to) start grinding up maize into flour for tortillas. Those are the little pancakes that everybody eats for breakfast, lunch and dinner. (It) is hard work because it is still done by hand . . . If the children are old enough she'll send them off to get some water, but if not, she has to go herself. Water is one of our biggest problems . . . diseases from bad drinking water are one of the biggest killers in El Salvador . . . If it's harvest time, everybody goes off to work on the big plantations . . . (but) if there's no work on the plantations, and often there isn't, there's still plenty of work to do. She looks after the animals; goes down to the river to wash the clothes; collects firewood for cooking; looks after the family's few crops; cooks the dinner; sews clothes . . . "*

Salvadorean women suffer in the knowledge that half of their children may die as infants. The infant mortality rate is 63 deaths per 1,000 births (compared with 18 deaths per 1,000 in England). There are fewer than three doctors and 17 hospital beds per 10,000 people, and two-thirds of the country's doctors are centred round the capital, not the rural areas.

There is massive migration to the cities because of poverty and repression in the countryside. But most peasant women are unskilled and illiterate, and are forced to work as servants, street vendors, or prostitutes.

Miriam also said:

> *"The social structure is inhuman. It is important to say this, because, yes, machismo is a real problem, but nothing is ever going to change until we have the basic necessities of life: economic security, housing, health and education. We must join with our men who suffer too, as well as fight for our specific rights."*

The Association of El Salvadorean Women (AMES) was set up to support women in the struggle for liberation as well as continue the fight for the specific rights of women. Although women have joined the guerrilla armies, many women and men still believe that armed struggle is the man's arena. Women's efforts have tended to emphasise people's daily needs: housing, water, food, health.

----

3.   *Spare Rib*, "Women's Lives in El Salvador", No. 106, May 1981

EL SALVADOR

The country:
Area: 20,700 sq. km.
Main cities:
    Capital: San Salvador (pop. 50,000)
    Santa Ana (pop. 170,300)
    San Miguel (pop. 112,600)

The people:
Population: 4,436,000 (1979)
    Women: 2,400,000 (1980)
Rural: 59.8%
Annual rate of population growth:
    2.9% (1979)
Race: Predominantly mestizo
Language: Spanish

Guatemala

El Salvador
● San Salvador

Social indicators:
Life expectancy at birth: women, 64
    years; men, 60 years
Infant mortality rate: 60/1000 live
    births, 0-1 year
**Population without access to clean
    water:** rural, 66%; urban, 34%
Population without sanitation: rural,
    74%; urban, 21%
Adult illiteracy: 38%

The economy:
Gross National Product: US $1,820 million (1975)
    GNP per capita: US $750 (1981)
Distribution of Gross Domestic Production:
    (1978)
    Services: 50%
    Industry: 21%
    Agriculture: 29%
    Manufacturing: 15%
Economically active population (aged 15+):
    56.6% (1970)
    Women as % of total labour force: 20% (1980)
    Women employed in agriculture: 8% (1975)

The government:
Civilian Military Junta
Central government expenditure:
    (1979)
    Education: 23.3% of total budget
    Public health: 10.1%

BIRTH CONTROL:
LIBERATION OR REPRESSION?

My conversations with the women in El Salvador were coloured by the political situation. We rarely discussed politics, or if we did, the women were understandably concerned about who might hear what they had to say. One woman I spoke to in the health centre I was visiting asked me to erase the tape of our conversation before I left the building, for fear that it might fall into the hands of the police.

Most of our discussions about oppression therefore concerned their suffering as women in a culture where the philosophy of *machismo* is strong. The issue of birth control, and the negative attitudes held by many Salvadorean men to limiting their wives' fertility, is central to the lives of all Salvadorean women.

The health centre was in a small town in the eastern regions of El Salvador, and a week long course was being run by the church on the ovulation method of birth control.

Conditions in the health centre were difficult. With 20 participants, an equal mix of women and men, and 15 children under the age of six, learning was difficult, especially for the women. They were often absent during classes to look after their children. Water was always in short supply; the toilets usually stopped functioning in mid-afternoon; there was often not enough food; and the heat was stifling.

The week was designed as further information and training for people who had been using the ovulation method within their own families during the previous year. Some had been teaching in their villages. They were all, now, being encouraged to work as "promoters" in their own rural communities.

The use of this method depends on the woman's understanding and monitoring of the nature of the changes in the mucus secreted from her vagina. Then, according to a chart on which she records the changes, using a series of horizontal and vertical lines, and filling in spaces, she is able to tell on which days she is fertile.

At the beginning one man explained that he'd come to the course, because although he'd learned before and was working as a promoter in his village, a few of the women had become pregnant. "I need to know the method better", he said.

Another man said that his sister had wanted to come, but that her husband had refused to allow her to leave. The men said that the husbands had to be convinced that family planning was a necessary thing. The women said very little in the group discussions.

Success of the ovulation method depends on abstinence from sexual intercourse during the fertile periods. During a discussion on the advantages and disadvantages of abstinence, it became clear that as far as the group was concerned, enforcement of abstinence was essentially the woman's problem. Some of the men did agree that they should have no sexual access to their wives, but only during the unsafe days. The rest of the time, it was their "right" to have sexual relations whenever they desired.

A number of women said abstinence was impossible, because their husbands often came home drunk, and would beat them if they didn't agree to have sex. They also said that if the woman tried to refuse too many times, the man would go off, and find another woman..

The women on the course had many stories to tell about their experiences with the government's highly abusive programme of family planning. Many of the women had been refused all treatment in the government health clinics unless they agreed to use contraceptives. Women with IUDs who had gone to the health centres because they were having problems with the device, were told to go away until their specified time for a checkup, often not for several months.

One of the nuns said that most of the clinics in the country have minimum quotas of sterilisations to be performed, and packages of pills to be distributed each month. She quoted a doctor as saying that he would lose his job if he didn't meet the quota.

In rural nutrition classes women had been recruited as volunteers for sterilisation. Packages of birth control pills had also been distributed free to women who couldn't read or write, with no medical consultation whatsoever.

One woman told the story of giving birth in the public hospital in town:

"They told me that if I wanted to be sterilised after having my baby, I could stay in the hospital for five days to rest. If I said no, they told me that I had to leave right away.

"I didn't want to be sterilised, so I had to leave within 24 hours, ride a bus for two hours and then walk for five kilometres to my house, with my new baby."

Isabel, 43, was one of the women attending the course. Between the classes, we had a chance to talk about her activities in her village and her own particular struggles as a woman.

I had 17 children, but only 10 are living. The first one had something wrong with his stomach, and another died of dysentry. Two died before they were born. Another had a problem in his head. One died when he was just seven days old, and another at five months. They both had fevers.

I got married when it was very deprived here. It wasn't the way it is now. Now there is education for young couples who get married. The priest who married us said that we should be ready to receive all the children that God wanted to send us. We didn't know anything else, and so we didn't look for ways to have less children. Year after year, I had children. It was just endless.

My husband said to me that if I didn't want a big family, he would go and find another woman. He didn't have any education or training in anything. I had to agree since I thought it was my duty. We had agreed to be married for the rest of our lives, and so . . . .

I didn't really want to have so many children. As soon as you had one child, you sat down to rest, and you became pregnant again. I had a very bad time with the pregnancies, and I had to look after the other children as well. They just kept coming, one after another. There was nothing I could do.

When I had the children, I had them on my own. No one helped me since there was no nurse or doctor. I was afraid of the hospital and doctors. You are — as a *campesino* — it is because of shame and embarrassment. With the last child, it was very difficult, and I got sick. After a while, they had to take me to the hospital. They said they would have to operate.

I don't know if they sterilised me or not. The operation was around here (the vaginal area), and even though I said I didn't want to be sterilised, I don't know what they did. They said, "No, we are just going to operate for the problem you have." But since then, I haven't had any children, and they didn't really explain what they did.

That is why I am involved now, helping the community. Because if they did

sterilise me, I don't want them doing it to my neighbours and other women I
know. I think it is important for the women here to learn about the methods
of family planning through the church. So I decided to come on this course,
so I could understand everything, and go back and teach it. I can advise
others that this is better than getting sterilised.

Here women serve as both men and women. In the house, we do everything
— cook, clean, wash, iron, grind corn, look after the children. But when we
have to work in the fields, we do that too. If we have to plant, or plough —
whatever it is — we do it. The life of the women in El Salvador is hard. You
give birth to the children. You look after them and your husband. You go to
the fields to work. You come back. You prepare the food for the family.

Having children isn't bad . . . it is good, because children are useful. They
help you in work. I have six girls, for example. My husband comes home and
wants to eat, and they serve him.

But I am lucky, because my husband is a good man. There has always been
an understanding between us. If I have to go out, he doesn't say, "Don't go".
He lets me go. He doesn't mind that I am here, for example. He understands
that women are human beings and that we have rights too. When I go out, he
stays at home, and I'll be at home, if he wants to go out. When he comes
back, I am pleased to see him. But everyone isn't like that. If more families
were like that, it would be fine, but they aren't.

I think I have a better life than other women. My husband is a man who
understands things. He feels the same as I do, and the rest don't. They feel
. . . of course they have feelings, but not the same as a woman. If my
neighbours' husbands were like mine, life would be much better.

There are some women who I am trying to help as a friend. We talk about
life, and how men and women should live together. A father shouldn't ignore
his children. He should care for them and look after them. He shouldn't
drink through the week. The men only earn 20 colons (80p) a day, because
work here isn't worth much. The family waits for this money, because they
don't have anything else. If the men drink, there is no food.

That is what I tell the women. They don't want their husbands coming home
drunk and beating them. The man gets home, and says, "Where is the
food?" She says, "I haven't cooked anything". "What have you been doing,"
he shouts. And she says, "You didn't give me money, so I couldn't buy anything".

"So what am I going to eat?" "But if I don't have anything what can I do?",
she says. So he hits her. It is terrible. But I am lucky. We have been married
for 23 years, and . . . we are poor . . . but we don't fight.

I think that women here need some help so they can live with more respect
and think they are worth something. You have to talk to them and explain
things. What we need most is some kind of work, so we can help our
husbands. There is nothing here — no way of earning a better life. All of the
campesinos should have land to grow things on and fertiliser to make the
land richer. But we don't have these things. We have no land, and no work.

I don't want my daughters to live the way I have lived . . . having so many
children . . . with no work and no money . . . spending their whole lives being
poor. With the little they have learned so far, I want them to learn more —so
they know how to find work . . . so they will be able to give their children a
better life. They are studying now, even though we can't do much for them.
We are very poor, and I can't really teach them. I would like them to have a
skill or something so they can work.

I was in school for three months — nothing more. In three months, I only
learned a little bit, but I understood a lot more. My parents were very poor.
My brothers and sisters only went for three months too — we had to work on
the land. We couldn't go to school.

All of my children are in school. I have four boys and six girls. Three of the
girls are already *señoritas*, and the other three are still very young. They are
learning to run a house, and make tortillas, cook, clean, mend clothes. They
have to learn all that. In school they are learning to read and write. I am
teaching my sons to respect women — not to be like the rest of the men here.

My mother's life was very different. It was much harder for her. After all the
work in the house, she would have to go up to the mountain with an axe to
chop trees, to make railroad ties. It was very hard work. And she used to do
all sorts of other things — making rum, baking bread. She did whatever she
could so we would have enough food. She had 20 children, but only 11 of us
are still living. Even though our lives are hard now, hers was harder.

Our lives here today are much more difficult than in other countries. I think
they have laws so young children don't have to work. But not here — they all
have to work. From the time they are young, they grow up knowing they have
to work hard just to live.

I have tried to teach myself lots of things, but I haven't got a paper saying I can do them. I can sew, and bake bread, and I help women to give birth. You have to fight to better your own life. No one else is going to do it for you. We are going to try and form a group of women to work together in our village, like the women in the bakery cooperative. They have a good group; they are all very enthusiastic — the way they work together. They are earning money to help their families.

If you are earning money, your family eats better. Instead of just eating rice and beans, they have eggs and milk. You and your children dress better too.

But for real change, you have to work with the women and the men. I think you should form groups of women and men — to let them talk and think together. To change, we have to get to know other people who have studied and know more than us, so they can teach us, instead of deceiving or cheating us. We had people here before, who promised all kinds of things, but in the end, they did nothing. So people here aren't interested anymore. But if there was someone they could respect, the men would work and change, and think about being better people for their families and the community.

I want to set up a group in the village like the cooperative bakery. I think we need to start with something like CARITAS (World Food Programme).[4] I have asked the priest to help us. Because the people will come for the food, and when they come for that, you can give them classes and talks.

I can't really do it on my own. I want to help the community. So many children don't have enough food. They wander around without clothes. Their fathers have nowhere to work.

Almost all the women here see the necessity of doing something about the children. They know that having more children will just make life so much more difficult.

The men don't like it though. They say, (lowering her voice), that people will talk if they don't have children. Even so, there are lots of women who are trying to make their husbands more aware. But the men say that they want to have relations with their wives, and that if their wives don't want that, then the men will have to go and look for someone else.

Many women say they would rather have all the children that come than be

----

4.   For more information about the World Food Programme see page 197

sterilised. The operation takes all your strength away. You are all still in one piece, but your body and mind aren't as strong as before.

I am trying to work against what the doctors are saying. They say it is much better to have the operation — that you will live better. And I say that that is wrong. You don't live better. You suffer, and it changes you.

In our village, they are building a health centre — but I think that they want to sterilise all the women. Someone from the health department came to see me. They came twice. They asked me what I was learning on this course, and whether I understood it all. "Yes," I said. "You are very intelligent," they said, "and it would be good if you could work with us and help us so there wouldn't be so many children in the village."

"Of course," I said. They asked me about the method, my children, was I going to work with the nun, and would I work with them too? "We could put a small health post right here in your house, and we could bring contraceptives and you could teach the women and help them."

So even though I agreed, I won't do it, unless the community agrees. I think contraceptives are bad for women. They give you cancer and all kinds of illnesses. So I will tell the women they mustn't accept these things.

I help where I can. The women seem to listen to me, although some say bad things about me. There is a saying here, "No one is a prophet in their own land".

Several women gave me some money so I could come here to the course. They know that I will be able to help them, and I won't deceive them.

It is all slow work. I hope that if the women can set up a cooperative, it will show the men a good example, and they will follow. But the women have to begin. Maybe we could set up other industries — if we work together, I think we would succeed. But we have to find some capital from somewhere.

It makes the women stronger when they are working together. They know that instead of being prisoners in the house, they can go out to work. That is a change for them. It won't make them stronger than their husbands. They won't ever tell their husbands what to do.

In the USA, I know it is different. No one is any bigger or smaller than anyone else. Everything and everyone is equal. But here we all have to fight for things because there isn't enough for everyone — well, not enough for the poor people.

THE BAKERY COOPERATIVE

The next group of women I met were involved in the bakery cooperative that Isabel talked about. Their village had no market, and no water system. Water for drinking, cooking and washing had to be fetched by the women at least once a day, and sometimes twice, from a source an hour's walk away, at the bottom of a steep hill.

For the past several years, a team from a Catholic diocese in the United States had been working in the community. They had been very active in promoting a leadership development programme amongst the men in the village. Recently, however, they had started a new programme with the women. One of the priests told me that politically it was safer to work with the women.

Using the CARITAS, or World Food Programme as a base, they established a series of classes for women in health, nutrition, childcare, and leadership development. By coming to the classes, the women were entitled to receive free food — oil, rice, milk powder, flour and other grains — surplus donated by the United States government.

CARITAS has always come under a lot of criticism from the politically active clergy and development workers throughout El Salvador. The clergy say that this kind of programme promotes "rice Catholics", worshippers who come to Church just to get the food.

"Soup-kitchen" dependency is the other by-product. It works against any efforts of the people or the nation to become self-sufficient at meeting their own dietary needs. The women in the CARITAS class said that without the free food, many of their children would go hungry. With the high malnutrition rate among children under five in El Salvador, their eagerness to receive the food from whatever source is understandable. And so the vicious cycle of dependency and exploitation continues.

The bakery had been going for about six months and had 12 members.

The community worker assisting the women spoke to me about how important the bakery was for them:

> *"Most of the women have to spend all their energy on just getting enough food to eat for that day. And for women who are raising families alone, the cooperative is their only source of income. Many women are abandoned by their husbands, or their husbands have more than one family, and there is never enough money for both.*

"We have tried to concentrate on the dignity of the women, and their importance as full members of the community. Many of the women we work with now actually leave the village to go to other areas for a day. Some women had never left the village before. Now they have learned to speak and express themselves. When we first came, the men would answer for everything. It was a real battle to get the women to talk. Now the women speak up, and often disagree with the men.

"And it is all a learning process for them. For example, when we first started the cooperative, they were so anxious to start, that they didn't really consider the cost of things, or different recipes. And after a while, they realised that they weren't making as much as they thought, and they were losing money. Their first reaction was to cut their own salaries. But that is just what any wealthy land owner would do when income drops. So they looked at the situation, chose better recipes, and didn't cut salaries."

I met with five women from the cooperative and the CARITAS classes. They ranged in age from 20 to the early 40s. All were married and had several children each. They told me how the classes and the cooperative had started.

MURA: It all started with the classes run by the priests — the "Family of God" classes, where we learned that it would be better to live in a more united way — women and men working hand in hand together.

When I started to work in CARITAS, it was originally just to get the food; that is why we all got involved. But after a while we all wanted to work for change — how to educate our children and how to teach the mothers to keep house better. We had talks about hygiene and health. At the end we were all working as teachers in the programme, but there were problems. The people running CARITAS didn't want to pay us for all the work we were doing.

So we started to think about what else we could do, and we decided that we needed a bakery here. There wasn't one product that was produced and consumed here in the village. We saw that the bread that we ate daily was brought in from somewhere else, and we had to buy it. And the money that we spent on the bread left the village.

So we thought that it would be much better if the money stayed here, and it would help us in the bakery, as well as the whole village. That was our idea. And we wanted to set up a cooperative so we could work together. That was important for us, too. There isn't much work here for our husbands, and they need our help with money for the household. This is a poor country, and we have to develop ourselves. So with both the wife and husband working, things would be much easier economically.

FRANCISCA: Every Sunday, we have a meeting together to plan for the week ahead. We decide who needs to work, whether we need flour or sugar, and whatever else has to be done. We plan everything for Monday. Everyone is supposed to come to the meeting — there are about 12 of us. If you can't come, you have to send a little note saying why you can't come, and saying which days you want to work in the week.

I'm the coordinator. I was elected because I was the only one who knew how to bake bread. I used to go around to all the shops to get the orders for the day, but now that we make French bread, too, I don't have time to go. One of the young girls does that.

The accounts are done by the man who is the coordinator of the school for boys. I do the receipts of what we pay and receive each day, and I give him the receipts. He is trying to teach us to do all the book keeping.

MARIA: I think the cooperative is a good thing, because now when the women want work, there is work to do. If they don't know how to make bread, we can teach them. So we are all learning things, and helping the community. Now there is fresh bread every day, and people don't have to buy it from outside the village.

MURA: The cooperative was formed from women who had already learned how to work together. If a group like this was formed from people who weren't well prepared, it would soon fall apart, because they wouldn't have the force or the understanding of how to work together and solve their problems together. In the classes, we got to know each other. You must always have some kind of classes to prepare people.

When you learn something new, you are able to work, and you are much stronger. But we do still have problems, because there are some who say that those of us working in the cooperative don't have anything to do in the house. But they don't understand that we are trying to help ourselves and the village, too. We have all learned a lot, and we just have to learn to be stronger to withstand the criticism.

Still there are so many women who think that they are only objects to serve their husbands, have children, look after the house, and nothing more. And this is the majority of women. I don't think we are going to win that battle quickly, or even in two or three years. It will only be little by little . . . by talking about the dignity of women. We have to start with the very young women and teach them that they aren't here just to serve men. They must realise that they are people with equal dignity and value.

Before in El Salvador, most of us weren't married by the Church. We lived together without getting married. There were lots of children that were abandoned. The men usually had more than one woman, because they were men and could do what they wanted. They were free in that sense, and the women were not. There are lots of men who still think that way. So we are trying to teach the young people, both girls and boys that each person must know her or his own dignity and worth.

There are some men who won't even let their wives leave the house, because they say they don't know where they are going, and they are suspicious. The majority of men are very jealous.

BERTA: Some husbands say they don't want their wives wasting time in the meetings. And some of the women say they have no time . . . that they are working hard in their houses, and can't join. But I live quite far away, and I can manage it. I make the effort because I want to work here.

There is no other work for women — only washing and ironing clothes for other people. I think that we in the cooperative are better off because we have our own money, and we have the chance to talk and work together. Both of these things are important to us. A woman without money doesn't have the chance to do anything. And if she can't think for herself, she is worse off still.

Before the cooperative, we didn't earn anything. We stayed here, and we didn't learn anything either. Every now and then, there would be work picking cotton in the fields. We would earn three colons (60p) a day, but the work was very hard.

JUANA: Now we work from 7 a.m. until about 5 or 6 p.m., and we earn four colons (80p) a day in the bakery. The coordinator earns two colons more per day than the other members. While we are here . . . those of us who have older children . . . they help us. I have a daughter of 16. She looks after her younger brothers and sisters in the morning, and she goes to school in the afternoon, when the other children have returned from going to school in the morning.

I think there should be more work for women away from the house. When you are alone in the house, you wash, cook, go to the mill (to grind corn for tortillas). You don't earn anything or learn anything. None of us can read and write, so the cooperative was good for us. All we had to do was learn how to bake bread.

One problem here, at least for poor people, is that to find work you need a mountain of paper. You need blood tests, lung tests, birth certificate, police recommendations — and if you don't have everything, you can't find work. But even if you have all that, you still can't find work.

And when the children finish school, and look for work, they are told that they need three years of experience. How can they get experience if they can never get a job to start working? They need to get a good recommendation, too. Because we are poor, our children don't have good clothes or good shoes.

They don't look very good, and they can't present themselves well. People don't want to give them jobs.

I want my children to be able to study, to find steady work, to find a husband who won't leave them, who will maintain them, and who will treat them well . . . so they can work together. The classes have helped us a lot. They have taught us how to change. For example, if we hadn't gone to the classes we would never have been able to come and talk to you.

BERTA: Some men, I think, are afraid that their wives will become stronger than them as they learn more. But if the men go to courses, too, then they understand what is going on — that they can learn, and that it is important. If they don't go to the classes, they don't learn anything, and they are afraid, and won't let their wives leave the house.

That is true for the family planning classes too. If the men don't come to the meetings to learn, they won't let their wives learn anything either. Both the woman and the man must be involved. Here we are learning the natural method — when the woman is damp or humid, then the seed could grow, and that is the dangerous time. If the wife and husband don't come together to the classes, they won't understand how to use the method.

Before the classes, we didn't use any family planning, because we didn't know anything about it. We wanted to use something, because we didn't want to carry on having so many children, but we didn't know what to do. In the clinics, they had pills, or you could have an operation, or have something put inside of you. But our husbands didn't want us to do any of that. You see, men here think that if women have operations, or use the pills, then they will go and live with other men. So they wouldn't give us permission to use anything. But now, it is different, because with the natural method, they understand what it is all about, and they aren't so jealous.

MURA: We were the first ones to learn about family planning. But we learned that we mustn't fight with our husbands about it. What I tried to do was to change a little bit — to be a little nicer, more attentive, so as to give him the confidence in the idea of family planning. Before we knew nothing about it — we didn't know how our bodies worked, or anything. And so I tried to teach my husband a little bit about it. He went to courses too, and started to realise that it was necessary.

Not everyone is agreed about using it. You know that using the natural method is very difficult, and takes a lot of effort. If the husband is a little drunk

... the men here ... they think that because they are men, they must rule and dominate the women. So even if a woman wants to use some control, she can't if her husband decides otherwise.

I have eight children, but two are married already. I had 10 altogether, but two died. The first had an infection, and died, and the other died when I was six months pregnant.

My youngest child is eight and we didn't want to have any more. We didn't know what to do, because no one had taught us anything. If there had been someone to tell us about the contraceptives, we would have used them. Now I use this method because it is so much better than pills. With this method, young couples can have children when they want to, and with the pills — they make you weak and hurt your body. The method we use is more difficult, but it doesn't harm your health. For a couple like us, it is better not to have any more, because we couldn't educate them, or give them a good life.

I have two girls, and the rest are boys. I want to teach the boys that girls are worth the same as the men. I want my sons to learn to treat their wives like people, and not like slaves. And I want to teach my girls that they must be strong people, and good mothers and teach their children properly. Some women don't realise that they have the right to be treated with respect and dignity. They say that they will suffer through with their husbands until the end, because they are afraid they won't find another one. They are afraid to be alone.

"Yes, my country is very beautiful, but the truth of the way people live here is very ugly."
—Cecilia, 21, a teacher

GUATEMALA

Guatemala is the third largest Central American country and is nearly the size of England. Over two-thirds of the country is mountainous and 62% is covered in forest and tropical jungle. There are two coastlines, one on the Pacific and the other on the Caribbean.

Over three-quarters of Guatemala's seven million people live in the rural areas. Fifty-five percent of the population are Indian, and live mainly in the West-Central highlands. The rest are *ladinos*. This term is used to describe Guatemalans who have a mixture of Spanish and Indian blood, as well as culturally assimilated Guatemalan Indians. There are few Guatemalans of pure Spanish descent.

Before the Spanish conquest, Guatemala was populated by several Indian cultures and groups, of which the most outstanding were the Mayas; "the most brilliant aboriginal people on the planet" according to one anthropologist.[1] The Mayan system of social and economic organisation was very sophisticated, and its scientific and cultural achievements very advanced. But the Mayan civilisation, originating in 100 AD, was already in decline by the time the Spaniards arrived.

The fate of Guatemala's Indians at the time of the conquest was similar to that experienced by Indians in the Andean countries. Their lands were seized and they were forced to give labour and service to their new rulers. Thousands died from overwork, ill treatment and disease. From the conquest

---

1. Dr Sylvanus Morly in *Four Keys to Guatemala*, by Vera Kelsey, *et al*; Funk & Wagnalls, New York 1961, p.1.

to the present day, Guatemala's Indian population have experienced only subjugation, exploitation and repression. Although there are many poor *ladinos*, the Indian population represents the poorest strata of society.

Land distribution

The Guatemalan economy is based on the export of cash crops. Since the 19th century the main export has been coffee and bananas, supplemented more recently by cotton, fresh meat, sugar, vegetables and citrus fruit. Seventy-two percent of the land, owned by a tiny 2.1% of the country's land owners, is given over to cash crop cultivation, while 91.4% of the land owners, mostly Indian, own a mere 21.9% of the land.

The Indian's land is usually poor and infertile, and rarely provides sufficient food or purchasing power for survival. It is estimated that at best, the small holdings produce only enough corn and beans, the staple diet, to last for six months of the year. So, the peasants are forced to seek seasonal work on the plantations. Thus, the nature and system of land tenure ensures that the big land owners have a cheap supply of labour at harvest time.

The economic and political power of the land owning elite is immense and jealously guarded. As in most other Latin American countries where land has been the basis of wealth, the land owners have relentlessly opposed any agrarian reform.

In 1952, a moderate agrarian reform was introduced by a liberal reformist President, Jacobo Arbenz. It affected only 16% of the country's idle, cultivatable land which had been in private hands. The land owners' fear of the agrarian reform was reinforced by the fact that it was accompanied by an unprecedented mobilisation of the peasantry.

The United States was equally distressed. The agrarian reform had also included 380,000 acres of land owned by the American company, United Fruit. Since the beginning of the century, this corporation had come to own some of the country's prime agricultural land, with almost complete control over the production and export of bananas. Because of the expropriation of United Fruit land, and the encouragement of peasant and worker unions, Arbenz was accused of being a communist. In 1954, he was overthrown in a CIA-backed coup. The new government of Castillo Armas reversed all his predecessor's progressive measures and, with a vast influx of American aid, and the support of the Guatemalan army, the small ruling class re-established its control.

This relatively mild challenge to their domination has never been forgotten. Ever since, the resulting fierce anti-communist force has ensured the suppression of any signs of peasant organisation and resistance as soon as they appear. In the 1960s, however, a guerrilla movement did emerge in Guatemala. It was quite small and never succeeded in mobilising the Indians into a revolutionary movement.

In suppressing the guerrillas, the Guatemalan army was backed by large amounts of US military aid. Training was available for the Guatemalan army to develop techniques aimed at eliminating all those suspected of opposition to the government. The campaign of terror launched by Colonel Arana Osorio in the late 1960s is estimated to have cost the lives of up to 8,000 people, many of them ordinary peasants with no links to any opposition movement.

At the same time as the regular army launched this campaign, a number of death squads appeared, with names like the White Hand, and an Eye for Eye, dedicated to wiping out "communism". These death squads, still active today, are made up of members of the army and security forces as well as memeber of ultra right wing parties such as the Movement of National Liberation (MLN). The death squads kidnap, torture and murder anyone suspected of supporting social change. In the late 1960s and early 1970s, an estimated 25,000 people died at their hands. In 1981, Amnesty International published a report showing that the death squads had direct links to the Presidential palace.[2]

Industrialisation and tourism

While official violence was being organised against the Guatemalan people, the country's economy was undergoing changes. Industrialisation began to take place, stimulated by the formation of the Central American Common Market (CACM) in 1961. American companies soon penetrated the most dynamic sectors of the country's industries. But this growth of industrialisation failed to keep pace with the ever growing number of unemployed.

Another change in the economy was the increasing emphasis in the rural areas on export crops. Under the influence of US-inspired development plans for modernising and diversifying agriculture, more and more land owners turned away from growing food for local consumption to growing cash crops for export. Thus, in a country where 80% of the children under five suffer from malnutrition, food is actually exported.

According to the National Bank for Agricultural development, most of the

2.   *Guatemala: A Government Programme of Political Murder*, Amnesty International Report, 1981.

credit available for agricultural projects went to the large land owners, exporting cash crops, rather than to the small farmer growing for domestic consumption. Between 1964-73, 41.4% of available credit went to cotton farmers, 36.3% to coffee farmers, 8.8% to sugar farmers, and only 2.9% to the producers of corn, beans and rice — usually the *minifundistas*.

In the 1960s, tourism also became a growth industry. Guatemala is a beautiful country, and its Indian culture and Mayan ruins attract thousands of European and North American visitors. In 1979, it was estimated that half a million foreign tourists visited Guatemala.

But the tourists tend only to see the beauty, and not the ugliness. Guided tour packages frequent the developed "tourist spots" rather than those areas where the majority of the population live in poverty and squalor. Army raids are timed to avoid the visits of tour buses. Recently, Alvaro Arzu, the national tourism director said, "Violence is no obstacle for the growth of tourism in Guatemala".[3]

Heading for civil war

While economic changes took place in the 1960s and 1970s, the structure of exploitation remained the same, and the fanaticism and ruthlessness of the small ruling class increased. Since General Lucas Garcia became President in 1978, an estimated 5,000 people have been seized without warrant and killed. An article in the *New York Times*, in August of last year, pointed out that:[4]

> "since January, 63 student leaders, 41 university professors, four priests, 13 journalists, 38 opposition party officials, dozens of labour leaders, and hundreds of peasants have been killed. In all, right wing terrorists have assassinated some 2,000 people in the last year."

There have also been a series of massacres such as the one that occurred in May 1978 in the eastern town of Panzos. The Indians had come to the town to discuss with a government official the settlement of a land dispute. Instead of the meeting, the army opened fire on the crowd. Over 100 Indian women, men and children were killed. It is said that there are no political prisoners in Guatemala because they are all dead.

———————

3.   *New York Times Magazine*, "Guatemala: State of Siege", August 24, 1980, p.20
4.   *New York Times Magazine, op cit,* p.19

This kind of repression, together with increasing poverty, has mobilised the Indian population to fight for its survival for the first time in Guatemala's history. Although peasant organisations and other opposition movements grew considerably in the 1970s, the most recent significant development has been the expansion of the guerrilla movement, due mainly to large-scale recruitment amongst the Indian population.

Guatemala is heading rapidly towards civil war. The military has long been in partnership with the ruling elite in suppressing opposition. But now, in spite of being well-equipped by Central American standards, the army is weak and demoralised. Corruption in the higher ranks and increasing losses at the hands of the guerrillas are responsible. In addition, the army is finding it difficult to recruit soldiers amongst the Indian population which, up to now, has made up over 90% of the army.

The *New York Times* last year described this "recruitment" process:[5]

> *"Inducted from their villages, Indian draftees are tied up for days, then given a humiliating form of training that includes being forced to insult their parents and their Indian heritage and to pledge blind loyalty to the army. They are instructed repeatedly that the Communists are the enemy."*

But now, for the first time, the army is having to look to the *ladinos* for recruits, relying on their racial prejudice to maintain the war against the Indians.

The role of the United States is another major factor in the escalating confrontation. Guatemala is the most important country in Central America for American investment. The recent discovery of substantial deposits of oil has increased Guatemala's economic importance to the United States. For these reasons alone the United States would be reluctant to lose the country to the opposition movement.

But equally important is the refusal of the Reagan administration to view the conflict in Guatemala as anything more than "Soviet expansionism" in its "backyard". Rather than support the attempts of the Guatemalan people to achieve social justice by challenging the vastly unequal distribution of wealth and power, it has maintained its external intervention to support the repressive activities of the current government, in much the same way as the CIA assisted the coup in 1954.

---

5.   *New York Times Magazine, op cit,* p.13

Third class citizens

The Indians of Guatemala are deeply traditional, maintaining their own languages, culture, dress and tightly knit family and social structures. Religion plays a major role in their lives, and they have adapted orthodox Catholicism to include their own gods and traditional beliefs. The Indians speak 23 different languages, and 100 different dialects. Many of them cannot communicate with each other unless they speak Spanish, Guatemala's official language.

Over half of Guatemala's people are illiterate, with a higher percentage of illiteracy amongst the Indians, and higher still amongst Indian women. Most women do not even speak Spanish, let alone read or write it.

Although there are many poor *ladinos*, they have adopted the Spanish language and culture and are therefore socially acceptable, save for their poverty. The Indians, however, are the second-class citizens, subject to racial prejudice by the *ladino* population, wealthy and poor alike.

The Indian women are the third-class citizens. Isolated by their inability to read, write or speak Spanish, and taught from childhood that they are inferior to men in every respect, the women are completely trapped by their lack of education and their own belief that they know nothing, and can do nothing.

The role of the rural, poor *ladina* (female) and the rural Indian woman is severely restricted. They rarely leave their villages, indeed rarely leave the their houses, and never without their husband's permission. Most of their time is spent cooking, washing, looking after their children and weaving the traditional clothes for their family or for sale.

Living conditions are not good. They live in huts with mud floors, and no water or electricity. Infant mortality exceeds 100 per 1,000 live births. Four out of five children are malnourished, and adults are constantly afflicted with stomach parasites.

Children have a very short "childhood". From birth, they are dressed identically to their parents, and once they reach the age of six or seven, they work as adult members of the family — the boys in the fields and the girls at home. Schooling for the girls is non-existent or very limited — one or two years — while the boys are often sent until they are at least literate. Wife-beating is common, and seen as a husband's right.

The main source of cash work available to the Indian women is weaving. Tourism has increased the women's opportunities to bring money into the home through the sale of their weaving. But in many cases, the result has been that the women can no longer afford to weave for themselves and their families. They revert to wearing factory-produced clothes, or wear their traditional costume until it is threadbare.

The cost of the yarn, and the time taken to weave the garments means that this aspect of the women's work is now devoted primarily to generating income rather than replenishing the family's clothing supply. Even though the money they earn is not very substantial, they need the cash obtained through tourist sales. One *huipil* (traditonal woman's blouse), taking up to three months to weave, will be sold for £10 to an individual tourist or a shop. The shop will, of course, resell the garment at a mark up of 300-400%.

A more reliable market for the weaving, with higher prices being paid to the women for their work, has evolved through the establishment of cooperatives. A national federation of artesan cooperatives, Artexco, was set up by the government with the help of Peace Corps volunteers during the last 10 years. There are now about 17 legally affiliated cooperatives throughout the country. But while providing a better market, they have not changed the nature of decision making at village level. Over 90% of the cooperative members are women, but both the village cooperatives and the national federation are controlled by men. It is often said that if there are 20 women in a room, and one man, it will be the man who makes all the decisions.

Only a few women ever participate fully in the management and decision-making. In one or two villages visited, the cooperatives were providing a springboard for other activities for women, with an emphasis on literacy, consciousness raising and leadership training. This, however, was the exception rather than the rule, and has since been stopped by the present government's reign of terror.

Throughout the interviews with the women, any discussion of their participation in politics either at a local or national level was rare. This was due partly to my being a stranger, and therefore somewhat suspect given the political tensions. But the other predominant factor was that this was one of the aspects of community life closed to women. We did talk about their own powerlessness and oppression, but for so many, this was the norm, *la costumbre* (the custom). The man was the head of the family, and all rights accrued to him.

GUATEMALA

The country:
Area: 108,889 sq. km.
Main cities:
    Capital: Guatemala City (pop. 800,000)
    Quetzaltenango (pop. 268,000)
    Huehuetenango (pop. 14,000)

The people:
Population: 6.95 million (1981)
    Women: 3.5 million (1980)
Rural: 70.6% (1979)
Annual rate of population growth: 3.2%
Race: 55% Indian or Mayan extraction, remainder ladino and mestizo
Language: Officially Spanish, over 20 major Indian languages

Social indicators:
Life expectancy at birth: women, 59 years; men, 57 years
Infant mortality rate: 83/1000 live births, 0-1 year (1975-80)
Population without access to clean water: rural, 84%; urban, 11%
Population without sanitation: rural, 82%; urban, 66%
Adult illiteracy: women, 62%; men, 46%

The government:
"Elected" Military Government
Central government expenditure: (1979)
    Education: 12.4% of total budget
    Public health: 8.9%
    Housing: 2.6%

The economy:
Gross National Product: US $6.6 billion
    GNP per capita: US $900 (1981)
Economically active population (aged 15+): 50.8% (1970)
    Women as % of total labour force: 14% (1980)
    Women employed in agriculture: 7% (1975)

"I'D NEVER MET ANY INDIANS BEFORE . . ."

Racism is a major force at work in defining the nature of the relationship between Indians and *ladinos* in Guatemala. The two groups do not mix, except for one to serve the other. Most urban *ladino* families have Indian servants. Many *ladinos* believe that Indians are unintelligent, prone to alcoholism and not worthy of any respect as human beings. Jobs with any kind of power and influence within the country, in the private or public sector, are held by *ladinos*. Almost all the professional areas of work are open only to *ladinos*. Essentially, the country is run by *ladinos* for *ladinos*.

The Indians view the *ladinos*, and their world, with mistrust and suspicion. Historically, because of the conquest, and presently because of their racist attitudes and more privileged position in society, the *ladinos* are responsible for much of the suffering, deprivation and humiliation experienced by the Indians. The objects of scorn and ridicule, symbolically and literally, the Indians are pushed to the back of the bus or simply left standing by the side of the road.

The Indians are denied access to the education system too. Half of all children in Guatemala between the ages of six to 18 are not enrolled in school; the majority are Indian. Because of the way they are treated and because of their own wariness of the *ladino* culture, Indian children, especially the girls, spend more time working in the fields or at home than they do in school. Since most Indian children do not speak Spanish, the official teaching language until they arrive at school, they are at a learning disadvantage at the beginning.

What is taught in the schools usually has more relevance to the urban, *ladino* society than to the needs of the rural Indians. Parents cannot afford to clothe or equip their children to attend school. Many Indian villages are without schools, and the children have to travel to be educated. Parents are often loathe to let this happen, even if they could afford it. "The school" in the rural area is often no more than a mud hut, without electricity, without tables and chairs. Most of the teachers are *ladinos* from the town, and very few are happy about being assigned to a remote village. They rarely speak the local language of the Indians, and many carry with them the racial prejudice which they have been taught as children.

Cecilia was a 24 year old, unmarried ladina, *who grew up in a small town, but who chose to work as a teacher with the Indians in a remote highland village. She told me what it was like for her, as a young, relatively sheltered woman to face the problems of dealing with a level of poverty and a set of cultural traditions previously unknown to her.*

It was both a frightening and awakening experience that helped sensitise her to the needs and plight of the Indians, especially the women. At the same time, it shaped her perspective on the broader political issues that all Guatemalans face on a daily basis.

First, I'll tell you a short story. When I left secondary school, I was very happy. My life was composed of parties, movies, seeing friends and studying. But I guess I finished studying at 18 without really knowing anything.

When I left secondary school, one of my teachers asked me if I wanted to work in a very remote mountain village in the north as a teacher for two months. The regular teacher was sick, and they needed a substitute. I agreed because I thought two months wasn't a very long time.

So a week after I finished studying, I left town to go to this village. I didn't know it at all, and when I got near and asked where I was to go, someone said: "Well, you have to walk towards the north of the mountain, and you'd better take two people to help you find it."

Anyway, we had to walk for three hours and finally we arrived. What a surprise! They were all *Indigenas* (Indians), and all the children were waiting for me.

I didn't speak Mam (Indian language), and I didn't know anything about their lives. I'd never met *Indigenas*. I only knew the town where I had lived and gone to school. I had been well prepared to teach children in the cities, who could speak Spanish and who were all the same age, but these children didn't speak Spanish very well.

All the children were of different ages and grades — from the first up to the fourth, and children from six years up to 16. And I was only 18. It made a very strong impression on me.

It wasn't a school. It was only a room with a door, and no windows. It was awful. The only light for everyone came through the one door. I was used to a school with facilities.

When I arrived, the community didn't really accept me. They said: "This is the teacher? She's just a small girl." And when I said "Good morning", no one would even answer me.

But after a week, the fathers of some of my students came to my house with presents. They brought beans, potatoes and corn. I couldn't understand why, until they said that I was teaching the children things that were very interesting.

The regular teacher was 50 years old, and taught them all the correct things in primary school — geography, mathematics, science. But I prefer to teach what is more realistic and important to them, and what is within my reach. For example, if I'm teaching about rivers and plants, we'll go and study the things in our community. And I guess the parents came to thank me. I felt better because the separation between us wasn't so great.

The other thing I realised was that I would have to know a lot of things, because the teacher was the only one with education in this place; the only one who knew a little bit. If someone was sick, they'd come to the teacher; if someone wanted advice, they'd come to the teacher; if someone died, or if they wanted to sell their land, the teacher was the one they would turn to. From five in the morning, in my house near the school — "knock, knock" on the door — "*Señorita*, please help me. Would you write a letter, or send a telegram for me?" Every day, there was something.

It is very important to be the teacher in the school. Because after school, at four o'clock, I'd go to visit the parents of my students, to talk about how things were going. I had much more to do with the mothers, because when I arrived, they'd be making tortillas, I'd help them and we would get to know each other. They had a lot of confidence in me. And they knew they could ask for help.

Mainly they needed economic help, and also . . . well, it was important if they had moral or emotional problems to have someone to talk to. If their husband or sons behaved badly, or if their husband had another woman, they would be very upset. They would talk to me, and sometimes cry: "My husband won't give me any money", or, "He's always drinking. I don't have money to buy food."

And you know, if the teacher had been a man, they would never have gone to him. They would *never* talk to a man, or tell him anything. But it depends on the woman, too. They won't go and talk to just anyone. They do talk amongst themselves, when they go to wash at the river; they share their problems, sometimes.

There wasn't a lot I could do. I didn't have much money, but if they needed medicine, I'd buy it, and give it to them. Or if they needed advice, I'd try to be ready to help them however it was possible.

I knew girls of 16 or 17 who had three children. I asked why they had so many children. I said I was 18 and didn't have children. They said: "We aren't intelligent. We are women." I said, "It isn't true. I'm a woman, young like you. I am studying. I am a teacher, and I am a woman. I can do these things."

As a teacher, I had influence over them — the young group of girls. Every now and then, I'd meet them all together to talk about things that young people should know — menstruation, what happens to a woman's body. But the boys didn't like being taught by a woman. And the men didn't like it either, because everyone said: "This woman is coming to open everyone's eyes, and this is not good." They were afraid that the young people would start to have sexual relations very quickly.

But I used to wash my clothes in the river, and I had a chance to talk to all the women and girls there. At the river, they talked a lot. It was a good opportunity for they asked a lot of questions. But in the classes — nothing.

I had a real problem in the school When I was explaining a subject, and asked for opinions, the girls would *never* give their opinions. They would only laugh. "Maria, what do you think about this?", and she would only laugh with her hair across her face, like this. It was like talking to a wall. The boys were the only ones who would answer — never the girls. They think that they are less intelligent than the boys.

I think the problem comes from the family. It seemed to me that the mother transmits this to her daughters: "You must respect your husband. The men are the ones who go out to work. We women were born to stay here and look after the men." The father tells the sons: "You are the man of the house; you have to be the one who makes the decisions."

Indigenas believe that the girls have to be in the house all the time, but not the boys. They think it is important for the men to go to school, but they don't have enough money to send all the children. They have to choose which and how many children will go, and usually, it is the boys who go. I had 65 students and only 16 were girls.

The women really live like slaves. They don't realise or understand what is happening in their lives. Getting married is not a real choice for them. It is the custom to get married. They have to get married, and then they have to have children one after another. I've met many mothers who shouldn't be mothers, in my opinion. They don't love or care for their kids. They feed them and that is all. But they get married and then they have the children. That is what they were born for, many of them think.

Most of the Indian women here think about getting married, and keeping much the same way of life. It is a closed society and they carry on much the same way as their parents.

I'll tell you a story of a woman who had a four-year old son with pneumonia. He was very ill. I went to see her. She asked me to come. I said: "You must take him immediately to the nurse. He needs help quickly." And she said, "But my husband is not here in the house and if he's not here, I can't take the boy anywhere. If my husband knew that I'd taken my son to the nurse without his permission, he'd beat me." Her husband was working on the coast, in the coffee plantations, and in three days, the boy died.

Most of the women were almost all the same. They were all under the influence of their husbands or fathers. I knew one girl who was 24 and wasn't married. She was sick with tuberculosis, but she wanted to get married. They all wanted to get married . . . but didn't know why. It was the only experience they had — to get married and work in their own houses.

The young girls used to ask me how people got married in town, and I would explain it to them. Then they would tell me about their villages. "Here, our fathers receive money when we get married. If the girl is a virgin, she brings Q100 (£50).[6] If she isn't, then it is Q50, and with children only Q25."

But the interesting thing is the sale. The fathers are selling their daughters to

_____

6.   Q = Quetzal, the Guatemalan currency.

other men. Then I realised that the men wanted more girl children so they could get the money. But they won't sell them to just anyone. They have to make sure they know the boy well — that he is a good person. They have their own rules and morals about this.

There was no family planning in the village. They didn't know anything about it. They would only talk about sex as a secret, and only amongst the adults, not to the children, or the young girls. Many younger girls would come to see me, because they couldn't talk to their mothers.

They just wanted someone to listen to their problems, someone to talk to. But I think that a real change would frighten them, because all their lives they are subjected to the rule of their husbands. They only know what their mothers did before them.

The work of the women is to look after their families and do weaving. The weaving is really a part of their daily work. When they have one or two hours free from everything else, they use it to weave. And the money they get from the weaving, they use to buy things they need. They don't usually give it to their husbands. They are supposed to use it to buy food or things for the house. If the women do the work, they keep the money.

But even so, it isn't really independence. It is only a small amount of money that they have to buy the food with. It is only four or five Quetzales (£2-£2.50) per week. I spoke to one woman who made a beautiful *huipil* in one year. It was beautiful and she sold it for Q14 (£7). That isn't real liberty. But it does mean that she might be able to buy chickens or hens for the house. Some women go to the market to sell vegetables and other things. They probably have more independence, because at least they have permission to leave the house. Other husbands won't let their wives leave the house.

A few young women in the village are already studying in the secondary school for *Indigenas* in another town. There aren't many, but in the future, their children will know more, and little by little a very slow change might come about.

But I think that the most important thing is conscientisation. And the teachers must learn the language of the *Indigenas*. Then they could come to the villages to teach the women. The women would then have a little more confidence if they could speak the same language. It wouldn't be a rapid change but they could start by giving a few courses. They could help them form cooperatives to market the weaving.

If you could organise the women into groups, each day they would become stronger. If they could all work together and sell together . . . and begin to leave the house more . . . if little by little they saw what women can do in other places and saw that they are capable of doing more. I don't know what the husbands would say. You would have to teach them, too.

In this country, there is a lot of repression against all citizens. It doesn't suit the government that anyone, no matter which race, whatever group or class, comes together, because this won't help the government. If you start to educate the women, they might start to act or complain. They could say that they don't like this or that. But the government doesn't want this to happen. So, no matter what kind of organisation, *ladinos*, *Indigenas*, rich, poor — they try to destroy them so as not to upset the power the government has. Most people are afraid that if they do anything serious, they'll die or be tortured. If you fight, you might well die. Is it worth it or not? The word "liberty" means nothing here really, and even less for the women.

People here say that the problem is women having too many children. But for many people, the idea of not having all the children you can is a strange thing. Birth control hasn't come from God; their parents didn't live this way; it is a sin. They don't really think about whether they want children. They simply come from God. They have sex, and then one day they get pregnant, and they accept what comes.

But you know, the problem here is not with family planning. The problem is not that the *Indigenas* are having too many children. Guatemala could produce everything we need. The problem is the distribution of the land. In the United States, people don't have to worry about the land to build houses for their families. There is land here too, but most of it is owned by 20 families while the rest of the people have almost nothing. So the people with many children have a problem; but if they had land, it wouldn't be a problem. In other countries, like the United States, they don't worry too much about large families. It isn't a problem for them. Only here in poor countries, where we have nothing.

THE MEN SERVED THE WOMEN DINNER . . . ONCE

The weaving cooperative that I was visiting had a membership of 50 women and 18 men and had been going for about two years. It had been started by a few of the men in the village, with the help of two foreign nuns and a Peace Corps volunteer. These same three people were still living in the village, and still working with the cooperative. Using the project as a base, in spite of the danger of potential government opposition, they had also set up classes in literacy, nutrition, health and gardening.

These activities helped develop a desire to learn more. This was slowly affecting life in the village, as attitudes towards *la costumbre* began to change. One of the nuns told me about an event that had taken place earlier in the year:

> *"We were having a special dinner for the annual general meeting of the cooperative. As usual, all the men sat down, and were served by the women. But then, when the men were finished, they told the women to sit down, and the men served them. It may seem like a small incident, but that was a big step forward."*

There was also a new awareness and excitement for the women that came from the realisation that they could learn something: that at the age of 60, a woman had learned to write her name for the first time in her life; that they could grow new kinds of vegetables, such as beets, carrots, celery and radishes; that they had learned to make new garments in the cooperative.

The women began to develop a sense of confidence and pride in their work. This change in attitude was made very clear to me after I bought a *huipil* from the cooperative's office.

I had it with me when I went to talk to a group of women in the house of Miriam, the vice-president of the cooperative. She looked at the *huipil* and showed it to the other women, who all started talking to each other in Cakchiquel, the local Indian language.

Miriam turned to me, and said, "You take this back to Martin, (the Peace Corps volunteer), and tell him that he should know that we don't sell weaving that isn't well done, and tell him that Miriam said so." All the women nodded in agreement.

My *huipil*, it seemed, had not been up to the standards set by the cooperative, and should not have been accepted from the weaver, much less sold. I dutifully returned it, still surprised at the force of this woman in a country where women rarely voice their own opinions, and almost never tell a man, especially a *gringo*, what to do.

There was one point, however, where *la costumbre* still reigned supreme. That concerned the amount of money paid to men and women cooperative members. Although working with different kinds of looms, the women using traditional backstrap, or stick loom, and the men the big, foot-powered, pedal looms, they worked more or less the same number of hours per day. But all the women were adamant. The men had to earn more, and the men did not disagree with this policy.

At the beginning when the men were learning how to use the big looms, the women had been earning more. "There were lots of fights when the women earned more, and the jail was full," the Peace Corps volunteer said with a laugh. "Now the men are earning more and the jail seems to be a lot emptier than it used to be, so the men and women must be fighting less."

For one or two women, the cooperative had been the opportunity to develop as leaders. A couple of women had been sent as delegates to a meeting of all the artesan cooperatives in the country. They came back and reported to the group on what they had experienced. And they were surprised to find that they were not the only ones with problems in the work. They used to think their difficulties arose because they were stupid, and had no education, they said. It was a revelation to find other people, who were educated, having similar problems.

Miriam was one of the most interesting women in the village. She was, in many ways, quite exceptional. She was the first woman in the cooperative. She was active in the church, yet used birth control pills, thereby going against the teachings of the church. She was on the executive of the cooperative, and had travelled as a delegate to a national cooperative meeting, away from the village.

She had also set up her own "finishing factory" apart from the cooperative. When I went to visit her, there were about a dozen women, sitting and sewing collars onto shirts that were to be sold in the cooperative. This was apparently a controversial issue within the cooperative as Miriam hired other women in the village, non-cooperative members, to do this piece work, paid them at a lower rate than the cooperative, and then turned the finished work in, collecting the higher rate herself.

She was also in charge of the cooperative's "yarn store". Since it had been transferred to her house, they had made a £50 profit, whereas the year before, when the men were looking after it, they had made a loss of £200.

Miriam came from a very poor family, and had nine brothers and sisters. She was 33, married, with six children. She had had a difficult time with her husband initially. He was also a leader in the community and the church. Being quite strong-willed, she had many arguments with him, and he often beat her. Nevertheless, she went to evening classes held by the nuns, and learned to read, write and speak Spanish. Eventually he did accept her freedom to go out and study as much as possible.

Helena also had strong views on what the cooperative meant for the women. She was 34 years old, married and had six children living. Another child had died the year before with measles. Helena was also active on the executive committee of the cooperative, although she, herself, did not actually do much weaving.

MIRIAM: I was in the first group that started the cooperative, two years ago. There were six men and two women. The nuns, and a Peace Corps volunteer helped us start it. We were the first two women, Helena and I. Then there were 18 and now there are 50. There are only 18 men. It is harder for the men, because they don't know how to weave, and they have to learn how to use the big foot looms.

Before the cooperative started we sold our weaving to tourists who came here, or to tourist shops. But we didn't earn much. Only after the cooperative started did we realise that we had been losing money. We worked every day and only made about 25 centavos (12p). We'd spend 1.50 Quetzales (75p) on thread and sell the weaving for Q2.50 (£1.25), and it would take days to make. The shops would sell it for double that price, but we didn't know. Now we are earning every day. We can sell our things, buy more thread and still have a profit. Before when we worked, we had nothing.

HELENA: Life is better now. We make shirts, blouses . . . we turn them in . . . we get paid, buy more thread, and actually make a profit. Women in the cooperative earn about Q30 (£15) a month.

I think that the men should earn more, because they do actually produce more. We can work all day and not produce as much, so it seems fair. They use the big looms and we use our small ones.

It is still the men who run the cooperative, even though there are three times as many women — because the men have studied more, and the women . . . well . . . we don't know anything. It is only the men who know all the things you have to do — money, banks, orders . . . .

MIRIAM: It is the custom here for the man to earn more. The man has to earn more, otherwise there would be lots of fights. The woman must be behind the man. It may not be fair, but that is the way it is. We would never demand more. We aren't like the women in the United States who shout about what they want. Because the men would get angry. Most of us are content with earning about 90 centavos (45p) a day, while the men earn Q2 (£1) — more than double. Some women want to earn more, but the men would have to earn more too, and we can't afford it yet.

People used to say that the men worked harder than the women, because they had to go to the fields, but I think it is equal. I work very hard too. At least when the man is finished, he can rest. The woman can't rest. She has to work all the time.

HELENA: The women here do have one big problem. If the husband comes home, and his wife isn't there with his coffee, he gets angry and shouts at her. He is tired, and he wants his food. Luckily, my husband is different. I explain to him what I'm doing and why. The nuns have spoken to him, too. Every Sunday, we have meetings at 3 in the afternoon. They don't start on time, and we often don't finish until 6.30 or 7 p.m. My husband doesn't say anything. He understands much more than some husbands. But I do get everything ready, and my children give him his coffee if I'm not here. That way, I can go to the meeting, and he still gets his coffee.

I went to a meeting with Miriam and one of the men in the cooperative for a day to Quetzaltenango, and then to another town . . . and my husband wasn't there. He had gone to work for a month on the coast. When he came back, I told him that I had had to go away to get more orders, and take weaving and see people. And he wasn't angry . . . not even when I had to go away again for two days.

At the first meeting we went to, we learned that the weaving had to be done of very high quality and turned in on time. We had to come back and tell all the other women in the cooperative. If things aren't well done, and ready on time, we lose orders and can't sell the work. It would be our own fault.

The things we used to sell before the cooperative didn't earn us much money, and we always used to make the same things. But now, we get much higher prices and make lots of different things. My children used to work in the fields collecting onions, for 25 centavos (12p) for one or two hours. But when they learn to weave, they will be able to earn more still.

Some things are changing, but it is all very slow. And in a way, my life is the same as my mother's was . . . we have children now in the same way that our mothers had us years ago. It is the custom . . . you get married; you have children; and that is all. When I had my first child, my mother told me that she was just the same when she had me, and that is the same for all women. That hasn't changed at all.

And my mother never earned very much. Because when I was nine or ten years old, there was no work for my mother, and not much money. Now there is a lot of work for women to do. So that is different.

My mother never used to go out. I go out all the time . . . I am meeting people and sitting in meetings and seeing new places. She never did that. It isn't the custom for women to be out of the house too much.

MIRIAM: "Liberty . . . independence" . . . those words don't really have much meaning to us. We are more equal now to the men, but we are still studying, and many women still don't know anything. The road is not open for women, here. We stay in the house most of the time; we are lucky to have the classes that we do have. Slowly the children are learning a bit more . . . but it is all very slow.

I hope my daughters will have a better life. It is much more open for them now, than it was for me when I was young. I couldn't stay in school. But now we know that the children need to study — the girls too. Both girls and boys have brains and need education. Only the women haven't been fighting for these things. But if you fight, one day, you will learn and win.

Many of the mothers and fathers here are frightened that their children will leave the village, and won't come back, or that something will happen to them. So they don't like them to go to other places. This is more true for the women, especially the younger ones.

HELENA: When I was a child, I went to school for two years, but I didn't learn anything — nothing. The teachers didn't do anything. They made us do drawings all the time, to waste notebooks and pencils. So my father said that it was better to stay at home and work than go to school.

My children don't go to school either, but they understand a bit of Spanish. You see, I don't think the schools are very good. The teachers are always drinking and shouting at the children. We are thinking of setting up our own school through the cooperative.

I want to learn to read and write. I can write my name already, but I can't read. I can teach some of the other women a bit of writing, in the classes we have. Little by little, I'm learning. When I was married, I was very shy and didn't say much. If you had come before, I would have run to hide in the house. I would have been afraid. Now, I can talk to you, and I'm not afraid.

MIRIAM: We live more correctly now. Before, it was always a battle between the women and men — well, in my house anyway. We used to fight a lot. The women had no studies or courses, and we didn't have . . . we didn't know anything. We thought women were slaves to the men. But then with the classes of the nuns, we learned that it should be different, and the woman is worth as much as the man. Before women thought they had to stay in the house. We couldn't work, or earn money or learn. But now we are doing all those things.

Now there aren't so many women who are slaves. They get more respect now. There always used to be fights between the husbands and wives. If he was angry, he would beat his wife. Before the women didn't know anything. They thought this was a man's right. Everyone had very closed minds. Now, it is different because both women and men are having classes, and the men are thinking in better ways.

We have other classes for the women on food, cooking better, eating healthier foods. The nuns showed us how to grow new kinds of vegetables like carrots, onions and beets. We never used to use these things, and some people say they don't taste good, but for those of us who use them, they give us more ideas to cook with, and they are healthy.

We are also having classes on how to take better care of our children and classes in reading and writing Spanish. So many women don't know how to read or write, or how the numbers work. But with the help of the nuns and Martin (the Peace Corps volunteer), they are learning a little.

But we still have lots of problems. I'd like to have more studies for the women. I think we should all know how to read and write and to speak Spanish. And we should know more about cooperatives, so that the other women who know how to weave could set them up too, in other parts of the country.

HELENA: The nuns are teaching us all kinds of things about good food, and cleaning the kitchen. But so many women aren't interested. They say that those of us who go to the courses, don't have any work to do and that is why we have time to go to the classes. They say that they are too busy to waste time that way.

I don't know why they say that. It couldn't be just their husbands, because the courses are between 2 and 4 p.m. So the women would be back before their husbands got home.

Some women have said at the courses, that it would be better to give more education to the men because they are the ones who are in charge, and they should always know more. But I think that is ridiculous.

We're trying to change things in the cooperative. But even the women who speak Spanish still don't do anything. They let a couple of us do all the work.

Most women used to be afraid of going to meetings or speaking or saying what they thought. We didn't know anything. Now with the cooperative, and all the classes, things are changing slowly.

MIRIAM: The women still don't talk much in the meetings, because they aren't used to talking in groups in public. They get frightened. They want to speak, and they can't. Most of them speak Cakchiquel, and many of our meetings are in Spanish, and they don't understand what is going on. That is why we are having classes. Before women never went out to meetings. Now they are seeing new things.

In the meetings, we talk mostly about the work. We talk about how long it takes to arrange the thread, and weave the cloth, and how much thread it takes. We try to figure out together how much to charge so that everyone agrees. We give out the new orders, and we arrange for new classes to teach the women how to use a measuring tape.

Now we are thinking that we would like to learn how to make new kinds of designs in the cloth. We would like to have classes and learn, so that we could sell more things. We would also like to learn other kinds of work — perhaps with the big looms, that the men use. I think it is important to learn new things, and to make new things. If we can't sell them, we have to find other things to do. Many of the men think it is a good idea that their wives are earning money, and learning, but there are still some who don't want their wives to come to the meetings.

It is the same with the practice of birth control. Some men are against it. But there are some who think that it is important to learn how to use these things, because life is so difficult now that things are so expensive. If the children want to go to school, they need pencils and notebooks. It is impossible to buy these things if you have many children. So some men think that it is very important. But no one will say that. It is not open. If someone came from far away, to teach us, we could study and talk about it; but if not, we'll stay where we are without knowing anything. Even this new nurse — if she had classes, we would go, but she doesn't say anything. And we are too frightened to ask for these things.

No one knows if they are going to have a child or not. Just suddenly you are pregnant, and there is another child in your life. They don't think about it, or talk about it. That is what life is like for women here. We don't know what we are doing, or how the babies come. We should learn.

HELENA: I did hear about some ways not to have children, but most people don't know anything about it. And I don't really know anything about it. I did hear that the nurse had a meeting to talk about these things, but I didn't go.

MIRIAM: Here, girls get married very young and then right away they are pregnant. Some people have 12 or 13 children. People don't use birth control very much. It's like I have been saying. We haven't studied things like that and women are frightened by things they don't know. We are beginning to talk about it . . . about how to use the pill. I would like to use something, because I don't want any more children than the six I already have. We aren't earning enough money.

But I don't talk to the other women about it. I am afraid to mention it because a lot of people are not using family planning. They think it is better to have lots of children.

Before when I used to take the pill, I had lots of problems, and got very sick. That's also why I didn't want to talk to others about it. I was afraid they might get sick too.

We used to have a nurse here. She was very good and would talk to the women about how not to have children, and many women would go to her. But she left, and the new one is not very good. I don't go to her.

I don't know how many were taking the pill. When the other nurse left us, she left us alone. When I got sick, I became frightened. My period came two to three times in the month, and then it didn't come at all. The nurse gave me an injection to help it come, but I decided to stop taking the pill, and then I had my last child. But I don't want to take them again, because they frighten me.

Perhaps you could come and give some classes for the women here, in the things that we don't know . . . to help us learn. A lot of women are afraid, because they think taking something will harm them or the baby, if they have another one.

It is difficult to talk about it because it is the custom not to talk about these things with women or girls who haven't had children yet. It is a closed subject really, and I am afraid to talk about it too much too.

For me that is the most important thing we have to learn now, and to develop our work and earn more money. If children come every year and a half, the mother can't work at her weaving. And she can't come to meetings or classes because of the children.

THE HEALTH PROMOTERS

For peasant women, dealing with the problems of ill health in Guatemala is a two-fold battle. Before gaining access to the information that would help to improve health, women first have to break free from the conditions imposed by their husbands preventing them from learning new things.

Attending courses, leaving the village, coming into contact with new ideas was much easier for women whose husbands had that kind of experience first. For many men, this happened through the church, and the more radical priests and nuns encouraged these men to "send" their wives along. One American nun said:

> "The women's activities depend very much on the husband. And men here are just like men all over the world. If they are insecure, they will feel jealous and threatened at the thought of their wives learning something new. They want to dominate. So in order to get to the women, you have to start with the men. We start with the catechists or the community leaders. And then they want their wives to know more about health and cleanliness, or how to cook different kinds of foods."

The one man I interviewed, an Indian community worker, said:

> "I've seen that a few women would like to attend the literacy classes, but if the husband gets home, and she isn't there, then he gets angry and will probably beat her. But my wife, for example, can go out. Except that we have very small children, so she can't go to the classes in the evening and leave them alone. She didn't go to school. Her father didn't want her to go. But I am trying to teach her a little bit at home."

Thus, even in families where the husband had a more progressive attitude to his wife's growth and development, her job in the family, that is, looking after the children, restricted her ability to have new experiences and learn from them.

In keeping with *la costumbre*, however, the women tended to accept this situation, and even tried occasionally to look on the bright side. As one Indian woman said:

> "Other slaves are totally locked up, and can never leave; but we can ask our husbands for permission if we want to go somewhere."

Juana, Gregoria and Maria were three women who were able to break from the traditional pattern. They had come to attend a health promoter's course, in a hospital some distance from their village. Anna, Maria's mother, had come along to keep an eye on her daughter. Maria was 20, and her mother was 47. They and Gregoria, who was in her late 20s, were all Indian women from the highlands. Juana was a ladina, and also lived in the northern regions of Guatemala. She was 30, married and had three children.

For Maria, it was her mother, and for Juana and Gregoria, their husbands, who recognised the value of learning the basis of improving health and nutrition standards both at home and in the village. Each of the women had been supported in their desire to know more and to teach others. They explained to me why they had wanted to come to the course, and why they were the only women there.

MARIA: We came here as representatives of our communities to learn something about medicine, so that when we go back, we can give classes to our *compañeras*, so they can learn too.

JUANA: In the first course, there weren't very many women. There were only four women out of about 30 people. On another course, there were only two out of 25. It is always the same.

GREGORIA: Many women don't have any confidence, so they don't try out new things. Their husbands probably wouldn't give them permission to come anyway. Also lots of women wouldn't have any interest in coming to a course.

But my situation is different. I didn't really want to come, but my husband was interested in my learning more, so he said I should come to study more about health. It was hard for me to get here, because I live so far away.

My husband is looking after the children now. He told me to come because he didn't want me to miss the course. "Don't worry," he said. "You go. I'll make the tortillas, look after the children, and arrange lunch."

So I am here for a whole week, and my children are with my husband. I can't go home during the course, because it is about three hours to walk to my house. There aren't any buses.

JUANA: My village is about half a day's walk from here. I am in charge of a group of women, and we are learning about nutrition, health, hygiene, how to avoid illnesses, and how to cure them if they come.

We only had one midwife in our community, so I offered to study to be a midwife, to help the community. But most people, especially women, don't want to get involved.

Many women can't afford to pay a lot for a midwife. Most charge Q10 (£5) for each child, but I charge less, because I know they are poor. If they can't afford what I charge, they pay what they can. While I'm working, if the woman has an older daughter she comes to my house to look after my family.

I know one midwife who charges more if it is a boy. She charges Q10 for a girl, and Q15 (£7.50) for a boy. I don't think that is right. All the children should be equal.

GREGORIA: The rest of us don't really earn any money in our work. Sometimes we get a little bit — some days, yes, and others, no. We buy the medicine, and when we sell it, we make a little bit of money. But people in the village are very poor. We all work as volunteers because we want to help the community.

JUANA: Most of us on this course had to give up quite a lot to come. I had to give up a lot . . . we are very poor, and I'm afraid that my children don't have enough food to eat because we had to save money so that I could come here.

One of the nuns said that she wanted me to come to the classes, because I am helping women in the community. I told her that I didn't have much money. I have to get a letter from her so I can try and get some money from the community when I return. I wasn't elected by them, so I don't get any help from them. I don't know what will happen.

MARIA: I was elected by my community . . . they will help me with the expenses, and I will go back and teach and work for the people.

ANNA: My daughter now can give good advice, and maybe even encourage other women to come along and learn.

JUANA: Women don't really know about their bodies — all they know is that they get pregnant, and then they have the baby. Some women have as many as 12 children, and that is why they are so poor. They can't look after them. It isn't really a question of whether they want them or not . . . they just have them.

In my village, almost everyone is a *ladino*. But the women do think about having children, and they talk to me about it. They say, "I'm pregnant again, and my other one doesn't even walk yet . . . what am I going to do?" I don't know what to tell them. There are two nurses, but they don't do much, and the doctors don't come to the village very often.

GREGORIA: In my village, the *ladinos* use family planning, but the Indians don't. One reason is money. The Indians can't afford it. The pills and injections all cost money.

MARIA: The *Indigenas* want to have children. "How do you know how many are going to die," they say. "It all depends on God." And if their wives won't give them all the children they want, the men will go and look for other women who will give them more children.

GREGORIA: I don't think that the women want to have so many children, but they don't really know what to do. Or their husbands don't want them to use any control. That is what happened to me. When my first child, who is 10 now, was two years old, I said to my husband that I didn't want to have any more children. So I said I wanted to take pills not to have any more.

He said to me, "Women taking those pills always have other men." So he wouldn't let me take them. Then after the second one — we are having classes now, and we are seeing examples of other ways to live. And my husband has seen that you don't have to have so many children . . . that they suffer because you can't feed or clothe them. We aren't rich . . . we are quite poor. He is a community promoter, and now, thanks to God, we have only two.

But I still don't take anything. We just sleep separately. (The other women laughed.) We never sleep together, because I am afraid if we did we could have more children, and they would suffer. I really don't want any more, but my husband still won't let me use the pills.

Men here are very jealous, and don't even want their wives to go out. I think women and men should be more equal.

Men do have more opportunities here. People say that women are not worth as much as men, but I think women have the same dignity as men. In my house, we discuss things, and try to come to an agreement with each other.

MARIA: For anything to happen — to change — both the women and men have to have confidence in each other and in what they are learning. If the men aren't in agreement, the women will never be able to do anything. For one to change, the other has to do the same.

But women aren't very independent . . . they are dependent on their husbands. Many men treat their wives very badly . . . they beat them and there is nothing they can do.

JUANA: I don't think it is good to be dependent . . . the only way to change it is to teach the men to respect the women as their equals, with the same rights in the house. The nuns say these things, and when the men are here on the course, they all agree, but when they get home, it is totally different. They behave the way they always have.

Although I guess it is changing a little. When I lived with my parents, we suffered a lot. We didn't have clothes, food — nothing. Now I have three children, and they don't suffer the way I did when I was young. Their life is better because I work, and earn more money than my parents did. I sew clothes.

I bought a sewing machine, and I work from my house. My husband works in the fields, so we only have what he harvests. I earn the money that we need, and I keep it to buy things for the house and the children.

If a woman doesn't have her own money, she has to get it from her husband, and then she is totally dependent on him. And that is why my parents suffered. My mother didn't work; she always had to get money from my father.

MARIA: I think you have to be able to work so you can earn money. But if a woman has been in her house for 15 years, she doesn't know how to work.

And sometimes women stop looking after themselves. After the first child comes, and after the second and third, women have so much to do, looking after the family, making the food, that they don't even keep themselves clean . . . they get dirty and messy.

I have been thinking . . . I could work; I could get married; I could go to school. In my village, most of the girls get married very young — at about 14 or 15 years old. If there is a girl who hasn't got married by the age of 16 or 17, they say it isn't so easy to find a husband. They have to stay with their parents or they become pregnant, and have children without a husband.

I did go to school for two years. I can read but not write. Boys go to school longer than girls. If you are the first girl in the family, you have three years to go to school, and then you have to look after the rest of the children. The boys can't work until they are older, so they go to school longer.

And the parents, the mothers, say too, that the boys are worth more than the girls, so they have to go to school to learn more.

ANNA: Well, I don't think that is true, but that is what people say. Who knows what luck your children will have? My daughter didn't have a lot of time at school because I was quite ill and we live far away from the school. I needed her to help in the house, cooking and looking after her father. But now her sisters are studying. One is 15, and in the third grade, and the other is 18, and in the first year of secondary school.

Education is very important. I only went for three years, and my husband didn't go at all. But I want as many of my children to study as is possible.

GREGORIA: I went to sixth grade. I wanted to go on further, but my father didn't want me to go on. I would have had to go away to school, and he was afraid that I would be out at night with boys in the school . . . and he didn't want me to do that.

ANNA: You know, we have courses and teachings, but we don't seem to be able to do much. We don't have the capacity to do many things. We are poor, and we don't have many ways of changing, of making life better. And my question to you is, "How do you do it; how can we learn more, and earn more money, so we aren't so poor?"

JUANA: My question is the same. I have been thinking about it. How do we learn enough to come out of the slavery that we are in? For it is like slavery — often we are attached or tied to our own customs. We are our own enslavers. We don't know how to earn even one centavo, to help our families. We need to be able to learn to guide ourselves and others better. I don't want my children to have the same life as I have had. So my question to you is about whether you could help us, or tell us how to orient ourselves.

MARIA: We are still fighting to change our circumstances. We are spending a lot of time, and our own money to come to a course like this. But it seems to me that we are always spending and never gaining.

Dominga, at 32, with five children, was a woman who also showed a high degree of independence, and a strong desire to learn. She worked with a nun, Sister Maria, visiting remote villages in the northern highland region to teach the ovulation method of birth control. As the nun did not speak the various Indian languages, Dominga translated for her.

Because of her own independence and her husband's support, Dominga travelled with the nun to El Salvador to attend a family planning training course. Her husband was to have gone with her, but as he had been drinking and was incapable of travelling, she went on her own.

She described her initial involvement with Sister Maria and her husband's reaction to her working "away from home".

I started work with the nun when she came to the village to give her first course on family planning and I went to listen. I translated for her. She liked me and asked me to help her with the second and third courses. The second time, she invited me to attend a course in El Salvador.

I knew a bit about health and birth control from a priest who is a friend of my husband's. Then some nuns came to the village — they were nurses. And the priest knew me quite well. He called me and asked if I wanted to work in the clinic. I was 13 years old then, and I worked with them for six years. So I learned a little about medicine — how to give injections and intravenous. I learned a lot from the nuns.

I had to leave school early. It was the way things were before. My father took me out of school so another younger sister could start school. And I stayed home with my parents doing things in the house — washing clothes, making tortillas.

I was 12 years old, and I was angry with my father, because it was my sister that went to the fifth grade, and I couldn't. I really liked school, and I wanted to study more. I asked him why I couldn't study more — my mother never said anything to help.

There were 13 children in our family. I don't think my mother wanted to have so many children, but they didn't know a thing about birth control in those days. There was no medicine, nothing to take, no one to talk to about not having children. My father did go to consult with a priest, and he said it was a sin to take pills, and that it was against the church. And because there was no other way — nothing else to do — they carried on having children.

Her life was very different. She couldn't speak Spanish. She never went to school. She didn't know any *ladinos*. She wanted to have *ladino* friends, and learn to speak Spanish, but she couldn't. She worked all the time with my grandfather and grandmother.

It was always my father who decided about things like whether we would go to school. But about things in the house — it was the two of them together.

My husband is good to me. Other husbands won't ever let their wives go out, but he lets me go out alone. He let me come on this course. I think that is because he loves me a lot. If he didn't love me, or was angry with me, he wouldn't let me go. He has confidence in me, and that must come from love. He knows that I am a special woman, and that I want to learn. So he will let me go, and he will stay with the children. Other men won't do that.

He also had to leave school early because he was an orphan and had no father. He had no land. We were both very poor. But my father gave us a small bit of land to build our house. Then my husband found some work as a bilingual promoter for the government. He teaches children to speak, read and write Mam (Indian language) and Spanish.

He worked for 11 years as a teacher, and then he was promoted. He goes out to the *aldeas* (outlying areas) to supervise other promoters. I suggested that I could go out with him to teach other people about family planning.

He said yes, that it was a good idea. But I don't have any sixth grade. I only went to the third grade, so I am going back to school at night. I hope to get my fourth grade this year.

It is much more difficult for other women. Two of my sisters both work. One works as a seamstress, and makes trousers, and the other works as a teacher. But they are both single. Married women can't work outside the home. That is the way it is for them. I know some women who are married and who work in the hospital as cooks. They have husbands and families. But they can't find anyone to look after their children — or they have to pay to have them looked after. And they don't see their children very much, because their families live far away.

I think there should be a house where the children could be looked after so the women could work more. Then they wouldn't have to worry about their husbands getting angry, or leaving their children.

I wanted to work . . . well . . . I had to. We needed the money. But it is good for a woman to earn money. You are helping your husband to maintain the house and family. If you don't earn any money, then you have to rely on your husband. And if he drinks, he won't give you very much, or sometimes, he won't give you any. Then where do you get the money for food and clothes?

Many women earn money by selling their weaving. In some cases, they keep the money for themselves. In other cases, they have to give it to their husbands. If the husband is a good man, and shares his money with his wife, then she will probably do the same. But if he is selfish, she probably will be too. The women must keep some money because they need to buy food and clothes for the children.

In my case, my husband and I respect each other. We share, and are equal. We have an understanding with each other, and many couples don't have this. There are many people who think that men are worth more than women. But I think that we have the same value. We can work — equally.

I want my daughters to know that they are equal to men — that they have the same value. And I hope they will be able to find work, because that would be good for them — to earn money and learn. But that will still depend on whether their husbands allow them to work.

WHERE THE GRINGOS HAVE BEEN...

For some peasant women in Guatemala, change had come through direct participation in training programmes or cooperatives. Often, other forces for change were less clear and less direct. At another weaving cooperative I visited, I had a sense that the lives and attitudes of many of the women had been affected by contact with foreigners passing through the village.

Each of the women I talked with had had a reasonably close personal contact with one or more *gringos* who had been present in force in the village for several years. They were Peace Corps workers, doctors, nurses, casual travellers settling down to live for several months, literacy workers, bearers of aid for earthquake victims,[7] itinerant interviewers and anthropology PhD candidates, looking for material.

In this one small village, there were two rival women's weaving groups. Each group had had the assistance of foreigners at the beginning. The first had been established initially with the help of a Peace Corps volunteer. Later they had the help of another American woman who came to live in the village. The second group, a cooperative, had been set up a few years later in competition with the first, but with some of the original members, and with the help of yet another Peace Corps volunteer.

Both groups suffered from competition within their own village, as well as with other cooperatives throughout the country. Orders were falling off, and most of the women expressed a real fear about their inability to solve the problem on their own, after most of the *gringos* had left.

For other women, there was a more lasting benefit from their contact with foreigners. As most rural women only go to school for one or two years, few know how to read and write Spanish. However, a number of women had studied with an American girl who came to live in the village, and offered literacy classes. Without those classes, most women said they would be just like all the other women in the area who knew nothing.

More than one was very keen that I stay on to give classes, too. "But," I said, "my Spanish isn't very good. I don't think I could teach very well." That

————

7. In February, 1976, Guatemala was struck by an earthquake of violent proportions. In this village and the surrounding province, most of the peasants' homes were destroyed.

didn't matter, they said, because they wanted to learn English, so they could talk to the tourists, as well as answer the letters for weaving orders that were written in English.

Here, more than in most other villages, the general feeling seemed to be that whatever the *gringa* thought, had, or did, it was better than any Guatemalan, especially a woman, could ever achieve.

For most, the experience of meeting foreigners had been positive, even though the women were left with difficulties that they could not resolve on their own. No one wanted to attach any blame to the foreigners coming in, establishing a new project and leaving within a year or two. In fact, one woman and her 18 year old daughter accepted this as one of the basic differences they saw between themselves and American women.

> Mother: *"I think it is very good that you are travelling and visiting lots of places and meeting lots of people. It is good to learn about how other people live, before you get married."*
>
> Daughter: *"You people from the US earn a lot — so all of you can travel. But here we earn nothing. Women in your country have work, but here, the women have no work; they have no money; and they can't go anywhere. And if their husbands don't have work, it is worse. They have nothing at all . . . only a lot of children to look after . . . with nothing."*

The other interesting aspect of this village, possibly attributable to the indirect influence of foreigners, was that one of the weaving groups was run by a family of single sisters. Three single women running a business were considered unusual in a country where:

> *". . . girls get married so young — at 14 years old — and then they have a baby immediately. From then on, you have one load strapped to your back, one on your head, your baby inside and children around your feet."*
>
> —A woman in the market

Rarer still was a second set of unmarried sisters, who, at 23 and 28 years old, had come to work with the other, older single sisters:

> *"We didn't want to get married either. Life is much more peaceful this way. Getting married means problems . . . having children, raising them, maintaining them.*
>
> *"People are always talking . . . they say that it is because we are lazy that we are single . . . that we don't want to look after a husband and children. But you have to be so understanding if you have a husband. You have to understand and accept everything he says, and it isn't easy to respect everything men do.*
>
> *"Women here don't know that there are other ways to live. That is why many girls get married. They don't know that there is another way. For many, it is the only thing to do . . . they are young and silly, and think it will all be wonderful."*

Guillerma, 34, was one of the sisters running the business and in charge of most of the finances. She still dressed in her traditional clothes, but had travelled for several months to the United States and Europe with one of the American women who had helped her establish the business.

Although she did not say much about this experience, she was noticeably more at ease with the many foreigners visiting the village than other peasant women of her age. She explained to me that her life before meeting the Americans was not very different from that of other young Guatemalan Indian girls.

Many years ago — about 15 years ago — a girl from the Peace Corps was living here in the village. She started giving us classes in how to cook — making cakes and other things. I was about 19 at the time.

We started to talk about the weaving that we all used to do. and she suggested that we might make some different things and sell them. I told her one of my ideas for something to make and she said it was a good idea. So we made some samples. Then my sister suggested other new things to make that we could sell. Everything we made, we sold to the Peace Corps volunteers. They always used to come here to the village.

We set up a club for women in the village to weave new things to sell to the tourists. Then there was Interfair, a big exhibition in Guatemala City, and we went to participate. By then, there were lots of other women in the club, and we sold more than Q100 (£50) — our first time there!

Soon after that, it was *Todos Santos* (November 1st — the Day of the Dead) and we sold Q500 (£250) worth of weaving to all the tourists who came to the village for the fiesta. We didn't have a shop; we just sold from the house.

We were afraid at the beginning. It was only because of the Peace Corps girl that we started. We couldn't . . . we wouldn't even go to Guatemala City on our own. It was only when she said, "Let's go," and we went with her. We were terrified.

She taught us everything — how to send packages and find orders, how to deal with banks. And each time the Peace Corps volunteer changed, the new one would help us, and would teach us how to keep records, and save some money, and open a bank account. Now we are all right on our own. We have our own business now, although there is more competition these days. It was better before; we used to be able to sell more.

Before the volunteer came, we didn't think about doing things like this. But then she came, and taught my sisters and me how to work and earn money, and we did very well on our own. What more did we need? We didn't have to get married, and then we decided that we didn't want to.

We like it as we are here, all of us single. Many men and husbands here are very jealous and don't let their wives leave the house; and if you can't leave the house, you can't do anything. And you can't tell beforehand whether they are going to be jealous or not. So I don't really think it is worth the trouble, or the risk to get married.

I am single, and I have the right to go when and where I want. I don't have any problems with anyone. That is the way my three sisters think too. One of my sisters was married, but she is separated now.

Women are supposed to stay in the house — cooking, cleaning and looking after the children. But if they could go out, they could earn more. If they stay in the house all day, they learn nothing, and they earn nothing.

I think that everyone should have the right to do what they want — it isn't just the men who can walk around and say what they think. The women can too. But the men make it very difficult.

Some women, and many men, say that the men are worth more. But for me, these people don't really think. For me, both are equal. Men have to eat; women have to eat.

There were eight children in our family, and all my brothers went to the sixth grade. You see, here, that is the way it is. Girls aren't important enough to go to the sixth grade. My parents too said that it was more important that my three brothers went to school.

We were very poor. Each of the girls went for two years. Of course, we forgot how to read and write. When we were young, it wasn't important. What could we think? We were young and silly, and thought that our parents were right. But then when we were older, our thoughts changed, and we wanted to study more, and learn what we never had a chance to learn.

Then an American girl came here, and rented our house to give classes in reading and writing. We went to her school, and I learned to write my name. We started to go every day. Now we know how to read, and we can write a little bit, too.

I think that studies and school are most important. But there is another thing. The girls get an education; some carry on, and some don't. They look for boyfriends, and when they get together, they decide to get married. Then the parents won't send the girls to school any more, because they say it isn't worth it. So the girls lose their studies this way.

If you work before you get married, often you can carry on earning. But if you get married before you work, then you never have a chance, and you lose everything.

I think it is because of the parents. They haven't taught us much — how to understand and learn about what you could do in life. But it is slowly changing.

Another problem here is that the men have to earn more than the women, regardless of the work. My sisters always grow potatoes, and they look for men and women to harvest the potatoes. The women work harder and get paid less. The men just dig them out of the ground and the women come along and collect them. That is much harder work. The men earn Q2 (£1), and the women earn Q1.25 (62p). The women have to carry them after they collect them, too. The men just leave them lying there. What do you think of that?

I think that if a woman works and a man works, and if it is the same work, they should get paid the same. If the woman works harder, she should get paid more. She has that right. But that will never happen here in Guatemala. It is impossible.

What is important to me is to be able to go out and know different people and places. That is how I want to live my life. I have another sister who is married, and she hardly ever comes here. She can't leave the house. She has a big family, with six children, and she has a lot to do. We always have to go to her house to see her.

Anna was vice-president of the other group of weavers who had formed the cooperative. She was 30, married and had three children. Having come from another village, pre-dominantly ladino, *where they did no weaving, her mother-in-law had taught her the techniques of weaving. She was an independent woman, a* ladina, *with strong, slightly racist views as to why the Indian women were much more disadvantaged.*

I have quite a good life. I have my work with the cooperative, and if I want to go out, I go. I have my own money, and my husband doesn't say anything. But there are so many who are awful. They are always scolding their wives, and they never let them leave the house. If the man says she can't go out, she never leaves. And for sure, if she doesn't have her own money, and he doesn't give her much, her life will be miserable.

Money is the most important thing to be free. With money you can do what you want, and you feel more peaceful about your family. If you don't have anything to buy them good food, and if you can't give them what they need for school, you feel very bad. It is hard to watch your children suffer.

When I was a child, I only went to school for two years. But there was a *gringa* here, and she said she wanted to help the women in the village — because they couldn't read or write. She went to the Ministry of Education, and they gave her pencils and notebooks and she taught us.

We told her what times were best, when our husbands weren't at home . . . so we said from 9-11 in the morning. By 9 o'clock, you have finished cleaning, and the men have left, and at 11 you can go home and make lunch. All the cooperative members came to study daily for three months. And we learned a little bit.

Whenever I was in the cooperative shop, I carried on reading. I know that if you don't practise, you don't learn.

Most children here in the village go to school, at least to the third grade. My three children are in an evangelical college. One is 10 years old, and in third grade. One is eight, and in second grade, and the smallest is six and in first grade.

Here in Guatemala, we have never been used to this idea of having small families. But some Americans came to live here and taught us about birth control. Some families I know have 15 children. They can't feed them. They can't go to school; they don't have proper clothes. It is much better to have only a few and give them a good life. I don't agree with sending one child to school and not the other. Either they should all go, or none. So when I heard about family planning on the radio, I went to see a doctor. On the radio, they said that it wasn't good to have so many children and that there were ways of not having so many. I use injections, now — every three months.

I think there are quite a few who are looking after themselves. Doña Elvira uses the coil. But I am a little afraid of that. I heard of a woman who lived here in the village, and she had one. But it started to come out and they had to operate. I don't want that to happen to me.

The other women use pills, but I don't want to. I am very forgetful, and I could never remember to take one every night. You know, when I get sick, and go to the doctor, and he tells me to take a pill every two hours, I always forget.

But with the injections, at least, I have to go to the doctor's office, and it is done for three months. It costs Q3.25 (£1.63) each time. It isn't a lot.

I started to do this six years ago, after my last baby. I was thinking the other day, that I would probably have five children now, because I used to have one every two years.. But this way, I only have three, and now that they are older, I can work, and they don't bother me.

My sister-in-law wanted to use birth control, but her husband didn't want her to.. And she asked me to take her to a doctor so that her husband wouldn't know. Each time the appointment comes, I get worried that he will find out. But she is 25, and already has three children.

I don't think the Indian women in the *aldeas* use anything. They wouldn't even know about it. They are very ignorant about these things. They don't understand many things outside their daily lives. Those that do know about it, think that it is a sin not to have children. And their husbands won't let them use birth control. They say it is for God to decide, or they say that their wives will run off with other men.

Life in the *aldeas* is so much more difficult than in the village. There, the women have to go to the fields for everything. They have to go and look for wood to start the fire to cook the food. They don't have water in the house. They have to go and look for it, and then carry it. The men don't do any of that. They don't have electricity — they can't work at night.

Here in the village, each house has water, and most of us have electricity so that we can work at night, and earn more.

I think that the cooperative is a good thing, especially for the women in the *aldeas*. They can't speak Spanish; they can't go to the capital to sell their work. They have big families, and it is impossible for them to go anywhere, even if they had the confidence to do it. So they only come here to the village on market day, and leave their weavings, and collect their money. We calculate exactly what it costs them for thread, wood, time . . .

At the end of the year, we calculate what the profit is, and those women who have worked most, get more of the profit.

I talk to women from the *aldeas* when they come to leave their weaving and sell their vegetables. I say to them, "Would you like to go to the capital when we sell the weaving? You could see what it was like." And they say, "Oh, you can go, but we can't. Our husbands won't let us. Who will make the food?" I say, "Let the older children do it," and they say, "but if we aren't there when our husbands get home, they hit us." Many of the women say that their husbands beat them.

I don't think you can tell people what to do . . . but I think that what they need most in the *aldeas* is a group or an organisation — so they could have a teacher who could teach them how to take care of their children and house — and learn better health. But there is no teaching or learning at all.

Their houses are filthy. I don't have animals because they are dirty — but they have animals eating on the same floor as they do. And that isn't very good.

In our meetings, the women who come from the *aldeas* hardly ever say anything. They are frightened to speak. We ask what their opinions are, and what they think is what the women before them thought. "I agree," they say, because they don't have one thought that comes from their own mind. They never say, "I don't agree with you; I think we should do this".

If I say I think we should do a certain project, and then ask them what they think . . . "*Si*" (yes) . . . only that one word that they know. But on the other hand, members from here — if I don't explain or speak well, they will complain and speak up.

The women from here have more opportunity to talk in groups. But in the *aldeas*, people live far apart. They don't leave their houses much except to go for water or wood. They talk within their families, but they are still not used to giving their opinions about the things we discuss in the cooperative.

We have such problems in the cooperative, even though we have fought a lot to change it. Whenever we have a meeting, the men say, "*Compañeras*, please give us an idea or an opinion of what you think about this or that. We aren't the only ones with tongues to speak. We aren't the only ones who can think. We aren't the bosses of the cooperative. It is for all of us. You must say what you think. If you say you always agree, we won't grow."

We try to take the women members to the capital, not just for an outing, but to see what we have to do. Often we have to go to offices, or see the government, to talk about the cooperative. We take them, not so that they can talk right away, but so that they can learn and begin to understand how to talk, think and explain.

Before I joined the cooperative, I was afraid to speak to anyone or give my opinion. I was like all other women. I spoke, but only to agree with what other people said. I could never have spoken to someone like you.

Then we had some classes about cooperatives from another organisation. When they taught us in class, the teacher would say, "Tell me what you think". You had to answer; you couldn't hide and you wouldn't know when they were going to ask. Little by little, I have become more able to speak and say what I think without being afraid.

I know four or five women from the *aldeas* who speak up a little now. Before they didn't say anything, but now, they give their opinions. They do it in Cakchiquel, because they can't speak Spanish.

There are always some women who don't talk in the meetings, but as soon as they leave, they talk about what they don't like. I think that as soon as women become stronger in themselves — to speak in meetings — they must be different at home as well.

I feel things are changing, and that it is better now, but that is probably because I am working and earning money. My mother worked — she cooked and washed the clothes. She didn't have the freedom to think that she could leave the house when she wanted. Every time she went out, she had to say where she was going — because she always had to ask my father for money.

But my life is different. Whenever I want to go somewhere, I have my money, and I go. If I want to take the children to another village, or the capital city, I take them. I go to the capital alone — for work. My husband can't go because he is working here. I go to buy the cloth that we need in the cooperative, because it is cheaper there. And if I am not back by the time he comes home, he never says anything. Sometimes I don't even say I am going. Or if I am behind in my work, and the meal isn't ready, he says: "Don't worry; I'll wait," and he never shouts.

If he were different, my life could not be so good. I think that it is all right for a man to scold if he has a reason, but if not, then I think it is wrong. They don't have that right automatically. And women should be able to speak up too. I don't believe that a woman is a slave to the man, and has to stay at home because he says so. If my husband beat me, I wouldn't stay here for one minute, even though my father taught me that you have to obey your husband and do what he says. My father didn't want me to marry my husband, but I wanted to. I loved him, and my father said, "All right, go ahead, but the day that he beats you, don't come home and tell me that you are leaving". And I said that I wouldn't, and I haven't.

It is very rare here for women to be single. Everyone gets married. My other sister-in-law was married, and has a child, but is separated from her husband. She left her child with her mother and went to find work. Now she is back and works at home.

There are some sisters here in the village — who are all single. But that is very rare. They are all single, and depend only on themselves, and their own business for support. People talk a bit because they are single. But people will always talk. They don't understand that it is a choice these women have made. I think it is better to be single than live like a slave locked in a house, and never able to leave.

The only problem of being alone and not married, without children, is that there is no one to look after you when you are old. If you can't work, who will buy your food, or look after you, if you are sick? If you are dying, who will pass you a glass of water? My daughter says she is never going to get married. She says she will always stay with me so I won't be alone.

But then if you are single, like you, you don't have any problems. You don't have to think about your family. What are we going to eat for breakfast, for lunch, for dinner; is there enough money for the children to go to school? It is much better to be on your own.

"All this experience has taught me what I know. And there is no better experience, no better school than you get in the factory or fields. That is where you truly learn what the reality is."
— Aida Hernandez, Peru

POOR AND FEMALE

Although the women interviewed were separated geographically by thousands of miles, and culturally by different languages and traditions, their concerns and experiences were remarkably similar. In spite of regional differences existing within countries, down to differences between families in one village and sisters in one family, the women repeatedly described one factor common to them all: their oppression — at work, in the community and in the family. They shared, too, a belief in their own inferiority and saw themselves as having no real choice for change in their lives.

The oppression of Latin American peasant women is not simply the result of a set of complex economic and social circumstances that make, and keep, them poor. It also functions through the roles conferred on them and attitudes directed towards them by virtue of their sex. They are oppressed because they are women.

Work the same, suffer more and get paid less

The forces of oppression operate effectively at every stage of the peasant women's lives, from childhood through to adulthood. The most immediately obvious element is the sexual division of labour — the kind of work demanded of women and their low status as workers.

Long, unpaid hours are spent cooking, cleaning, washing, and caring for children. These are coupled with cultivation of the family's small plot and shepherding any livestock they have, and form part of the women's double or even triple day of activity.

These "responsibilities" were seen to be different from the "real work" men did. Women tended to refer only to paid employment as "work" and this concept was a major factor in the belief that women were only there to serve. Even working as a member of a cooperative or as an agricultural labourer was seen by the women as only "helping" their husbands, rather than contributing to the maintenance of the household on an equal basis.

Women also "helped" their husbands by raising and selling small animals, or through the production of handicraft work which they sold to tourist shops or craft cooperatives. The women alone marketed their handicraft work, as well as any buying or selling of produce in the local markets — any produce, that is, that was of little value. Major sales were not entrusted to the women. The men carried out these "important" transactions in larger markets away from the village.

In some areas, even when working as hired labourers, women did not actually get paid in cash; they received "wages" in kind — vegetables, grains or credit at the community or cooperative store. The women were not happy about this since they all needed money but said there was little they could do about it. When they did receive cash it was inevitably less than the men received for the same work. Usually both women and men justified this by saying men were stronger, worked harder and accomplished more in a given eight-hour day of labouring. In only one out of more than 50 different villages and cooperatives I visited were women paid the same as men.

Only a few women agreed with the views expressed by Lourdes, a woman working in an agricultural cooperative in southern Peru:

> "Women work equally as hard as men, or even harder. But the men don't believe this. The men say they must earn more. But I don't think that is fair . . . we should get paid the same. The rest of the women just sit silently and agree with the men. They don't see that it isn't right that we work the same, suffer more, and get paid less."

Despite the assumed "incapability" of the women, in many villages for several months of the year, they had to carry the entire responsibility for all aspects of the family's well-being. When the men left to search for work elsewhere, the women became both mothers and "fathers", since the men rarely sent any money back during this time. In fact, the men often supported a second family during the time they were away. When they did return, the women said that the men were, once again, "in charge".

Sabina, a 22 year old Peruvian woman with a young child, who was separated from her husband, pointed out:

*"Here they think that whatever the man says or thinks, the woman
has to do. Whatever he orders, it is our duty. They think because
they are men, the ones who earn money, they can dominate us."*

The issue of access to, and control of, the household's income produced
varied responses. Occasionally, a woman would say that her husband gave
her all the money, and that she was in charge. But she then hastened to add
that this was very rare. Usually the women were only allowed to keep the
small amounts of money they, themselves, earned from any sales of animals,
cheese, eggs and handicrafts. As one woman said:

*"Without money, you are nothing. I keep the money I earn. I don't
even let my husband smell it."*

And by the same token, he kept the money he earned, usually a much larger
amount. This meant that she was then dependent on him for cash to buy
food and clothing. But many women said they could compete neither with
the local canteen where the men got drunk, nor with their husbands' general
lack of understanding about the cost of supporting a family. As Sabina said:

*"When a woman earns her own money, she can manage and buy
what she and the children need. The men just think about beer . . .
they don't worry about clothes or food. They just give you what they
think things cost. They think it is still like it used to be.*

*"I think that some of the men here should spend a week at home
so they could realise what it all costs, and what it is to try and look
after a family without any money . . . just so they would know what
it is like. And then they might never complain again."*

The word "independence" usually arose only when women were talking
about the small economic freedom that earning and keeping their own
money gave them. It seemed a misuse of the words, however, to talk about
economic independence. True, the women were no longer totally subject to
their husband's decisions about whether to hand over money. But the
amounts that were being talked about were small compared to their needs.
As Felipe, a Peruvian woman of 30 with six children, said:

*"It is difficult to think of changing things when you have so many
children, and you can't even give them enough to eat. It doesn't
make sense to talk about a better life, unless your children are
eating well, have shoes, and are getting an education. I work in the
cooperative as a cook, earning about 250 soles (50p) a day. And my
husband works in the fields. He earns more, but we still can't feed
our children properly."*

We used to be afraid

With no industry in the rural areas, no transportation and lacking skills, the women had little hope of finding work outside the home or the fields. Their usual options of doing laundry or working as servants merely perpetuated their servitude to long hours and very low wages. Participation in a cooperative offered an avenue for change.

Whether agricultural cooperatives set up by a reformist government, or craft cooperatives encouraged by enthusiastic young foreign volunteers, the initial objective was usually the same — at least for the peasants — to create more work and to increase income.

Although a laudable intention at first glance, there has been some criticism of the cooperative movement as merely a subtle form of government control by introducing reforms designed to provide a steadier, marginally increased income, thus raising people slightly from their level of subsistence living. The effect of this, critics say, is to tranquilise any potential grass roots demands for real, structural change — that is, a challenge to the system and a redistribution of wealth.

This was borne out, to an extent, by comments of the women. When I asked whether their lives had changed through participation in a cooperative, they almost all said, "Yes, it has made a difference; we have work and more money now." It was often difficult to move beyond that in the discussion, because their poverty and need for employment and economic gain, however, minimal, were what most concerned them.

Nevertheless, in every cooperative I visited, there were always one or two women, who said that for them, the cooperative had been a clear learning experience — that in addition to having a steady income, they had, through participating in meetings and discussions, lost their initial terror and felt able to speak up and give opinions; or they had learned something about book keeping or marketing; or they had gone to a cooperative meeting in another town where they met people with problems similar to their own. Meeting other people had allowed an exchange of ideas and led to a new awareness that they were not alone, and, more importantly, a realisation that they could learn to resolve some of the problems facing them.

Even though initially most women could only identify more money as the major change in their lives, the cooperative had, in fact, come to mean more than a reliable market for their products. They said they enjoyed coming together; it was the only legitimate reason they had to leave the house, talk to other women and hear new ideas.

For some it was the first step in understanding the value of solidarity and self-help, and in realising that they were not stupid . . . they could learn. But this awareness only occurred in the few cooperatives where there was an emphasis on the value of learning and participation as well as on economic growth. Where the cooperative's primary goal was only to generate income, there was usually little change in the women's self-perception or understanding of their situation.

The cooperatives occasionally served as vehicles of political education as the women came to learn the benefits of working collectively and sharing skills and resources. But, again, unless this was actively and clearly promoted by the cooperative leaders, there was little change in understanding.

The philosophy of cooperativism is very different from the traditional way of working and producing in the village, that is, through the nuclear or extended family. In a remote village in northern Ecuador, women told me how their efforts to set up a rabbit-producing cooperative had failed:

"Everyone wanted to have their own rabbits to look after, instead of keeping them cooperatively. No one would trust anybody else."

Women who were cooperative members were occasionally accused by other villagers of being communists, or at least were subject to jealous gossip and suspicion. Women who hadn't joined the cooperative often said, "That sort of thing is only for women who have nothing else to do in the house".

The husbands of women in cooperatives were both suspicious and jealous. In every group there were stories of women whose husbands had refused to allow them to join. At a meeting of a mixed cooperative in central Ecuador, which produced jelly from the local apple crop, a woman came to the door in tears, and said:

"My husband told me that I can't come to work in the cooperative any more. He says I have to stay home and do what I am supposed to do." And then she said, laughing and crying at the same time: *"But I'll still come when he goes off to the fields for a couple of days."* After she left, one of the the men in the group said, *"It would have been better if she had been born the man and he the woman. We want to support her, but there is nothing we can say against her husband. It is his right to decide what she should do."*

In one village, the women had organised a meeting for their husbands to explain what the cooperative was all about and what it could mean for the future growth of the village. This, plus the new economic gain for each family often convinced the men of the project's value. A number of women chuckled as they told me how their husbands' attitudes had changed when they realised the women were bringing money into the house. And it usually did mean an increased sense of self-respect, however small, for the women, because they were "helping" or contributing.

But consistent with the usual oppression and denial of women's skills, very few were involved in the management of their cooperative. Only where there was an entirely female membership, (so there could be no men in management roles), or where there was an emphasis on female participation, usually at the instigation of a "professional" worker, were the women allowed any kind of management responsibility. The reasons for their lack of involvement were as always: no one would vote for a woman leader; the men always dominated the meetings and decision-making; the women were illiterate, and couldn't read the necessary documents; they had no time to come to meetings; they were afraid to take on the obligations of leadership; or their husands simply said "no". The prevailing norms of male domination and female inferiority made it impossible for women to participate.

We aren't allowed to speak

Outside of their traditional roles as wives and mothers, women were excluded from most other aspects of community life, except for participation in cooperatives or communal village work parties, or village *fiestas* and religious activities.

In some villages, women were not allowed to vote on community issues, in others not allowed to speak, and the ultimate restriction, not even allowed into the room where the men of the village met. Most of the women were convinced that this was really not their affair. They had been taught they had nothing to contribute. They repeated their husbands' words: "Who will do the cooking; who will look after the children? And what do the women have to say anyway?"

Other women disagreed with this attitude, but were so disabled by the fear of reprisal that they lacked the confidence and therefore the ability to alter the situation. Given that they were likely to be beaten by their husbands, or ridiculed by men and other women alike for speaking up and giving their points of view in meetings, the women didn't dare take the risk.

The accepted norm was that women were to be suppressed; any attempt at asserting themselves was deserving of physical punishment, or at the least, laughable. It was suggested by some women that they should have meetings and discussions without the men. When men were around, women rarely spoke or participated at any level.

Learning is difficult

As many women said, especially those who were experiencing change in their self-image or their role at home, the process was a slow and difficult one. They said that unless some special consideration was given to women in development projects, they were ignored or intimidated. The training and resources were always directed towards the men, and the only role the women played was to provide the food for course members.

The women believed this was because women weren't worth teaching. This is reinforced by much of the development work in Latin America today. Development still means "for the men" in most of the planning, programming and implementation.[1]

Even where there were special women's projects, the women had difficulties. Women in courses in health, literacy, new craft skills or leadership development talked about barriers to their learning, ranging from their fear of anything new to not having any time. This last point was a particular problem for single mothers, who, as the sole supporters of their families, could take no time off to go to classes.

Women also talked about the difficulty of learning when surrounded by children. Learning to hold a pencil, the first step to literacy, became impossible while constantly tending a small baby, let alone two or three. A number of women suggested a creche where the children could be looked after for a couple of hours.

Fear arose repeatedly as the single greatest barrier to learning. Carmen, a Peruvian, with three children, and already a widow at 24, said:

> *"I never learned to read or write because I couldn't go to school, but I don't go to the reading and writing classes here in the cooperative either. They enrolled me, but I didn't go. I'm not very clever and I can't learn things. I went for two days, and then no more.*
>
> *"There are women and men in the classes, and they started to take one woman and one man to give examples to the class. If you don't know the answer, you can't say anything. Everyone looks at you and the men laugh, and it makes you feel stupid and ashamed. So I don't go any more."*

Peasant women who did not speak Spanish, (the majority in Guatemala, Peru and Bolivia), had a further barrier to overcome. The language of the learning materials and of the teachers on many of the courses was Spanish. Women who couldn't speak Spanish became frightened and confused so that even the translation into their own language was less than effective.

The same problem arose when development workers went to the villages. Many "professionals" do not speak the local Indian language. With the best will in the world, these workers could not overcome the barrier to confidence that this created.

----

1. Barbara Rogers in *Domestication of Women* (Kogan Page, London, 1980) presents a thorough and convincing account of the discriminatory impact of the partriarchal development process on women of all classes in the Third World.

A number of women also said that they and others couldn't learn as fast as they were "expected to":

> *"You have to explain things very clearly to the women. They aren't used to classes because they spend all their time in the house and the* chacra. *They don't read, and they often don't understand what is going on. It takes a long time for them to learn new things."*

Unfortunately, as some women pointed out, the development workers came out once or twice for short visits, and went away, never to be seen again.

It seems an ironic paradox that the effect of some educational or training programmes is to reinforce in the women the feeling that they are incapable of learning. The constraints of time and financial resources, inappropriate learning materials, workers who can't speak the women's native language — all are problems to be overcome. But surely, the first step must be to ensure that these factors do not compound the problem by confirming the belief of the peasant women that it is *their* fault that they cannot learn.

In a similar vein, contact with foreigners, mainly volunteers coming to the villages, sometimes reinforced a feeling of inferiority and the myth that foreigners are the experts. "You are not stupid like us," the women would often say to me. It was difficult to overcome this belief in their own inadequacy unless the women already had some understanding of the factors of oppression which were determining and limiting their lives.

There were positive aspects to these encounters, however. For many women, it was the first opportunity they had to exchange ideas about different lifestyles and value systems. Meeting young women and men who had ideas different from their own about the role of women in society did plant seeds for the long-term struggle towards liberation.

Other sorts of changes were even less obvious. Learning to write gave confidence; having more information about how to look after their families gave support; membership in a cooperative taught solidarity.

Taught to be inferior

The women were trying to unlearn a lesson they had been taught from the earliest possible age: the lesson of subservience and inequality. From the moment of birth, women are considered inferior beings. In Guatemala, midwives charge more for delivering boys. In Peru, a family will give the midwife a sheep worth £10 for a boy, but only two hens, worth £4, for a girl.

Maria, a 25 year old Guatemalan teacher, said:

> *"My baby is due in six months. I don't want to have a baby girl . . . I want a boy. Women lead such terrible lives. They suffer and are*

*treated badly by the men. Things are bad enough in this country
with the government the way it is. I don't want my daughter to have
to fight all her life to make simple choices."*

For young girls, their role is reinforced as they grow up, through their
personal experiences, the role and attitudes of their mothers and the nature
of their parents' relationship. Little girls of three and four years old "play"
with dolls strapped to their backs in preparation for the job of motherhood.
The "play" turns quickly to the serious responsibility of looking after their
younger brothers and sisters.

Without exception, the women told stories of how either they, their
sisters or their girl friends, had little chance to go to school because they
were girls and therefore not worth educating.

Even where that attitude was gradually changing, young women who did
become literate complained that they had forgotten how to read and write
because they never got a chance to practice. They didn't need those skills to
carry out the tasks ascribed to them.

Literate and illiterate women alike made it clear that education was the
only opportunity their children would have to change the pattern of their
lives. Without an education, young girls would be caught in the same trap as
their mothers, with the only learning they received coming from the home.
In fact, a number of young girls accused their parents of having "taught
them to be submissive and shy" so they would never challenge the role
model set out for them.

Better to be single than a slave?

All women agreed that for them, marriage was really a confirmation of a
woman's primary purpose — to serve a man. First it was her father and
ultimately, her husband. There was some disagreement, however, about the
inevitability of marriage; that is, some women said there was a choice. But
these women were rare, and for most, the pattern of relationships with
young men was predetermined, led inexorably to marriage, and immediately
after to children.

For some, the children came without the husband, and this meant a still
lower status within the community. The position of a woman without a man
was not desirable, to the point where few women said they would encourage
their daughters to remain single.

Whatever doubts they expressed about the oppression of married life,
they and their daughters lived, first and foremost, to be wives and mothers.
Women cited foolishness, not knowing any better, lack of other opportunity
and wanting to get away from their parents as reasons for having married.

Only a few dared risk breaking from the norm. The strength to be different, to stay single, often came from having moved away from the village to study or work, or from experiencing other lifestyles and values through contact with teachers, foreigners or city-dwellers. As Rosita, a 19 year old Guatemalan girl, said:

> *"I don't want to get married yet . . . maybe later, but I want to finish school first. I left the village to go to school because the school here doesn't go past third year of primary. Other girls are afraid to leave the village for anything, let alone to study. But they are just afraid of change. If you want to study and learn, then you will make an effort to go wherever you have to. But if you don't go to school in the first place, then you will never leave, and you will never change."*

Her mother supported her in this decision:

> *"I miss her a lot, but if she wants to study, then she has to go away. And I want her to learn and have a profession. For those who don't study, there is nothing. All they can do is weave. Like me, I never went to school, and I can't do anything but weave."*

But many mothers, even though desperately wanting their children's lives to be different from their own, did not want to risk the danger of letting their daughters leave the village to work or study. Again the young girls learned the lesson of their female handicap. It was not a problem for the boys who would often leave to find work elsewhere. But the girls could be "taken advantage of" — they often became pregnant, and, as an unmarried mother, a burden and a shame to their family.

If I'd known about birth control, I wouldn't have had so many children

The complex issue of birth control most often came up when women asked if I knew how some people managed to have only one or two children. Every woman I spoke to, with one exception, wanted reliable information about how to control her own fertility. The fact that most women had been forced to have more children than they wanted was the most damning evidence of the suffering and loss of human rights experienced by peasant women under the rule both of their husbands and the political factors controlling their lives.

Fear and despair surrounded my discussions of birth control with the women. Fear of the church, fear of doctors, fear of their husbands, fear of their neighbours' knowing, fear of the potential damage to their own bodies — all this stopped women from taking the necessary steps to control or plan the birth of their children.

Girls accused their mothers of not explaining anything to them about sexual relations and birth control. Many women, now in their 20s, said they had known nothing about menstruation, let alone birth control. Older women said they had not even known it was possible to avoid having children. Many mothers also taught their sons and daughters that the number of children you had was something ordained by God, and therefore not to be challenged.

In many of the more remote villages, there was no information available about contraception outside the family network. This left the women no option but to have babies year after year, regardless of their own poor health, malnutrition, excessive work load and impoverished economic situation. Besides the force of their religious beliefs compelling them to reproduce constantly, having large numbers of children was the only way of assuring there would be enough children to work the fields and look after the parents in their old age. Given the high infant mortality rates, women could easily expect at least half of their children to die. Under these circumstances, there was not much chance of women making a considered choice to have fewer children.

Even where information was available, rumour abounded. Women told me that birth control pills were addictive, that you could go crazy, that your face turned black and you died, or that you couldn't work as hard if you used contraception. These rumours stopped many women from seriously considering family planning.

However, reliable information and access to contraceptive methods was rarely a clear path to independent choice. Husbands often forced their wives to have sex, foolishly believing that if their wives refused, it proved they were having an affair with someone else. The men often refused permission for the women to use birth control on the same jealous grounds. Women commented that the only way the men could maintain their wives' dependency was to keep them pregnant. Many men too, seemed to feel that their virility was challenged if their wives didn't have a lot of children.

Despite the Catholic Church's reactionary position on contraception, a few progressive clergy provided an opportunity for some women to break the never ending cycle of reproduction. By involving the men in discussions about the "immorality" of having more children than they could feed and clothe, priests and nuns encouraged the men to allow their wives to learn the various "natural" methods. But whenever abstinence was relied on as a method of control, the failure rate was high. The men could not be depended upon to honour the agreement, especially when drunk.

The methods most commonly used were the pill, the IUD and Depo Provera (DP). Many women refused to take the pill as they had become aware of the health hazards, but the use of DP was still widespread, despite its harmful side effects. This seemed due to its reliability, ease of use and lack of information about its dangers. Diaphragms were not known by any of the women, and were not on offer anywhere in the rural areas.

Only one or two women admitted risking the use of contraceptives without their husbands' knowledge. In all other cases, they said that the men had agreed. This was definitely more common in areas where the men had been included with their wives in the discussions and teachings about family planning.

But even when the husbands were in agreement, women did not really have "freedom of choice". They had to use whichever method was presented to them, either through the local clinic, nurse, neighbour, church or government family planning programme. There is a distinction to be made between choice and control. Choice presupposes access to, and understanding of, information and different methods. Control is imposed by restricting both access and information. Control is most characteristic of the family planning programmes that have been available to peasant women in Latin America.

It was left to a Guatemalan Indian man, a community development worker, to raise the explosive political aspects of birth control:

> *"They say it is better to have only two or three children because there isn't enough land. But who is it who is saying that there isn't enough land? There is plenty of land, but only a few people who own it all. And they want all the Indians to disappear, so they can keep all the land, and we won't be a threat to them.*
>
> *"That's why they keep sending so many people to Guatemala to talk about brith control, and teach it. We know that these things are not good for women's bodies. To me, it is a form of violence."*

The primary aim of many international and governmental birth control programmes has been to achieve a reduction in the overall birth rate in Latin America. It has not been to enable a woman to make a considered choice of the safest, most inexpensive, most appropriate and effective method of planning for her and her husband. Thus even where peasant women were freed of having to serve their husbands' wants, they were still being manipulated to serve another master.

The head of the house

A more direct form of violence towards women emerged in the nature of the relationships they had with their husbands. Not only were the women duty-bound to obey their husbands to the full, they suffered physical punishment if their behaviour became "unacceptable". Wife-beating was high on the list of rights accruing to men by virtue of their sex and position within the family. The women said there was little they could do about it.

It was generally accepted that the man was the head of the house. Dorilda, a 51 year old Guatemalan woman with four children, said:

> *"He knows more, and he can do more. Women and men should be worth the same, but the man is really in charge. And if the man is a little timid or cowardly, the woman can see that, and she has to help him, and teach him how a man should be in the house."*

So even when a woman was stronger and more capable than her husband, her role was to support him, at the same time denying her own needs and abilities. Her role as wife and mother demanded that she be passive and "in her place". From the crudest form of conditioning, such as wife-beating — through to the more subtle ways of devaluing women's intelligence and abilities, by denying them an education — women had been raised to believe in their own incapacity. It had become a conviction so deeply internalised that the inequalities or "wrongs" were not seen as such. They were *la costumbre*, and therefore, unchangeable. As Carmen, a Peruvian woman said:

> *"When you say you want to go out, the men say, 'I am a man; you are a woman. Women stay in the house and the men go out on the street. The man is the man,' they say."*

That kind of statement indicated more than a lack of confidence or a low self-image; it was that most of the women never even began to think of themselves as individuals who could create options and make choices. To them, the only option presenting itself each day, was to win or lose the struggle for basic survival for themselves and their families. The fight was not to challenge the factors of oppression, but to accept and endure them.

Man as enemy

On one level, the first of the women's oppressors that needs to be identified is the Latin American peasant man, and his embodiment of *machismo*. The men are culpable. Many women spoke about relationships with their husbands or *compañeros* which were defined in terms of the man's right to demand sex whenever he wanted it, his right to deny her the opportunity of using birth control, his right to beat her, or his right to earn more money than her, for the same work.

Obviously not all men beat their wives, nor do they all commit the myriad of sins of which they have been accused. Some women spoke of their husbands as "good men" with whom they had an understanding. They could discuss family issues and make decisions together. In addition, most of the development projects focussing on women had been started through initiatives taken by the male leaders of the community. Some women had been "sent" on health courses by their husbands, with the husband assuming all his wife's domestic duties in her absence. Unfortunately these men seemed to be notable as rare exceptions to the norm. And as people familiar with the struggle for women's liberation in the industrialised world know, the "loving support" women receive from men can often be as effective a shackle in making sure that women stay in their place.

In any case, there is no denying, given the evidence articulated so clearly by the women that *machismo* is one of the ruling forces in their lives. And it is as true for the men as for the women, that unless they are active in taking positive steps to break down these factors responsible for women's oppression, it will continue. Without a change in the attitudes of the women and the men, peasant women will be forever denied their rightful places as human beings with pride, self-confidence and self respect.

Defenders of the predicament of the Latin American peasant man say that the only dignity left to him is the opportunity to prove that he is head of the house, to be responsible for, and protective of, his family. It is a role which gives immediate satisfaction to his need for self-esteem.

But it is clear that it is his own oppression as a poor peasant which creates his desire for power and respect. It is a statement of fact, although not a justification of his behaviour, that he, too, is a victim. The peasant man is either landless or has a piece of land so small he cannot feed his family. He too has received an inadequate education, and so is semi-literate, because his parents were poor, and he had to work.

City-dwellers and *ladinos* ridicule Indian men to such an extent, that in Guatemala, the men have almost completely stopped wearing their traditional clothes. Going into town becomes potentially less humiliating if you are at least indistinguishable by your dress. He too is caught in the trap of having more children than he can support because he lacks reliable information about preventative measures, or fears what people will say, or actually believes his potency is in doubt if he has a small family, especially if there are no boy-children.

He too has been exploited for centuries at the hands of the wealthy both within his own country and from abroad. His subjugation is as thorough and effective as that of the woman with whom he lives, and the daughter and son whose lives he hopes will change. He still suffers the despair, as women do, of believing that major changes within his lifetime will remain unachieved.

Liberation is not selective

Critics denying the importance of feminism in the Third World, (and indeed in most other parts of the world), say that any attempt to separate the women's struggle from this larger battle for social, political and economic justice, "the class struggle", will be divisive and counterproductive. It is more important, they say, that the men and women work together, first to change the political and economic conditions in which we live. Once that battle is won, we can then turn our minds to the women's struggle.

There is little evidence, however, that a change in the economic system will automatically bring with it a change in the situation of women. Too often women have responded to crisis and joined the war, the march or the campaign, only to go back to the kitchen when the crisis is over.

New economic freedoms do not necessarily liberate women from their tightly defined sex roles. Even in our own economically 'developed' societies, women are in second place. Greater access to resources, higher standards of living, industrialisation — none of these have enabled a real liberation for women. We are simply more comfortable in our exploitation; the forces of discrimination are that much more subtle.

For peasant women in Latin America, a change in their economic situation might make it possible for them to attend courses in health, new skills training or leadership development; but as long as the men in that society have the power to say, 'No, you are not going to that class', the women will remain effectively locked into poverty and underdevelopment.

This denial of the importance of the women's struggle is only one more attempt to devalue women, trivialise their needs and convince them of the secondary nature of their demands for liberation, and focus attention on the unseen or distant holders of power. Why is international exploitation more vicious than that encountered within the community or the home? Justice in the form of political, economic and social change cannot be applied selectively. It is a contradiction in terms. The suffering of women at the hands of men cannot be justified in the name of a greater struggle.

The force of power as wielded by a Latin American peasant man beating his wife is as wrong and deserving of condemnation as the force of a multinational corporation stripping Bolivia of its mineral wealth. A male-dominated society which condones, in the name of a balanced population, the abuse of a woman's body so that she is denied the right of choosing when and how often she will give birth is as much in need of fundamental change as one which sanctions murder in the name of political stability. A system whereby some are denied their rights to a basic education and literacy because they are women is as unjust as one which denies others the right to work because they are black.

Showing real political insight, some of the peasant women stressed the importance of involving men in the struggle for the liberation of women. As peasants the women have already learned that those in control do not give up easily. One woman said that unless the men were involved in discussions about such issues as family planning, or the value of women's education and work, nothing would change, because: "they won't pay any attention to us".

They are right, and at least one Guatemalan man agrees with them. The Indian community worker said:

> "If one day the men wake up, women will be freer. Now they don't have much freedom. The men don't want them to have any liberty or freedom. We have to animate and liberate the men."

The culture of silence

But the true liberation of women will not be brought about simply by a change in the attitudes of men. There is no real liberation if the new equality for peasant women were to mean living with their men, equal in poverty and equal in suffering.

Paulo Freire, a Brazilian educator, outlined the fatalistic and submissive attitudes created and supported by social, economic and political conditioning which work together to ensure that the peasants remain imprisoned in poverty and suffering. Although Freire talks of the peasant classes as a whole, his argument is vital in understanding the plight of women as a still more oppressed group:[2]

> "The oppressed see their suffering . . . as the will of God — as if God were the creator of this 'organised disorder' . . . Self-deprecation is another characteristic of the oppressed . . . So often do they hear that they are good for nothing, know nothing and are incapable of learning anything . . . that in the end they become convinced of their own unfitness."

This leads to a "fear of freedom" and the "culture of silence". The key to change, according to Freire, is "conscientisation" — the process of identifying the man-made forces and mechanisms of their own oppression and discovering that within themselves exists the ability to learn and the power to effect change. The idea that inherent inferiority is the cause of the

—————

2.   Paulo Freire, *Pedagogy of the Oppressed*, Herder and Herder 1972, pp.48-9

problem gives way to an understanding of the ways, historically, peasants have been locked into a cycle of deprivation which they have been unable to break. It is a process of politicisation, not unlike the consciousness-raising process so central to the growth and strength of the women's movement in industrialised countries. It is a process that must also be central to the liberation of Latin American peasant women.

Alienated from the wider community by their illiteracy and mono-lingualism, isolated within the village by an overwhelming work load of domestic, child-rearing and agricultural duties, taught to believe in their own inherent inferiority — corroborated by an often authoritarian husband — most peasant women have been left completely trapped.

A reallocation of power

Freire chose the teaching of literacy as the means of liberation from that vicious cycle. There are other vehicles, but unfortunately none are acceptable to ruling power groups.[3] If the process of conscientisation were effective, peasants — both women and men — would become aware of all the forces of oppression determining their lives, not just the ones closest to home, or easiest to see. The result could be a real challenge, not only to a society dominated by men, but a society dominated by a small, wealthy elite, military rule, multinational corporations, and a well-entrenched international aid and development industry.

Development agencies have not, until recently, focussed on the particular concerns of women. They too, have promoted the assumption that the lives of peasant women would automatically improve with development. Yet, as Barbara Rogers clearly demonstrates in her book, *The Domestication of Women*:

> "Once substantial inequality has been established in a society undergoing 'development', the self-interest of those who benefit most, and have the greatest power, will tend strongly to perpetuate and increase the divisions."

The peasant women describe very clearly the examples of their "substantial inequality" in a male-dominated society.

The initial response of some development agencies has been a partial reallocation of resources towards special "women's programmes" which emphasise training in domestic and child-care skills.

This type of aid and skills training is important and necessary, but it is

___

3.   After the military coup of 1964, Freire was forced to leave Brazil as a political exile.

certainly not sufficient. It helps with the very real tasks that women have to carry out, and indeed, the women themselves say "yes" — they want to know more about nutrition, sewing and cooking. This is not surprising given that all the economic, educational and social forces have long been at work to limit their aspirations to those of basic survival and the fulfillment of their traditional roles.

Thus, the response is inadequate. As an end in itself, it makes the women better mothers and wives, but ultimately, it only increases their social and political marginalisation.

Development means improved nutrition, health, education and an improvement in the physical conditions of living; it also means economic change. But it must be defined, in the first instance, in terms of a woman's increasing ability to assume influence and control over all aspects of her environment — physical, economic, social and political.

Women must be enabled to develop a consciousness of their own potential, to discover their own capacity to learn and to participate actively and critically at all levels within their communities. The new generation of development programmes for women is attempting to meet these needs. They abound with recommendations about: legal change in the status of women; simple labour-saving technology for the tasks women are required to do; the inclusion of men in family planning education; promotion of women's cooperatives; the teaching of skills to earn money; the involvement of more women in the planning of development projects.

Each of these recommendations tries to tackle the problem of physical or economic poverty. But, as a former consultant to a programme of integrated rural development in Mexico has pointed out:[4]

> *"The intentions (are) admirable; but unfortunately a development programme is influenced less by good intentions than by the structure and culture of implementation."*

These programmes do not confront the underlying reasons for the underdevelopment of some, and the development, even overdevelopment, of others. They rarely take up the issues of power and control — the problems of social and political poverty.

Peasant women are not in charge of their own lives. Unless they have the opportunity to examine and challenge where authority and power lie at home, in the village and in their countries, there will be little real growth and change. Development must involve a reallocation of power.

————

4.   Barbara Rogers, "Discrimination in Development", *Spare Rib*, No. 100, November 1980, p.48

GLOSSARY

Aldea — Region outside the village centre in the countryside (Guatemala)

Alfabetizacion — Literacy teaching

Altiplano — High plateau lying at 13,000 feet above sea level between the two ranges of the Andes mountains

Asamblea — General meeting of the community (Andean countries)

Ayllu — Village and the land it owned under the Inca Empire

Aymara — Indian people living in the Altiplano region around Lake Titicaca in Peru and Bolivia

Cabuya — Sisal; inner fibre from the leaves of the century cactus plant (Ecuador); used for a variety of articles — sandals, mats, rope, sackcloth

Cakchiquel — Indian language (Guatemala)

Campesino(a) — Peasant, particularly poor peasant or agricultural worker

Campo — Rural area

Cargador — Stevedor; mover; men who work in markets carrying loads for stall holders or purchasers

CENCICAP — Campesino Education and Research Centre; government training centre (Peru)

Chacra — Small field in the mountains (Ecuador, Peru, Bolivia)

Chicha — Maize beer (Peru)

Chuño — Freeze-dried potatoes or other tubers (Andes)

Cholita — Scornful name for an Indian woman who adopts language, habits and dress of the *ladino* culture (Andes)

Colono — Poor peasant who pays the land owner with labour for the use of land

Communidad campesina — Modern Indian/peasant village community and its land

Compañero(a) — Comrade, companion, friend, spouse

Comunero(a) — Member of an Indian village community

Conquistador —Member of the Spanish conquest

Costumbre — The custom, the norm

Domestica — Maid, servant

Encomienda — System whereby Indian's labour and land was put at the disposal of Spanish estate-owners in the 16th-18th centuries

Espiral — Intra Uterine Device

Faena — Collective work party (Andean countries)

Fiesta — Feast day or holiday usually celebrated with a party or fair

Gringo(a) — Any foreigner, but especially a North American or European

GNP — Gross National Product

Hacendado — Estate owner

Hacienda — Large, privately owned estate

Hectare — 10,000 sq. metres = 2.03 acres

Huasipungo — System whereby peasant received a subsistence plot in return for services and labour for the land owner (Ecuador)

Huipil — Traditional Indian woman's poncho-style blouse (Guatemala)

IMF — International Monetary Fund

Indigena — Indian

Ladino(a) — Non-Indian; of mixed Spanish/Italian blood and Western culture

Latifundio — Large land holding

Latifundista — owner of a *latifundio*

Mam — Indian language (Guatemala)

Mestizo — Mixed blood Spanish/Indian

Minifundio — less than a subsistence land holding

Minifundista — Owner of a *minifundio*

Muchacha — Young girl; servant, maid

Naranjilla — A small fruit that looks like a fuzzy, orange-green crab apple. (Ecuador)

Oriente — Eastern region

Paisano(a) — Countryman/countrywoman

Patron — Landlord, boss

Quechua — Dominant Indian people of the Andes, especially Peru and Bolivia; their culture and language (that of the Incas)

Señora — Spanish equivalent of Mrs.

Señorita — Spanish equivalent of Miss

Sierra — Andes mountains region; highlands

Traje — Traditional dress of the Indians (Guatemala)

Yungas — Valley of tropical or sub-tropical climate in Bolivia

FURTHER READINGS ON LATIN AMERICAN WOMEN AND DEVELOPMENT

Esther Boserup, *Women's Role in Economic Development*, St. Martins Press, New York, 1970

Domitila Barrios de Chungara with Moema Viezzer, *Let Me Speak: Testimony of Domitila, a Woman of the Bolivian Mines*, Stage One Press, London, 1978

Perdita Huston, *Message from the Village*, Epoch B Foundation, New York, 1978

Perdita Huston, *Third World Women Speak Out*, Praeger, New York, 1979

Latin American and Caribbean Women's Collective, *Slave of Slaves*, Zed Press, London, 1980

Megan Martin and Susie Willett (editors), *Women in Nicaragua*, Nicaraguan Solidarity Campaign, London, 1980

NACLA Report on the Americas: Latin American Women, Vol. XIV, No. 5, North American Congress on Latin America, New York, 1980

June Nash and Helen Icken Safa (editors), *Sex and Class in Latin America*, J.F. Bergin Publishers, New York, 1980

Margaret Randall, *Cuban Women Now*, The Women's Press and Dumont Press, Canada, 1974

Barbara Rogers, *The Domestication of Women, Discrimination in Developing Societies*, Kogan Page, London 1980

Doris Tijerino, *Inside the Nicaraguan Revolution*, New Star Books, Vancouver, Canada, 1978

"Women and World Development", Parts 1 and 2, Nos. 88 and 89, 1980, *New Internationalist*, Wallingford, Oxford

Inter-Action

Inter-Action is the umbrella name for Inter-Action Trust Ltd and its nine associated charitable companies and trusts. They are all directed from a purpose-built centre located in the London Borough of Camden. A Council of Europe Report has described Inter-Action as "The most exciting community arts group (socio-cultural animation organisation) in Europe."

Inter-Action was founded in 1968 by Ed Berman to stimulate community involvement and to experiment with applying creativity to social needs. From the beginning there has been an emphasis on encouraging mutual-help projects in neighbourhoods, enabling more community participation. This inevitably results in the development of local pride and care as well as substantial cost-savings.

Inter-Action has followed a concept of "social enterprise", applying the initiative of creative persons from the arts, community work and business worlds towards the solution of social, educational and financial problems. Moreover, Inter-Action has followed a policy of helping to professionalise the charity and voluntary fields through its Advisory Service.

In the late '70s Inter-Action set up an international branch of its work — the Institute for Social Enterprise. This branch deals with the training of workers and helping set up local self-help groups outside of the UK, especially in Third World countries. Training and action consultancy take place either in the UK or on the ground abroad where practical projects are implemented with local people and trained workers.

WOW Campaigns Ltd

WOW Campaigns Ltd is a non-profit making company set up in 1980 to promote, support and further the objects and activities of War on Want, which is a registered charity.

Primarily a campaigning body, WOW Campaigns works to combat poverty, whatever its cause; to promote self-determination, self-reliance and freedom from racial, sexual and cultural discrimination in any part of the world.

WOW Campaigns conducts research into the causes of and ways of relieving poverty, oppression, distress, sickness, and discrimination, and works closely with grass roots organisations in Britain and throughout the world to promote economic, political and social change which will benefit those who are most disadvantaged.